KU-618-770

Jewish Quarter
JOSEFOV

Old Town
STARÉ MĚSTO

New Town
NOVÉ MĚSTO

PAGES 80–93
Street Finder
maps 3–4

PAGES 60–79
Street Finder
maps 3–4

PAGES 142–157
Street Finder
maps 3–6

0 metres   500

0 yards   500

EYEWITNESS *TRAVEL GUIDES*

PRAGUE

DK EYEWITNESS TRAVEL GUIDES

PRAGUE

Main Contributor: VLADIMÍR SOUKUP

DORLING KINDERSLEY
LONDON • NEW YORK • SYDNEY • DELHI
PARIS • MUNICH • JOHANNESBURG
www.dk.com

A DORLING KINDERSLEY BOOK

www.dk.com

PROJECT EDITOR Heather Jones
ART EDITOR Lisa Kosky
EDITORS Ferdie McDonald, Carey Combe
DESIGNERS Louise Parsons, Nicki Rawson

CONTRIBUTORS
Petr David, Vladimír Dobrovodský, Nicholas Lowry,
Polly Phillimore, Joy Turner-Kadečková

PHOTOGRAPHERS
Jiří Doležal, Jiří Kopřiva, Vladimír Kozlík, František Přeučil,
Milan Posselt, Stanislav Tereba, Peter Wilson

ILLUSTRATORS
Gillie Newman, Chris Orr, Otakar Pok, Jaroslav Staněk
•
This book was produced with the assistance of
Olympia Publishing House, Prague.

Reproduced by Colourscan, Singapore
Printed and bound by L. Rex Printing Company Limited, China

First published in Great Britain in 1994
by Dorling Kindersley Limited
9 Henrietta Street, London WC2E 8PS

**Reprinted with revisions 1994, 1995, 1996, 1997,
1998, 1999, 2000, 2001**

Copyright 1994, 2001 © Dorling Kindersley Limited, London

A CIP CATALOGUE RECORD IS AVAILABLE FROM THE BRITISH LIBRARY.

ISBN 0-7513-9405-X

This DK Eyewitness Travel Guide is updated annually.
In addition, regular updates and information on current events are
available on this Guide's own website at:
www.dk.com/travel
We value the views and suggestions of our readers very highly.
Please write to: Senior Managing Editor, DK Eyewitness Travel
Guides, Dorling Kindersley, 9 Henrietta Street, London WC2E 8PS.
Or contact us via: travelguides@dk.com
Even though every effort has been made to ensure that this book is
as up-to-date as possible at the time of going to press, some details
are liable to change. The publishers cannot accept responsibility
for any consequences arising from the use of this book.

CONTENTS

Rudolph II (1576–1612)

INTRODUCING PRAGUE

Outdoor café tables

Wallenstein Palace and Garden in the Little Quarter

Church of Our Lady before Týn

Czech beer-bottle top

Fiacre, Old Town Square

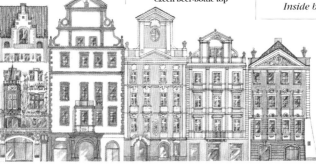

Baroque façades of houses at the eastern end of Old Town Square

How to Use this Guide

Planning the day's itinerary in Prague

THIS EYEWITNESS Travel Guide helps you get the most from your stay in Prague with the minimum of difficulty. The opening section, *Introducing Prague*, locates the city geographically, sets modern Prague in its historical context and describes events through the entire year. *Prague at a Glance* is an overview of the city's main attractions, including a feature on the River Vltava. Section two, *Prague Area by Area*, starts on page 58. This is the main sightseeing section, which covers all the important sights, with photographs, maps and drawings. It also includes day trips from Prague and four guided walks around the city.

Carefully researched tips for hotels, restaurants, shops and markets, cafés and bars, entertainment and sports are found in *Travellers' Needs*. The last section, the *Survival Guide*, contains useful practical advice on all you need to know, from making a telephone call to using the public transport system.

FINDING YOUR WAY AROUND THE SIGHTSEEING SECTION

Each of the five sightseeing areas in the city is colour-coded for easy reference. Every chapter opens with an introduction to the part of Prague it covers, describing its history and character, followed by a Street-by-Street map illustrating the heart of the area. Finding your way around each chapter is made simple by the numbering system used throughout. The most important sights are covered in detail in two or more full pages.

Each area has colour-coded thumb tabs.

Locator map

A locator map shows where you are in relation to other areas in the city centre.

A suggested route takes in the most interesting and attractive streets in the area.

1 Introduction to the area
For easy reference, the sights in each area are numbered and plotted on an area map. To help the visitor, this map also shows metro stations, tram stops, river boat boarding points and parking areas. The area's key sights are listed by category: Churches; Museums and Galleries; Historic Streets and Squares; Palaces; and Parks and Gardens.

The area shaded pink is shown in greater detail on the Street-by-Street map on the following pages.

2 Street-by-Street map
This gives a bird's eye view of the most important parts of each sightseeing area. The numbering of the sights ties in with the area map and the fuller descriptions on the pages that follow.

The list of star sights recommends the places that no visitor should miss.

PRAGUE AREA MAP

THE COLOURED AREAS shown on this map *(see inside front cover)* are the five main sightseeing areas – each covered in a full chapter in *Prague Area by Area (pp58–157)*. They are highlighted on other maps throughout the book. In *Prague at a Glance (pp36–57)*, for example, they help locate the top sights. They are also used to show some of the top restaurants in *Travellers' Needs (pp192–3)* and to plot the routes of the river trip *(p54)* and the four guided walks *(p170)*.

Numbers refer to each sight's position on the area map and its place in the chapter.

Practical information lists all the information you need to visit every sight, including a map reference to the *Street Finder (pp244–9)*.

Façades of important buildings are often shown to help you recognize them quickly.

The visitors' checklist provides all the practical information needed to plan your visit.

3 Detailed information on each sight
All the important sights in Prague are described individually. They are listed in order, following the numbering on the area map. Practical information on opening hours, telephone numbers, admission charges and facilities available is given for each sight. The key to the symbols used can be found on the back flap.

A timeline charts the key events in the history of the building.

A timeline charts the key events in the history of the building.

4 Prague's major sights
Historic buildings are dissected to reveal their interiors; and museums and galleries have colour-coded floorplans to help you find important exhibits.

Stars indicate the features no visitor should miss.

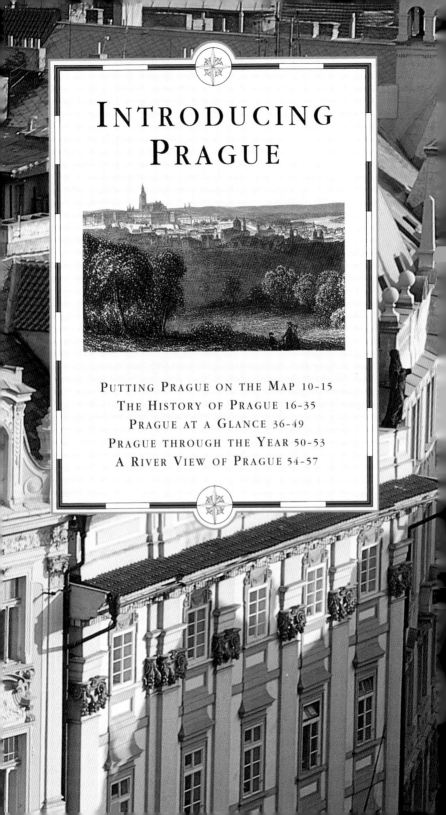

INTRODUCING PRAGUE

Putting Prague on the Map

P RAGUE HAS A POPULATION of just over 1 million and covers 500 sq km (200 sq miles) at its outer limits. It is the capital of the newly-formed Czech Republic and head of the region of Bohemia. Prague's geographical position at the centre of Europe makes it a convenient base from which to visit both the Bohemian countryside and many other major cities, such as Nuremberg, Vienna, Bratislava and Budapest.

GERMANY

Berlin

Dresden

Terezín

PRAGUE (Praha)

Karlsbad (Karlovy Vary)

Karlstein (Karlštejn)

Kutná Hora

View looking southwest over the Vltava

Nuremberg

Paris

Pilsen (Plzeň)

Vltava

Budweis (České Budějovice)

EUROPE

NORWAY

FINLAND

SWEDEN

UNITED KINGDOM

DENMARK

ESTONIA

RUSSIAN FEDERATION

LATVIA

LITHUANIA

REP OF IRELAND

NETHERLANDS

POLAND

BELORUSSIA

BELGIUM   GERMANY

Prague

CZECH REPUBLIC

UKRAINE

FRANCE

SWITZ

AUSTRIA

SLOVAKIA

HUNGARY

MOLDAVIA

SLOVENIA

CROATIA

ROMANIA

BOSNIA HERZ

SPAIN

YUGOSLAVIA

BULGARIA

ITALY

ALBANIA

MACEDONIA

GREECE

TURKEY

Danube

Linz

Salzburg

AUSTRIA

Graz

Europe

The Czech Republic, right at the heart of continental Europe, is completely landlocked. Prague, the capital, has one airport and road and rail links to neighbouring countries.

Drava

ITALY

Verona

PRAGUE AND ENVIRONS

Veltrusy
Neratovice
10
Lysá n.
Labem
Slaný
Kralupy
n. Vltavou
Brandýs n. Labem-
Stará Boleslav
Elbe
Švermov
Roztoky
Čakovic
Čelákovic
D11
Kladno
Horní Počernice
See next page
12
Úvaly
Český
Brod
Ruzyně
Unhošť
Řičany
333
Rudná
0 km   10
Zbraslav
0 miles   5
Beroun
Karlštejn
Jílové
u Prahy
Řevnice

Prague and Environs
*Most sights are in the central, historic area of Prague.
These are covered in detail on pages 58–157.
Important sights outside the centre and day
trips can be found on pages 160–69. For
road and rail networks, see pages 230–31.*

Oder
POLAND
Warsaw
Breslau
A4   8
3
Elbe
8
33
Cracow
CZECH
REPUBLIC
Ostrava
7
48
46
Brno
Morava
D2
303
53
VIENNA
D61
SLOVAKIA
A1
A21
BRATISLAVA
Váh
3
10
2
M3

Aerial view of Greater Prague

M1
BUDAPEST
A2
Rába
HUNGARY   **KEY**

Lake Balaton   Greater Prague

Airport

Motorway

Major road

Railway line

Country boundary

M7
1
0 kilometres   50
0 miles   30
Zagreb

Greater Prague

THE CITY OF PRAGUE IS MADE UP of five ancient towns *(see pp54–165)* with the Vltava, a tributary of the Elbe, running through the centre. In 1922 the greater Prague conurbation was formed. It incorporated 37 other districts and suburbs of central Bohemia. The greater Prague area is well served by public transport systems.

ČIMICE

ZÁMKY

BOHNICE

241

LYSOLAJE

TROJA

PŘEDNÍ KOPANINA

DOLNÍ ŠÁRKA

HOROMĚŘICKÁ

NEBUŠICE

HORNÍ ŠÁRKA

DEJVICE

STROMOVKA

BUBENEČ

240

7

Slaný

ŠÁRKA

EVROPSKÁ

STŘEŠOVICE

6

See next page

Autobusové Nádraží Hradčanská

Masarykovo nádraží

Vltava

600

Ruzyně

PATOČKOVA

BŘEVNOV

OBORA HVĚZDA

PODBĚLOHORSKÁ

BĚLOHORSKÁ

6

Karlovy Vary

MOTOL

PLZEŇSKÁ

5

KOŠÍŘE

SMÍCHOV

RADLICKÁ

4

5

Plzeň

STODŮLKY

JINONICE

RADLICE

PODOL

EREMIÁŠOVA

PROKOPSKÉ ÚDOLÍ

JEREMENKOVA

600

JIŽNÍ SPOJK.

29

K BARRANDOVU

SLIVENEC

CHUCHELSKÝ HÁJ

HODKOVIČKY

STRAKONICKÁ

VELKA CHUCHLE

4

MODŘANY

Strakonice

KEY

▨	Central Prague
▢	Greater Prague
✈	Airport
🚍	Coach station
🚆	Train station
▭	Motorway
▬	Major road
═	Minor road
—	Railway

0 kilometres   2

0 miles   1

Central Prague

PRAŽSKÝ HRAD A HRADČANY
PRAGUE CASTLE AND HRADČANY

JELENÍ • MARIÁNSKÉ HRADBY • KRÁLOVSKÁ ZAHRADA • CHOTKOVA

NOVÝ SVĚT • Brusnice

Šternberský palác Sternberg Palace

Klášter sv. Jiří St George's Convent

VIKÁŘSKÁ • JIŘSKÁ

Chrám sv. Víta St Vitus's Cathedral

Královský palác Royal Palace

Loreta The Loreto

HRADČANSKÉ NÁMĚSTÍ

KANOVNICKÁ

LORETÁNSKÉ NÁMĚSTÍ

LORETÁNSKÁ • ÚVOZ • K HRADU

NERUDOVA

LEDEBURSKÁ ZAHRADA

VALDŠTEJNSKÉ NÁMĚSTÍ • VALDŠTEJNSKÁ

VALDŠTEJNSKÁ ZAHRADA

VOJANOVY SADY

MALOSTRANSKÉ NÁMĚSTÍ

JOSEFSKÁ

Kostel sv. Mikuláše Church of St Nicholas

DRAŽICKÉHO NÁMĚSTÍ

MOSTECKÁ

VRTBOVSKÁ ZAHRADA

MALTÉZSKÉ NÁMĚSTÍ

VELKOPŘEVORSKÉ NÁMĚSTÍ

KAMPA

POHOŘELEC • STRAHOVSKÁ

Strahovský klášter Strahov Monastery

STRAHOVSKÁ ZAHRADA

LOBKOVICKÁ ZAHRADA

SCHÖNBORNSKÁ ZAHRADA

MALÁ STRANA
LITTLE QUARTER

SEMINÁŘSKÁ ZAHRADA

KARMELITSKÁ

ÚJEZD

RŮŽOVÝ SAD

PETŘÍNSKÉ SADY

VÍTĚZNÁ

MALOSTRANSKÉ NÁBŘEŽÍ

ŘÍČNÍ

STŘELEC OSTROV

CHOTKOVY SADY

LETENSKÁ

TOMÁŠSKÁ

SNĚMOVNÍ

U LUŽICKÉHO SEMINÁŘE

ČERTOVKA

KLÁROV

Orb and Cross
An important part of the royal coronation regalia, this orb is now kept at the Royal Palace at Prague Castle (see pp104–5).

KEY

▢	Major sight
ᴹ	Metro station
🚌	Coach station
🚋	Tram stop
🚋	Funicular railway
⛴	River boat boarding point
P	Parking
ℹ	Tourist information
✚	Hospital
🚓	Police station
✝	Church
✡	Synagogue
—	City wall

View of the Church of St Lawrence
Petřín Park offers outstanding views of Prague (see p141 and Three Guided Walks, pp174–5).

Painted House Façade
The Old Town has many Gothic and Baroque houses. Some have colourful mural paintings like this one in Old Town Square (see pp66–9).

Art Nouveau Statue
The New Town has many examples of Art Nouveau architecture (see pp148–9).

*Map labels:*

Svermův most

FRANTIŠKU

REVOLUČNÍ

Klášter sv. Anežky
St Agnes's Convent

NÁMĚSTÍ
CURIEOVÝCH

JOSEFOV
JEWISH QUARTER

Staronová synagóga
Old-New Synagogue

Starý židovský hřbitov
Old Jewish Cemetery

HRADEBNÍ

NÁMĚSTÍ JANA
PALACHA

Čechův most

DVOŘÁKOVO NÁBŘEŽÍ

PAŘÍŽSKÁ

LISTOPADU 17.

Vltava

KOŠÁRKOVO NÁBŘEŽÍ

Mánesův most

KŘIŽOVNICKÁ

VALENTINSKÁ

ŽATECKÁ

MAISELOVA

PLATNÉŘSKÁ

MARIÁNSKÉ
NÁMĚSTÍ

U RADNICE

MALÉ
NÁMĚSTÍ

STAROMĚSTSKÉ
NÁMĚSTÍ

Staroměstská radnice
Old Town Hall

OVOCNÝ
TRH

BÍLKOVA

DUŠNÍ

U OBECNÍHO DVORA

VĚZEŇSKÁ

KOZÍ

DLOUHÁ

MASNÁ

RYBNÁ

KRÁLODVORSKÁ

Karlův most

STARÉ MĚSTO
OLD TOWN

SMETANOVO NÁBŘEŽÍ

ANENSKÉ
NÁMĚSTÍ

BETLÉMSKÉ
NÁMĚSTÍ

HUSOVA

SKOŘEPKA

NA PERŠTÝNĚ

UHELNÝ
TRH

RYTÍŘSKÁ

PERLOVA

28. ŘÍJNA

NA MŮSTKU

NA PŘÍKOPĚ

NEKÁZANKA

PANSKÁ

V CÍPU

VÁCLAVSKÉ
NÁMĚSTÍ

JINDŘIŠSKÁ

RŮŽOVA

POLITICKÝCH VĚZŇŮ

NÁRODNÍ

SPÁLENÁ

JUNGMANNOVA

OPLETALOVA

VÁCLAVSKÉ
NÁMĚSTÍ

WASHINGTONOVA

WILSONOVA

ost Legií

Národní divadlo
National Theatre

OSTROVNÍ

VLADISLAVOVA

VODIČKOVA

ŠTĚPÁNSKÁ

VE SMEČKÁCH

KRAKOVSKÁ

MEZIBRANSKÁ

SOKOLSKÁ

LEGEROVA

SLOVANSKÝ
OSTROV

NA STRUZE

PŠTROSSOVA

V JIRCHÁŘÍCH

OPATOVICKÁ

ČERNÁ

KŘEMENCOVA

SPÁLENÁ

LAZARSKÁ

ČELAKOVSKÉHO
SADY

MASARYKOVO NÁBŘEŽÍ

NA ZDERAZE

MYSLÍKOVA

NÁPLAVNÍ

ODBORŮ

NOVÉ MĚSTO
NEW TOWN

ŽITNÁ

JEČNÁ

KARLOVO
NÁMĚSTÍ

NA RYBNÍČKU

HÁLKOVA

V TŮNÍCH

LIPOVÁ

Jiráskův most

JIRÁSKOVO
NÁMĚSTÍ

RAŠÍNOVO NÁBŘEŽÍ

DITTRICHOVA

RESSLOVA

VÁCLAVSKÁ

KARLOVO
NÁMĚSTÍ

GORAZDOVA

TROJANOVA

NA MORÁNI

VYŠEHRADSKÁ

U NEMOCNICE

KATEŘINSKÁ

KE KARLOVU

VINIČNÁ

Palackého most

PALACKÉHO
NÁMĚSTÍ

NÁMĚSTÍ POD
EMAUZY

BENÁTSKÁ

BOTANICKÁ
ZAHRADA

APOLINÁŘSKÁ

NA SLUPI

0 metres   200

0 yards   200

THE HISTORY OF PRAGUE

RAGUE'S POSITION at the crossroads of Europe has made it a magnet for foreign traders since pre-recorded times. By the early 10th century it had developed into a thriving town with a large market place (the Old Town Square) and two citadels (Prague Castle and Vyšehrad), from where its first rulers, the Přemyslids, conducted their many family feuds. These were often bloody: in 935, Prince Wenceslas was savagely murdered by his brother Boleslav. Wenceslas was later canonized and became Bohemia's best-known patron saint.

Prague coat of arms

During the Middle Ages Prague enjoyed a golden age, especially during the reign of the Holy Roman Emperor, Charles IV. Under the auspices of this wise and cultured king, Prague grew into a magnificent city, larger than Paris or London. Charles instigated the founding and building of many institutions, including the first University of Central Europe in Prague. The University's first Czech rector was Jan Hus, the reforming preacher whose execution for alleged heresy in 1415 led to the Hussite wars. The radical wing of the Hussites, the Taborites, were finally defeated at the Battle of Lipany in 1434. During the 16th century, after a succession of weak kings, the Austrian Habsburgs took over, beginning a rule that would last for almost 400 years. One of the more enlightened of all the Habsburg Emperors was Rudolph II. He brought the spirit of the Renaissance to Prague through his love of the arts and sciences. Soon after his death, in 1618, Prague was the setting for the Protestant revolt which led to the 30 Years' War. Its aftermath brought a serious decline in the fortunes of a city that would revive only in the 18th century. Prague's many fine Baroque churches and palaces date from this time.

The 19th century saw a period of national revival and the burgeoning of civic pride. The great public monuments – the National Museum, the National Theatre and Rudolfinum – were built. But a foreign power still ruled the city, and it was not until 1918 that Prague became the capital of an independent Republic. World War II brought occupation by the German army, followed by four decades of Communism. After the "Velvet Revolution" of 1989, Prague is today on the threshold of a new era.

View of Prague Castle and Little Quarter, 1493

◁ *St Wenceslas and St Vitus*, by Bartholomaeus Spränger, about 1600

Rulers of Prague

THREE GREAT DYNASTIES have shaped the history of Prague: the Přemyslids, the Luxemburgs and the Habsburgs. According to Slav legend, the Přemyslids were founded by Princess Libuše *(see p21)*. Her line included St Wenceslas and Přemysl Otakar II, whose death on the battlefield at Marchfeld paved the way for the Luxemburgs. This family produced one of Prague's greatest rulers, Charles IV, who was King of Bohemia and Holy Roman Emperor *(see pp24–5)*. In 1526, the city came under the control of the Austrian House of Habsburg whose rule lasted 400 years, until 28 October 1918, when Czechoslovakia gained its independence. Since then there has been a succession of presidents.

The mythical Princess Libuše

1346–78
Charles IV

1453–7
Ladislav
Posthumus

1310–46
John of Luxemburg

935–72
Boleslav I

1140–72
Vladislav I

1305–6
Wenceslas III

1230–53
Wenceslas I

1278–1305
Wenceslas II

1034–55
Břetislav I

900	1000	1100	1200	1300	1400

PŘEMYSLIDS

LUXEMBURGS

900	1000	1100	1200	1300	1400

972–99
Boleslav II

1061–92
Vratislav II

921–35 St Wenceslas

1173–9
Soběslav II

1197–1230
Přemysl Otakar I

1253–78 Přemysl Otakar II

1378–1419
Wenceslas IV

1419–37 Sigismund

1935–8 and **1945–8** Edvard Beneš

1740–80 Maria Theresa

1948–53 Klement Gottwald

1790–92 Leopold II

1953–7 Antonín Zápotocký

1526–64 Ferdinand I

1918–35 Tomáš Garrigue Masaryk

1957–68 Antonín Novotný

1564–76 Maxmilian II

1657–1705 Leopold I

1792–1835 Franz II

1458–71 George of Poděbrady

1637–57 Ferdinand III

1711–40 Charles VI

1835–48 Ferdinand V

1968–75 Ludvík Svoboda

| 1500 | 1600 | 1700 | 1800 | 1900 |

JAGIELLOS | HABSBURGS | PRESIDENTS

| 1500 | 1600 | 1700 | 1800 | 1900 |

1619–37 Ferdinand II

1516–26 Ludvíc II

1705–11 Josef I

1916–18 Charles I

1471–1516 Vladislav Jagiello

1848–1916 Franz Josef I

1611–19 Matthias

1975–90 Gustáv Husák

1576–1611 Rudolph II

1780–90 Josef II

1990 Václav Havel

Prague under the Přemyslids

EARLY CELTIC TRIBES, from 500 BC, were the first inhabitants of the area around the Vltava valley. The Germanic Marcomans arrived in 9–6 BC, and gradually the Celts left. The first Slavic tribes came to Bohemia in about 500 AD. Struggles for supremacy led to the emergence of a ruling dynasty, the Přemyslids, around 800 AD.

9th-century earring They built two fortified settlements: the first at Prague Castle *(see pp94–110)*, the second at Vyšehrad, a rocky headland on the right bank of the Vltava *(see pp178–9)*. These remained the seats of Czech princes for hundreds of years. One prince crucial to the emerging Czech State was the pious Wenceslas. He enjoyed only a brief reign but left an important legacy in the founding of St Vitus's rotunda *(see p102)*.

EXTENT OF THE CITY

◼ *1000 AD*   ☐ *Today*

Boleslav's henchman raises his sword to strike the fatal blow.

St Cyril and St Methodius
Originally Greeks from Salonica, these two brothers brought Christianity to Moravia in about 863. They baptized early Přemyslid, Bořivoj, and his wife Ludmilla, grandmother of St Wenceslas.

Second assassin grapples with the Prince's companion.

Early Coin
Silver coins like this denar were minted in the royal mint of Vyšehrad during Boleslav II's reign from 967–99.

Wild Boar Figurine
Celtic tribes made small talismans of the wild animals that they hunted for food in the forested areas around Prague.

TIMELINE

Bronze head of a Celtic goddess

623–658 Bohemia is part of an empire formed by Frankish merchant, Samo

600 AD		700

500 BC Celts in Bohemia. Joined by Germanic Marcomans in 1st century AD

6th century Slavs settle alongside Germanic tribes in Bohemia

8th century Tribe of Czechs settle in central Bohemia

Vyšehrad acropolis – first Czech settlement on the right bank of the Vltava

Sword and Helmet
St Wenceslas was buried in the southern apse of the rotunda of St Vitus. His sword and helmet were preserved as relics and today form part of the Cathedral's treasure.

Wenceslas seeks sanctuary.

A monk opens the door for Wenceslas.

Rotunda of St Vitus
Founded by Wenceslas in the early 10th century, the rotunda became a place of pilgrimage after the saint's death in 935. It stood where St Wenceslas Chapel is today.

Roman-arched windows

Curving stone walls

ASSASSINATION OF PRINCE WENCESLAS

In 935, the young Wenceslas was murdered on the orders of his brother, Boleslav. This manuscript illustration of 1006 shows the moment when the assassins caught up with the prince as he was about to enter the church for the morning mass.

Early Christian breast cross

921 Wenceslas becomes Prince of Bohemia

993 Bishop Adalbert founds monastery at Břevnov, near Prague

0
nasty of
emyslids
nded

870 Prague Castle founded

900

1000

863 St Cyril and St Methodius bring Christianity to Moravia

935 Wenceslas dies

920 Founding of St George's Basilica at Prague Castle

Bishop Adalbert's bejewelled glove

Early Medieval Prague

P RAGUE CASTLE STEADILY grew in importance from the beginning of the 12th century onwards. Prone to frequent fires, its wooden buildings were gradually replaced by stone and the area developed into a sturdy Romanesque fortress with a palace and religious buildings. Clustered around the original outer bailey was an area inhabited by skilled craftsmen and German merchants,

Initial letter D from the Vyšehrad Codex

encouraged to come and stay in Prague by Vladislav II and, later, Přemysl Otakar II. This came to be known as the "Little Quarter" and achieved town status in 1257. It was joined to the Old Town by a bridge, known as the Judith Bridge.

EXTENT OF THE CITY

▨ *1230* ☐ *Today*

PRAGUE CASTLE IN 1230

Sited on a high ridge, the Romanesque fortress had protective stone walls and easily-guarded gates.

St George's Convent and Basilica (see pp106–9 and p98)

The Prince's Palace grew into the Royal Palace (see pp104–5).

Entrance from Old Town

The White Tower gave access from the west.

Decorative Comb
This ornate, bone, fine-toothed comb was one of the relics of St Adalbert.

Site of Hradčany Square

External staircase

Vaulted ceiling

Living room

Romanesque Stone House
These three-storeyed houses were based around a very simple floor plan.

Ground floor

St Vitus's Basilica and Chapter House (see pp100–3)

Stone houses were built on what is now Nerudova Street in the Little Quarter (see p130).

TIMELINE

1040 St Adalbert's remains brought to Prague		**1110** Small German settlement in Prague	**1140** Strahov Monastery founded
	1092–1110 Reign of Bretislav II		
1091 Old Town marketplace first mentioned by travellers			
1050		**1100**	**115**
	1070 Vyšehrad becomes temporary seat of Czech princes	**1091** Great fire at Prague Castle	**1110–20** Reign of Bořivoj II
St Adalbert with a martyr's palm frond	**1085** Vratislav I becomes first King of Bohemia	**1135** Seat of Czech princes moves from Vyšehrad to Prague Castle	*Romanesque stone head from Judith Bridge Tower*

St Agnes
Sister of Wenceslas I, this devout woman built a convent for the order of the Poor Clares (the female counterparts of the Franciscans) (see pp92–3). She was not canonized until 1989.

WHERE TO SEE ROMANESQUE PRAGUE

Remains can be seen in the crypt of St Vitus's *(pp100–3)*, the basements of the Palace of the Lords of Kunštát *(p78)* and the Royal Palace *(pp104–5)*.

St George's Basilica
The vaulting in the crypt dates from the 12th century (p98).

The Black Tower was the exit to Bohemia's second town, Kutná Hora *(see p168)*.

Vratislav II
The Vyšehrad Codex, an illuminated selection from the gospels, was made to mark Vratislav's coronation in 1061.

Little Quarter Square

St Martin's Rotunda
This well-preserved building is in Vyšehrad (p179).

Little Quarter Coat of Arms
Vladislav II's portrait was incorporated into this 12th-century miniature painting.

Přemysl Otakar II
The last great Přemyslid king was killed in battle after trying to carve out a huge empire.

1233 Founding of St Agnes's Convent

1182 Romanesque construction of Prague Castle completed

1257 Little Quarter receives town status

1258–68 Strahov Monastery rebuilt in Gothic style after fire

| 1200 | 1250 | 1290 |

1212 Přemysl Otakar I receives the Sicilian Golden Bull, confirming the sovereignty of Bohemian kings

Sicilian Golden Bull

1278 Přemysl Otakar II dies at Marchfeld

1158 Judith Bridge built *(see pp136–9)*

Prague's Golden Age

Gift from Pope
Urban V in 1368

I N THE LATE MIDDLE AGES, Prague attained the height of its glory. The Holy Roman Emperor, Charles IV, chose Prague as his Imperial residence and set out to make the city the most magnificent in Europe. He founded a university (the Carolinum) and built many fine churches and monasteries in the Gothic style. Of major importance were his town-planning schemes, such as the reconstruction of Prague Castle, the building of a new stone bridge to replace the Judith Bridge, and the foundation of a new quarter, the New Town. A devout Catholic, he owned a large collection of relics which were kept, along with the Crown Jewels, at Karlstein Castle *(see pp168–9)*.

EXTENT OF THE CITY

▨ *1350*   ☐ *Today*

Charles IV wears the Imperial crown, set with sapphires, rubies and pearls.

**St Wenceslas
Chapel**
*Proud of his direct
descent from the
Přemyslids, Charles
had this shrine to
St Wenceslas built in
St Vitus's Cathedral
(see pp100–3).*

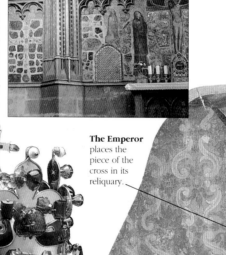

The Emperor
places the
piece of the
cross in its
reliquary.

St Wenceslas Crown
*Worn by Charles at his coronation
in 1347, the Bohemian crown was
based on early Přemyslid insignia.*

TIMELINE

1280 Old-New Synagogue
completed in Gothic style

*Town Hall, Old
Town Square*

1333 Charles IV
makes Prague
his home

1344 Elevation of Prague
bishopric to archbishopric

1305	1320	1335

1306
Přemyslid
dynasty
ends

1338 John of Luxemburg gives permission
to Old Town to build a town hall

*Portal of Old-
New Synagogue*

1310 John of
Luxemburg
occupies Prague

*Votive panel showing Charles,
Archbishop Jan Očko and
Bohemia's patron saints*

St Vitus by Master Theodoric
This is one of a series of paintings of saints by the great Bohemian artist for the Holy Rood Chapel at Karlstein Castle (c1365).

A jewelled reliquary cross was made to house the new relic.

University Seal, 1348
The seal depicts the Emperor offering the foundation documents to St Wenceslas.

Building the New Town
This manu-script records Charles IV supervising the building of the New Town during the 14th century.

CHARLES IV AND HIS RELICS
Charles collected holy relics from all over the Empire. In about 1357 he received a part of Christ's cross from the Dauphin. This mural in Karlstein Castle is thought to be the best likeness of the Emperor.

WHERE TO SEE GOTHIC PRAGUE
Prague's rich Gothic legacy includes three of its best-known sights – St Vitus's Cathedral (pp100–3), Charles Bridge (pp136–9) and the Old-New Synagogue (pp88–9). Another very important building from Charles IV's reign is the Carolinum (p65). Churches that have retained most of their original Gothic features include the Church of Our Lady before Týn (p70).

Carolinum
This fine oriel window was part of the university (p65).

Old Town Bridge Tower
The sculptural decoration is by Peter Parler (p139).

1348 Charles IV founds Charles University

1357 Charles Bridge begun

Sculpture of young Wenceslas IV by Peter Parler in St Vitus's Cathedral

1378 Reign of Wenceslas IV begins

1391 Bethlehem Chapel founded

| 1350 | 1365 | 1380 | 1395 |

1361 Wenceslas IV born, oldest son of Charles

1378 Charles dies

1348 Charles IV founds Prague New Town

Bethlehem Chapel

Hussite Prague

IN THE EARLY 15TH CENTURY, Europe shook in fear of an incredible fighting force -- the Hussites, followers of the reformist cleric, Jan Hus. Despite simple weapons, they achieved legendary military successes against the Emperor's Catholic crusades, due largely to their religious fervour and to the discipline of their brilliant leader, Jan Žižka, who invented mobile artillery. The Hussites split into two camps, the moderate "Utraquists" (see p75) and the radical "Taborites" who were finally defeated at the Battle of Lipany in 1434, paving the way for the moderate Hussite king, George of Poděbrady.

George of Poděbrady

EXTENT OF THE CITY
☐ 1500   ☐ Today

Nobles' Letter of Protest
Several hundred seals of the Bohemian nobility were affixed to a letter protesting about the execution of Jan Hus.

GOD'S WARRIORS
The early-16th-century Codex of Jena illustrated the Hussite successes. Here the Hussites, who included artisans and barons, are shown singing their hymn, with their blind leader, Jan Žižka.

Jan Žižka

The priest held a gilded monstrance.

War Machine
For maximum effect, farm waggons were tied together to form a shield. A chilling array of weapons were unleashed including crossbows, flails and an early form of howitzer.

TIMELINE

1402–13 Jan Hus preaches at Bethlehem Chapel (see p75)

1415 Jan Hus burned at the stake at Constance

1419 Defenestration of councillors from New Town Hall

1434 Battle of Lipany

The Taborites made lethal weapons from simple farm tools

1400	1420	1440

1410 Jan Hus excommunicated. Building of Old Town Clock

1424 Jan Žižka dies

1448 Prague conquered by troops of George of Poděbrady

1420 Hussites victorious under Jan Žižka at Vitkov and Vyšehrad

Jan Hus preaching

The chalice, symbol of the Utraquists

Satan Dressed as a Priest
Lurid images satirizing the corruption of the church were painted on placards and carried through the streets.

The banner was decorated with the Hussite chalice.

A variety of farm implements were used as makeshift weapons by the peasants.

Hussite Shield
Wooden shields like this one that bears the arms of the city of Prague, were used to fill any gaps in the waggon fortress's tight formation.

The peasant army marched behind Jan Žižka.

REFORMER, JAN HUS

Born to poor parents in a small Bohemian town, Jan Hus became one of the most important religious thinkers of his day. His objections to the Catholic Church's corrupt practices, opulent style and wealth were shared by many Czechs – nobles and peasants alike. His reformist preaching in Prague's Bethlehem Chapel earned him a huge following, noticed by the Roman Papacy, and Hus was excommunicated. In 1412 Wenceslas IV, brother of the Emperor Sigismund, asked him to leave Prague. In October 1414, Hus decided to defend his teaching at the Council of Constance. Even though he had the Emperor's safe conduct, he was put in prison. The following year he was declared a heretic and burned at the stake.

Jan Hus at the Stake in 1415
After suffering death at the hands of the Church on 6 July 1415, Jan Hus became a revered martyr of the Czech people.

1458 Coronation of George of Poděbrady *(see p172)*

1460

Chalice on the outside of the Týn Church denotes the Hussite cause

1480

1485 Hussite uprising in Prague

1487 First book printed in Prague

1485 King Vladislav Jagiello begins to rebuild Royal Palace at Prague Castle

1492–1502 Vladislav Hall built

1500

Vladislav Jagiello

The Renaissance and Rudolph II

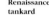

WITH THE ACCESSION of the Habsburgs, the Renaissance reached Prague. Art and architecture were dominated by the Italians who enjoyed the patronage of the Imperial court, especially that of Rudolph II. The eccentric Rudolph often neglected politics, preferring to indulge his passions for collecting and science. His court was a haven for artists, astrologers, astronomers and alchemists, but his erratic rule led to revolts and an attempt by his brother Matthias to usurp him. In the course of the Thirty Years' War *(see pp30–31)* many works of art from Rudolph's great collection were looted.

Renaissance tankard

EXTENT OF THE CITY

▨ *1550* ☐ *Today*

Fish pond

Dalibor Tower

Belvedere

Pergola

Rudolph II
A connoisseur of the bizarre, Rudolph was delighted by this vegetable portrait by Giuseppe Arcimboldo (1590).

Orchard

Formal flower beds

Lion House

Mosaic Desk Top
Renaissance table tops with Florentine themes of fountains and gardens were made at Rudolph's court in semi-precious stones.

Rabbi Löw
A revered Jewish sage, he was said to have invented an artificial man (see pp88–9).

TIMELINE

1502 Vladislav Hall built	**1526** Habsburg rule begins with Ferdinand I	**1541** Great fire in Little Quarter, the Castle and Hradčany	**1556** Ferdinand I invites Jesuits to Prague

1520	**1540**	**1560**

Vladislav Hall

Ferdinand I

1538–63 Belvedere built

1547 Unsuccessful uprising of towns of Prague against Ferdinand I

Charter for manglers and dyers

Sense of Sight
Jan Brueghel's allegorical painting shows the extent of Rudolph II's huge collection – from globes to paintings, jewels and scientific instruments.

Ball Game Hall

Tycho Brahe
The Danish astronomer spent his last years living in Prague.

A covered bridge connected the Palace to the garden.

ROYAL PALACE GARDENS

No longer a medieval fortress, Prague Castle and its gardens were given over to the pleasure of the King. Here Rudolph enjoyed ball games, exotic plants and his menagerie.

WHERE TO SEE RENAISSANCE PRAGUE

The Royal Garden *(p111)* preserves much of the spirit of Renaissance Prague. Paintings and objects from Rudolph's collections can be seen in the Sternberg Palace *(pp112–15)*, the Picture Gallery of Prague Castle *(p98)* and the Museum of Decorative Arts *(p84)*.

At the Two Golden Bears
Built in 1590, the house is famous for its symmetrical, carved doorway, one of the most graceful in Prague (p71).

Belvedere
The palace is decorated with stone reliefs by Italian architect, Paolo della Stella (p110).

Ball Game Hall
Beautiful Renaissance sgraffito covers the façade of this building in the Royal Garden, but it has been heavily restored (p111).

1583 Prague becomes seat of Imperial court of Rudolph II; great art collection begun

1614 Matthias Gate at Prague Castle built

1618 Defenestration of two royal governors from Royal Palace *(see p105)*

1580

1600

1620

A ten-ducat coin (1603)

1609 Publication of Rudolph's Imperial Charter on religious freedom

1612 Rudolph II dies

Baroque Prague

I N 1619 THE CZECH NOBLES deposed Habsburg Emperor Ferdinand II as King of Bohemia and elected instead Frederick of the Palatinate. The following year they paid for their defiance at the Battle of the White Mountain, the beginning of the Thirty Years' War. There followed a period of persecution of all non-Catholics, accompanied by the systematic Germanization of the country's institutions. The leaders in the fight against Protestantism were the Jesuits and one of their most powerful weapons was the restoration of Prague's churches in

EXTENT OF THE CITY

1750	Today

the new architecture of the Baroque, coupled with the building of many new churches.

A sculpture of Atlas (1722) adorns the top of the tower.

Mirror Chapel

Church of St Nicholas
This outstanding High Baroque church in the Little Quarter was the work of the great Dientzenhofers (see pp128–9).

Grape Courtyard

Measuring the World
Some monasteries were seats of learning. Strahov (see pp120–21) had two libraries built, decorated with Baroque painting. This fresco detail is in the Philosophical Hall.

Holy Saviour Church

TIMELINE

Old Town coat of arms – embellished with the Imperial eagle and 12 flags in recognition of the defence of the city against the Swedes

1620 Battle of the White Mountain			**1706–14** Decoration of Charles Bridge with statues
1627 Beginning of Counter-Reformation committee in Prague			
1625	**1645**	**1665**	**1685**	**1705**
1621 Execution in Old Town Square of 27 Protestant leaders	**1634** Wallenstein killed by Irish mercenaries	**1648** Swedes occupy Prague Castle. Treaty of Westphalia and end of Thirty Years' War	**1704–53** Building of Church of St Nicholas in the Little Quarter
	1631 Saxon occupation of Prague	**1676–8** New bastions built to fortify Vyšehrad	

Battle of the White Mountain
In 1620 the Czech army was defeated by Habsburg troops at Bílá Hora (White Mountain), a hill northwest of Prague (see p163). After the battle, Bohemia became a de facto province of Austria.

Observatory Tower

St Clement's Church
gave its name to the whole complex.

Italian Chapel

Monstrance
Baroque monstrances – used to display the communion host – became increasingly elaborate and ornate (see pp116–17).

CLEMENTINUM
The Jesuits exercised enormous power over education. Between 1653 and 1723 they built this College. It was the largest complex of buildings after Prague Castle and included three churches, smaller chapels, libraries, lecture halls and an observatory.

WHERE TO SEE BAROQUE PRAGUE
The Baroque is everywhere in Prague. Almost all the churches were built or remodelled in Baroque style, the finest being St Nicholas (pp128–9). There are also the grand palaces and smaller houses of the Little Quarter (pp122–41), the façades in the Old Town (pp60–79), and statues on churches, street corners and along the parapets of Charles Bridge.

Nerudova Street
At the Golden Cup, No. 16, has preserved its typical Baroque house sign (p130).

Charles Bridge
This statue of St Francis Borgia by Ferdinand Brokof was added in 1710 (pp136–9).

Maria Theresa

1740 Accession of Empress Maria Theresa

1748 Bohemian Chancellery loses last vestiges of power

1773 Jesuit Order dissolved

1784 Four towns of Prague united to form a single city

| 1725 | 1745 | 1765 | 1785 |

1757 Prague besieged by Prussians

1782 Convents and monasteries closed

1787 Mozart stays at Bertramka preparing for the premiere of *Don Giovanni* at the Estates Theatre (see p65)

Mozart at Bertramka (p160)

The National Revival in Prague

EXTENT OF THE CITY

☐ 1890   ☐ Today

T HE 19TH CENTURY was one of the most glorious periods in the history of Prague. Austrian rule relaxed, allowing the Czech nation to rediscover its own history and culture. Silent for so long, the Czech language was eventually re-established as an official language. Civic pride was rekindled with the building of the capital's great showpieces, such as the National Theatre which utilized the talents of Czech architects and artists. The Jewish Quarter and New Town underwent extensive redevelopment and, with the introduction of public transport, Prague grew beyond its ancient limits.

Emperor Franz Josef

Smetana's Libuše
Written for the scheduled opening of the National Theatre in 1881, the opera drew on early Czech legend (see pp20–21).

Days of the year

Months and zodiac signs revolve around the centre.

Old Town coat of arms

Rudolfinum
A major concert venue beside the Vltava, the building (see p84) *is richly decorated with symbols of the art of music.*

OLD TOWN CLOCK TOWER CALENDAR
In 1866, the revolving dial on Prague's most enduring landmark was replaced by a new one by celebrated artist, Josef Mánes. His studies of Bohemian peasant life are incorporated into pictures symbolizing the months of the year.

TIMELINE

1805 Czechs, Austrians and Russians defeated by Napoleon at Battle of Slavkov (Austerlitz)

1833 Englishman Edward Thomas begins production of steam engines

1818 National Museum founded

Restored clock from the east face of the Town Hall Tower

1848 Uprising of people of Prague against Austrian troops

1800	1820	1840	180

1815 First public demonstration of a vehicle driven by a steam engine

The battle of Slavkov

1838–45 Old Town Hall undergoes reconstruction

1845 First train arrives in Prague

1868 Foundation stone fo National Theatre laid

Expo 95 Poster
Vojtěch Hynais designed this poster for the ethnographic exhibition of folk culture in 1895. In the Art Nouveau style, it reflected the new appreciation of regional traditions.

WHERE TO SEE THE NATIONAL REVIVAL

Many of Prague's remarkable monuments, the National Museum for example, were built around this period. One fine example of Art Nouveau architecture is the Municipal House (p64), where the Mayor's Room has murals by Mucha. The Rudolfinum (p84) and the National Theatre (pp156–7) have gloriously-decorated interiors by great artists of the day. The Prague Museum has many objects from the late 19th and early 20th centuries as well as the original painting for Mánes' Old Town Clock.

December   Sagittarius

Municipal House
Allegories of civic virtues painted by Alfons Mucha adorn this Art Nouveau interior.

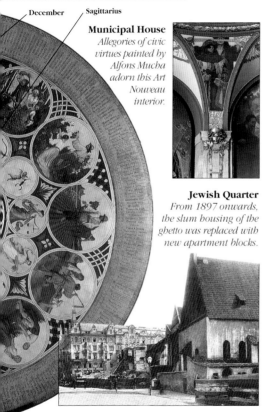

Jewish Quarter
From 1897 onwards, the slum housing of the ghetto was replaced with new apartment blocks.

National Museum
The Neo-Renaissance façade dominates the skyline (p147).

National Theatre
The décor has murals by Czech artists, including Aleš (pp156–7).

National Theatre

1881 Newly opened National Theatre destroyed by fire, then rebuilt

1883 Re-opening of the National Theatre

1891 Jubilee Exhibition

1884–91 Building of the National Museum

1883 First public lighting with electric lamps

1896 Proper city transport of electric trams starts

1912 Municipal House opens

1897–1917 Slums of Jewish Ghetto cleared

1914 World War I begins

1916 Emperor Franz Josef dies

1880

1900

Early electric trams

The satirical novel, Good Soldier Švejk, (see p154) explored the futility of war and the inept Austrian military

Prague after Independence

J UST 20 YEARS AFTER its foundation, the
Czechoslovak Republic was helplessly
caught up in the political manoeuvring that
preceded Nazi domination of Europe.
Prague emerged from World War II
almost unscathed by bombings, no
longer part of a Nazi protectorate but of
a Socialist republic. Any resistance was
brutally suppressed. Ultimately, the intellectuals spoke
out, demanding observance of civil rights. Denial of
such rights led these dissidents to unite and prepare
for the "Velvet Revolution". In the end, it was a
playwright, Václav Havel, who stepped onto the
balcony of Prague Castle to lead the country at the
start of a long and often difficult return to independence.

Letná Park metronome

1945 Soviet Red Army enter Prague
on 9 May to rapturous welcome,
following four days of uprisings.
In October, provisional National
Assembly set up under Beneš

1935 Edvard Beneš
succeeds Masaryk as
President. Nazi-funded
Sudeten German Party,
led by Konrad Henlein,
makes election gains

1920 Avant-
garde left-
wing artists
form Devětsil
movement in
Prague's
Union Café

1938 Munich
Agreement hands
over parts of
Republic to Hitler.
Beneš flees country

1952 Most famous of
many show trials under
Gottwald, Slánský
Trial sends 11 senior
politicians to gallows as
Trotskyites and traitors

Edvard Beneš

1918	1930	1940	1950

1918	1930	1940	1950

1924
Death of
Franz
Kafka,
author of
The Trial

1932 Traditional
gymnastic rally or
slet takes place at
Strahov stadium

1942 Tyrannical
"Protector" for
only eight months,
Reinhard Heydrich
assassinated by
Czech resistance

1955 Largest
statue of Stalin
in the world
unveiled in
Letná Park,
overlooking city

1958 Premiere of
innovative animated
film, *The Invention of
Destruction* directed
by Karel Zeman

1948 Communist
Party assumes
power under
Klement Gottwald;
announces
89% support in
May elections

1918
Foundation of
Czechoslovak
Republic. Tomáš
Masaryk first
democratically-
elected
President

1939 German troops
march into Prague; city
declared capital of Nazi
Protectorate of Bohemia
and Moravia

*Welcome Home poster, to
mark the president's return
on 21 December 1918*

1966 Jiří Menzel's *Closely Observed Trains* wins Oscar for Best Foreign Film, drawing the world's attention to Czech cinema

1989 Year of the "Velvet Revolution": growing civil discontent prompts demonstrations and strikes. Havel unites opposition groups to form Civic Forum. Temporary Government of National Understanding promises free elections; President Husák resigns and Václav Havel sworn in by popular demand

1968 Alexander Dubček elected to post of First Secretary

1990 First democratic elections for 60 years held in June, producing 99% turnout, with 60% of vote going to alliance of Civic Forum and People Against Violence

1962 Statue of Stalin in Letná Park demolished (replaced, in 1991, by a giant metronome)

1979 Playwright Václav Havel founds Committee for the Defence of the Unjustly Persecuted and is sent to prison

1992 Plastic People band perform at celebratory concert, 15 years after ban which resulted in Charter 77

60	1970	1980	1990

60	1970	1980	1990

60 Czechoslovak cialist Republic SSR) proclaimed

1969 Jan Palach burns to death in protest at Soviet occupation

1993 Prague is once again declared capital of Czech Republic

1967 First Secretary and President, Antonín Novotný, imprisons dissident writers

1977 Human rights manifesto Charter 77 drawn up after arrest of band, Plastic People

1984 Jaroslav Seifert, signatory of Charter 77, wins Nobel Prize for Literature but cannot collect prize in person

1968 Moderate Alexander Dubček adopts the programme of liberal reforms known as "Prague Spring". On 21 August, Warsaw Pact occupies Czechoslovakia and over 100 protesters are killed as troops enter Prague

1989 Canonization of St Agnes *(see pp92–3)* takes place on 4 November. Vatican commissions painting by dissident Prague-born artist Gustav Makarius Tauc for the occasion. Czech legend that miraculous events will accompany her elevation to sainthood prove correct when "Velvet Revolution" begins on 17 November

The coat of arms of the Czech Republic has the inscription "truth victorious" and the arms for Bohemia (top left, bottom right), *Moravia* (top right) *and Silesia* (bottom left)

PRAGUE AT A GLANCE

THERE ARE ALMOST 150 places of interest described in the *Area by Area* section of this book. A broad range of sights is covered: from the ancient Royal Palace, which was the site of the Defenestration of 1618 *(see p105)*, to cubist houses built in the Jewish Quarter in the 1920s *(see p91)*; from the peaceful oasis of Petřín Park *(see p141)*, to the bustle of Wenceslas Square *(see pp144–5)*. To help you make the most of your stay, the following 12 pages are a time-saving guide to the best Prague has to offer visitors. Museums and galleries, churches and synagogues, palaces and gardens all have their own sections. Each sight has a cross reference to its own full entry. Below are the attractions that no visitor should miss.

PRAGUE'S TOP TEN SIGHTS

Old Town Square
See pp66–9

National Theatre
See pp156–7.

Church of St Nicholas
See pp128–9.

Charles Bridge
See pp136–9.

Old Town Hall
See pp72–4.

Wallenstein Palace and Garden *See p126.*

Old Jewish Cemetery
See pp86–7.

St Vitus's Cathedral
See pp100–3.

Prague Castle
See p96–7.

St George's Convent
See pp106–9.

◁ Mucha's allegory of Vigilance in the Mayor's Room in the Municipal House *(see p64)*

Prague's Best: Museums and Galleries

WITH MORE THAN 20 museums and almost 100 galleries and exhibition halls, Prague is a city of unexpected and rare delights. Here, religious masterpieces of the Middle Ages vie with the more recent opulence of Art Nouveau and the giants of modern art. New galleries have opened since 1989 with many more temporary exhibitions. There are museums devoted to the history of the state, the city of Prague and its people, many of them housed in buildings that are historical land-marks and works of art in them-selves. This map gives some of the highlights, with a detailed overview on pages 40–41.

St George's Convent
Among the fine Bohemian art is St Jerome by Master Theodoric.

Sternberg Palace
The collection of European art here is outstanding, represented in works such as The Feast of the Rosary *by Albrecht Dürer (1506).*

Prague Castle and Hradčany

Little Quarter

The Loreto
The offerings of devout local aristocrats form the basis of this collection of religious decorative art. In 1721 this jewel-encrusted, tree-shaped monstrance was given to the treasury by Countess Wallenstein.

Smetana Museum
The life and work of this 19th-century Czech composer are remembered beside the river that inspired one of his most famous pieces – the Vltava.

Schwarzenberg Palace
The ornate Renaissance palace forms a handsome backdrop to the Museum of Military History's displays of weaponry and memorabilia.

V L T A V A

Museum of Decorative Arts

Five centuries of arts and crafts are represented here, with particularly impressive collections of Bohemian glass, graphic art and furniture. This carved and painted chest dates from 1612.

St Agnes's Convent

The collection of 19th-century Czech art includes Impressionist views of Prague by Jakub Schikaneder. This is Dusk on the Ramparts of the Castle.

Maisel Synagogue

One of the most important collections of Judaica in the world is housed in the Maisel Synagogue and other buildings of the State Jewish Museum. The displays include religious artefacts, furnishings and books. This illuminated page is from the manuscript of the Pesach Haggadah of 1728.

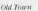

Jewish Quarter

Old Town

0 metres	500
0 yards	500

New Town

National Museum

The vast skeleton of a whale dominates the other exhibits in one of seven grand halls devoted to zoology. The museum's other displays include fine collections of minerals and meteorites.

Dvořák Museum

This viola, which belonged to the influential 19th-century Czech composer, is among the personal effects and musical scores on display in the charming Michna Summer Palace.

Exploring the Museums and Galleries

THE CITY'S MUSEUMS give a fascinating insight into the history of the Czechs and of Prague's Jewish population. Also a revelation to visitors unfamiliar with the culture is the art of the Gothic and Baroque periods and of the 19th-century Czech National Revival. The major museums and galleries are cramped for space, but plans are under way to put more of their collections on show in the near future.

Carved figure on façade of the Museum of Decorative Arts

14th-century *Madonna Aracoeli*, St Vitus Treasure, Prague Castle

CZECH PAINTING AND SCULPTURE

THE MOST IMPORTANT and wide-ranging collection in Prague is that of the National Gallery. Its holdings of Czech art are shown at three venues: works dating from the 12th to 18th centuries at **St George's Convent**; 19th-century art at **St Agnes's Convent** and 20th-century art at the Trades Fair Palace.

The **Picture Gallery of Prague Castle** is a reminder of Emperor Rudolph II's once-great collection. Alongside the paintings are documents and other evidence of just how splendid the original collection must have been.

For the best of the Castle's Bohemian art, you must visit the Gothic and Baroque works at St George's Convent. These include panels painted for Charles IV by Master Theodoric, and examples by Baroque masters Karel Škréta and Petr Brandl. Also within the Castle but currently without a permanent display space is the St Vitus Treasure, a collection of religious pieces including a Madonna from the School of Master Theodoric.

Centuries of Czech sculpture are housed in the Lapidarium at the **Exhibition Ground**. Among its exhibits is statuary formerly found on the Charles Bridge, and the Marian pillar that used to stand in the Old Town Square.

The collection at **St Agnes's Convent** includes works by Josef Mánes, the leading Czech 19th-century painter and ardent patriot. Works by 19th- and 20th-century Prague artists can be seen at the Prague Gallery. Its branches include the Baroque **Troja Palace**, where the architecture makes a marvellous backdrop. Exhibitions are drawn from the gallery's collection of 3,000 paintings, 1,000 statues and 4,000 prints.

The superb Centre for Modern and Contemporary Art at **Trades Fair Palace** represents almost every 20th-century artistic movement. Romanticism and Art Nouveau are both represented, as are the understandably popular 1920s figures of Otto Gutfreund. The development of such ground-breaking groups as Osma, Devětsil, Skupina 42 and the 12.15 group is also strikingly well documented.

EUROPEAN PAINTING AND SCULPTURE

PRAGUE ALSO OFFERS visitors an opportunity to view an exceptional range of master-pieces by Europe's finest artists from antiquity to the 18th century, at **Sternberg Palace**.

The most treasured work in the collection is the *Feast of the Rosary* by Albrecht Dürer, but other equally delightful works include many by 17th-century Dutch masters such as Rubens and Rembrandt, as well as Rodin bronzes.

The Centre for Modern and Contemporary Art at **Trades Fair Palace** has an outstanding collection of Picassos; and examples of work from almost every Impressionist, Post-Impressionist and Fauvist. Three notable self-portraits are those of Paul Gauguin (*Bonjour Monsieur Gauguin*, 1889), Henri Rousseau (1890) and Pablo Picasso (1907). Modern German and Austrian painting is also on show, with works by Gustav Klimt and Egon Schiele. The *Dance of Life*, by Norwegian Edvard Munch, is considered greatly influential upon Czech avant-garde art.

Commerce by Otto Gutfreund (1923), Trades Fair Palace

The other main venue for European art is the **Picture Gallery of Prague Castle**, which focuses on European painters of the 16th to 18th centuries. As well as Titian's superb *The Toilet of a Young Lady*, there are also works in the collection by Rubens and Tintoretto.

MUSIC

Two CZECH composers merit their own museums, as does Prague's much-loved visitor, Mozart. The **Smetana Museum**, **Dvořák Museum** and **Mozart Museum** all contain personal memorabilia, musical scores and correspondence. In the summer, concerts are held on the terrace of the Mozart Museum.

The Museum of Musical Instruments is in the process of finding new quarters. Seek it out if you can; it has many rare and historic instruments, and scores by composers such as Josef Haydn.

HISTORY

The HISTORICAL collections of the **National Museum** are held at the main Wenceslas Square building, and at Prague Castle. Of special interest in the former are displays which trace the development of Czech theatre. The artefacts at Prague Castle are housed in **Lobkowicz Palace** and focus on Czech life and culture.

Bohemian Baroque glass goblet (1730), Museum of Decorative Arts

The **Prague Museum** centres on the history of the city, with period rooms, historical prints and a model of Prague in the 19th century, made of paper and wood by the lithographer Antonín Langweil.

A branch of the museum at Výtoň, on the banks of the Vltava, depicts the way of life of a former settlement. Another at Vyšehrad records the history of this royal seat.

The exquisite Renaissance building of **Schwarzenberg Palace** is a fine setting for the battle charts, weaponry, uniforms and regalia of the Museum of Military History.

The Jewish Museum is made up of various sites in the Jewish Quarter, including the **High Synagogue**, **Maisel Synagogue** and the **Old Jewish Cemetery**. Among its collections are holy artefacts taken from other Jewish communities and brought to Prague by the Nazis as part of a chilling plan for a museum of "an extinct race". Another moving display is of drawings by children imprisoned in the Terezín concentration camp.

DECORATIVE ARTS

With GLASSWARE spanning centuries, from medieval to modern, porcelain and pewterware, furniture and textiles, books and posters, the **Museum of Decorative Arts** in the Jewish Quarter is one of Prague's best, but only a small selection of its holdings is on show. Look out for specialized temporary exhibitions mounted either at the museum itself or at other venues in Prague.

Many other museums have examples of the decorative arts, ranging from grandiose monstrances – including one with 6,222 diamonds – in the treasury of **The Loreto** to simple everyday furnishings in the **Prague Museum**. There is also a fascinating collection of pre-Columbian artefacts from Central America in the **Náprstek Museum**.

16th-century astrolabe from the National Technical Museum

SCIENCE AND TECHNOLOGY

A VAST EXHIBITION hall holds the transport section of the **National Technical Museum**. Ranks of vintage cars, motorcycles and steam engines fill the space, and over them hang examples of early flying machines. Other sections trace the progress of sciences such as electronics. Visitors can even tour a reconstruction of a coal mine. As befits the city where Tycho Brahe and Johannes Kepler studied the stars, there is a fascinating astronomy exhibition.

Prague's Best: Churches and Synagogues

THE RELIGIOUS BUILDINGS of Prague vividly record
the city's changing architectural styles, and
many are treasure houses of religious art.
But they also reflect Prague's times of
religious and political strife, the lives of
its people, its setbacks and growth as
a city. This map features highlights of
their architecture and art, with a more
detailed overview on pages 44–5.

St George's Basilica
*St George, sword raised to slay the
dragon, is portrayed in this late-Gothic
relief, set above the doorway of the magnificent early Renaissance south portal.*

St Vitus's Cathedral
*The jewel of the cathedral is the
Chapel of St Wenceslas. Its walls
are decorated with semi-precious
stones, gilding and frescoes. Elizabeth of Pomerania, the fourth
and last wife of Charles IV, is
shown at prayer in the fresco
above the Gothic altar.*

*Prague Castle
and Hradčany*

The Loreto
*This shrine to the
Virgin Mary
has been a
place of
pilgrimage
since 1626.
Each hour,
its Baroque
clock tower
chimes a
hymn on the
carillon of 27 bells.*

Little Quarter

V L T A V A

Church of St Thomas
*The skeleton of the martyr St Just
rests in a glass coffin below
a Crucifixion by
Antonín Stevens,
one of several
superb works
of religious art
in this church.*

**Church of
St Nicholas**
*In the heart of the
Little Quarter, this
is Prague's finest
example of High
Baroque. The dome
over the high altar
is so lofty that early
worshippers feared
it would collapse.*

Church of Our Lady before Týn

Set back behind a row of arcaded buildings, the many-spired twin towers of the church dominate the eastern end of Old Town Square. The Gothic, Renaissance and Baroque features of the interior create striking contrasts.

Old-New Synagogue

Prague's oldest synagogue dates from the 13th century. Its Gothic main portal is carved with a vine which bears twelve bunches of grapes symbolizing the tribes of Israel.

Jewish
Quarter

Old Town

Church of St James

Consecrated in 1374, this church was restored to new Baroque glory after a fire in 1689. Typical of its grandeur is this 18th-century monument to chancellor Jan Vratislav of Mitrovice. Fine acoustics and a superb organ make the church a popular venue for concerts.

Slavonic Monastery

These cloisters hold a series of precious frescoes from three Gothic masters depicting scenes from the Old and New Testaments.

New Town

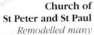

| 0 metres | 500 |
| 0 yards | 500 |

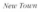

Church of St Peter and St Paul

Remodelled many times since the 11th century, the design of this church is now 1890s Neo-Gothic. This striking relief of the Last Judgment marks the main entrance.

Exploring Churches and Synagogues

Altar, Capuchin Monastery

Religious building began in Prague in the 9th century, reaching its zenith during the reign of Charles IV *(see pp24–5)*. The remains of an 11th-century synagogue have been found, but during the 19th-century clearance of the overcrowded Jewish ghetto three synagogues were lost. Many churches were damaged during the Hussite rebellions *(see pp26–7)*. The political regime of the 20th century also took its toll, but now churches and synagogues are slowly being reclaimed and restored, with many open to visitors.

High, Gothic windows at the east end of St Vitus's Cathedral

ROMANESQUE

Three reasonably well-preserved Romanesque rotundas, dating from the 11th and 12th centuries, still exist in Prague. The oldest is the **St Martin's Rotunda**; the others are the rotundas of the Holy Rood and of St Longinus. All three are tiny, with naves only 6 m (20 ft) in diameter.

By far the best-preserved and most important Romanesque church is **St George's Basilica**, founded in 920 by Prince Vratislav I. Extensive reconstruction was carried out after a fire in 1142, but its chancel, with some exquisite frescoes on its vaulting, is a Late-Romanesque gem.

The **Strahov Monastery**, founded in 1142 by Prince Vladislav II *(see pp22–3)*, has retained its Romanesque core in spite of fire, wars and extensive renovation.

GOTHIC

Gothic architecture, with its ribbed vaulting, flying buttresses and pointed arches, reached Bohemia in about 1230 and was soon adopted into religious architecture.

The first religious building in Gothic style was **St Agnes's Convent**, founded in 1233 by Wenceslas I's sister, Agnes. Prague's oldest synagogue, the **Old-New Synagogue**, built in 1270, is rather different in style to the churches but nevertheless is still a superb example of Early-Gothic.

The best example of Prague Gothic is **St Vitus's Cathedral**. Its fine tracery and towering

11th-century Romanesque Rotunda of St Martin in Vyšehrad

nave epitomize the style. Other notable Gothic churches are **Our Lady before Týn** and **Our Lady of the Snows**.

Important for its historical significance is the reconstructed Gothic **Bethlehem Chapel** where Jan Hus *(see p27)* preached for 10 years.

The superb Gothic frescoes found in abundance at the **Slavonic Monastery**, were badly damaged in World War II, but have been restored.

RENAISSANCE

In the 1530s the influence of Italian artists living in Prague sparked the city's Renaissance movement. The style is more clearly seen in secular than religious building. The Late-Renaissance period, under Rudolph II (1576–1611), offers the best remaining examples.

DOMES AND SPIRES

The domes and spires of Prague's churches are the city's main landmarks, as the view from the many vantage points will confirm. You will see a variety of spires, towers and domes: Gothic and Neo-Gothic soar skywards, while Baroque often have rounded cupolas and onion domes. The modern top of the 14th-century Slavonic Monastery, added after the church was struck in a World War II air raid, is a rare example of modernist religious architecture in Prague. Its sweeping, intersecting twin spires are a bold reinterpretation of Gothic themes, and a striking addition to the city's skyline.

Gothic

Church of Our Lady before Týn (1350–1511)

Baroque

Church of St Nicholas in th Little Quarter (1750)

The **High Synagogue** and the **Pinkas Synagogue** retain strong elements of the style: the former in its 1586 exterior, the latter in the reworking of an original Gothic building.

The Church of St Roch in the **Strahov Monastery** is probably the best example of Late-Renaissance "Mannerism".

Renaissance-influenced vaulting, Pinkas Synagogue (1535)

BAROQUE

The COUNTER-REFORMATION (*see pp30–31*) inspired the building of new churches and the revamping of existing ones for a period of 150 years. Prague's first Baroque church was **Our Lady Victorious**, built in 1611–13. **St Nicholas** in the Little Quarter took almost 60 years to build. Its lush interior and frescoed vault make it Prague's most important Baroque building, followed by **The Loreto** (1626–1750), adjoining the **Capuchin Monastery**. The father-and-son team, Christoph and Kilian Ignaz Dientzenhofer designed both buildings, and **St John on the Rock** and **St Nicholas** in the Old Town.

A special place in Prague's history was occupied by the Jesuit **Clementinum**. This influential university's church was the **Holy Saviour**. The Baroque style is closely linked with Jesuit teachings: Kilian Ignaz Dientzenhofer was educated here.

Klausen Synagogue (now the Jewish Museum) was built in 1689 with Baroque stuccoed barrel vaults.

Many early buildings were given Baroque facelifts. The Gothic nave of **St Thomas** has Baroque vaulting, and the once-Gothic **St James** went Baroque after a fire in 1689.

19th-century Neo-Gothic portal, Church of St Peter and St Paul

NEO-GOTHIC

During the height of the 19th-century Gothic Revival (*see pp32–3*), **St Vitus's Cathedral** was completed, in accordance with the original Gothic plan. Work by Josef Mocker, the movement's leader, aroused controversy but his **St Peter and St Paul** at Vyšehrad is a well-loved landmark. The triple-naved basilica of **St Ludmilla** in Náměstí Míru was also designed by Mocker.

Nave ceiling of the Church of St Nicholas in the Little Quarter

Baroque Neo-Gothic

Loreto (1725) St Peter and St Paul (1903)

Modernist

Slavonic Monastery (1967)

Prague's Best: Palaces and Gardens

P RAGUE'S PALACES and gardens are among the most important historical and architectural monuments in the city. Many palaces house museums or galleries *(see pp38–41)*, and some are concert venues.

The gardens range from formal, walled oases with fountains and grand statuary, to open spaces beyond the city centre. This map features some of the best palaces and gardens, with a detailed overview on pages 48–9.

Belvedere
The Singing Fountain (1568) stands in front of the exquisite Renaissance summer palace.

Royal Garden
Though redesigned in the 19th century, the Renaissance garden preserves much of its original character. Historic statues still in place include a pair of Baroque lions (1730) guarding the entrance.

Prague Castle and Hradčany

0 metres	500
0 yards	500

Little Quarter

South Gardens
Starting life as the Castle's defensive bastions, these gardens afford a wonderful view of Prague. First laid out as a park in 1891, their present design was landscaped by Josip Plečnik 40 years later.

Wallenstein Palace
Built in 1624–30 for Duke Albrecht of Wallenstein, this vast Baroque palace was intended to outshine Prague Castle. Over 20 houses and a town gate were demolished to make room for the palace and garden. This Fountain of Venus (1599), stands in front of the arches of the sala terrena.

Wallenstein Garden
The garden statues are copies of 17th-century bronzes. The originals were plundered by the Swedes in 1648.

Kolowrat-Černín Garden
In the Baroque period, several palace gardens with spectacular terraces were laid out on the hillside below Prague Castle.

Golz-Kinský Palace
The Kinský coat of arms adorns the pink and white stuccoed façade designed by Kilian Ignaz Dientzenhofer. The Rococo palace is now part of the National Gallery.

Jewish Quarter

V L T A V A

Clam-Gallas Palace
Four giant statues of Hercules (c1715) by Matthias Bernard Braun show the hero straining to support the weight of the massive Baroque front portals of the palace.

Old Town

Michna Summer Palace
This charming villa was designed by Kilian Ignaz Dientzenhofer in 1712. It now houses the Dvořák Museum. The garden's sculptural decorations are from the workshop of Antonín Braun.

New Town

Kampa Island
A tranquil waterside park was created on the island after the destruction of its original gardens in World War II.

Exploring the Palaces and Gardens

PRAGUE BOASTS an amazing number of palaces and gardens, spanning centuries. Comparatively few palaces were lost to the ravages of war. Instead, they tended to evolve in style during restoration or enlargement. Palace gardens became fashionable in the 17th century, but could only be laid out where there was space, such as below Prague Castle. More vulnerable to change, most have been reland-scaped several times. In the 19th century, and again after 1989, many of the larger parks and private gardens were opened up to the public.

Statue on Kampa Island

MEDIEVAL PALACES

THE OLDEST PALACE in Prague is the **Royal Palace** at Prague Castle. In the basement is the Romanesque ground floor, started in about 1135. It has been rebuilt many times, particularly between the 14th and 16th centuries. The heart of the Palace, Vladislav Hall, dates from the 1490s and is late Gothic in structure. Less well known is the **Palace of the Lords of Kunštát**. Here,

the vaulted ground floor of the 13th-century building survives as the basement of a later Gothic structure.

RENAISSANCE PALACES

ONE OF THE most beautiful Renaissance buildings in Prague is the 16th-century **Schwarzenberg Palace**. The work of Italian architects, its façade is entirely covered with geometric, two-tone *sgraffito* designs. Italians also

Bronze Singing Fountain in the Royal Garden by the Belvedere

worked on the **Belvedere**. Its graceful arcades and columns, all covered with rich reliefs, make this one of the finest Renaissance buildings north of the Alps. The **Martinic Palace**, built in 1563, was the first example of late-Renaissance building in Prague. Soon after came the **Lobkowicz Palace**. Its terracotta relief-decorated windows and plaster *sgraffito* have survived later Baroque modifications. The huge **Archbishop's Palace** was given a later Rococo façade over its Renaissance structure.

BAROQUE PALACES

MANY PALACES were built in the Baroque style, and examples of all its phases still exist in Prague. A handsome, if ostentatious, early Baroque

Southern façade of Troja Palace and its formal gardens

DECORATIVE PORTALS AND GATES

The elaborate gates and portals of Prague's palaces are among the most beautiful and impressive architectural features in the city. Gothic and Renaissance portals have often survived, even where the buildings them-selves have been destroyed or modified by renovations in a later architectural style. The period of most prolific building was the Baroque, and distinctive portals from this time can be seen framing many a grand entrance around the city. Statues of giants, heroes and mythological figures are often depicted holding up the doorways. These were not merely decorative but acted as an integral element of support.

Gateway to Court of Honour of Prague Castle (1768)

example is the **Wallenstein Palace**. Similar ostentation is evident in the **Černín Palace**, one of Prague's most monumental buildings. The mid-Baroque had two strands, one opulent and Italianate, the other formal and French or Viennese in influence. **Troja Palace** and **Michna Summer Palace** are in Italian villa style while the **Sternberg Palace** on Hradčanské náměstí is more Viennese in style. Troja was designed in 1679 by Jean-Baptiste Mathey, who, like the Dientzenhofers (*see p129*), was a master of the Baroque. The pairs of giants on the portals of the **Clam-Gallas Palace**, and the **Morzin Palace** in Nerudova Street, are a popular Baroque motif. The **Golz-Kinský Palace** is a superb Rococo design by Kilian Ignaz Dientzenhofer.

GARDENS

Tʜᴇ ꜰɪɴᴇꜱᴛ of Prague's palace gardens, such as the **Wallenstein Garden**, are in the Little Quarter. Though the style of Wallenstein Palace is Early Baroque, the garden still displays the geometric formality of the Renaissance, also preserved in the **Royal Garden** behind Prague Castle. The **South Gardens** on the Castle's old ramparts were redesigned in the 1920s.

Many more gardens were laid out in the 17th and 18th centuries, when noble families vied with each other to have fine winter residences in the Little Quarter below the Castle. Many are now the grounds of embassies, but others have been opened to the public. The **Ledebour Garden** has been combined with two neighbouring gardens. Laid out on a steep hillside, the **Kolowrat-Černín Garden**, in particular, makes ingenious use of pavilions, stairs and terraces from which there are wonderful views of the city. The **Vrtba Garden**, landscaped on the site of former vineyards, is a similar Baroque creation with statues and splendid views. Former palace gardens were also used to create a park on **Kampa Island**.

The many old gardens and orchards on Petřín Hill have

Ancient trees in Stromovka

been transformed into the large public area of **Petřín Park**. Another former orchard is **Vojan Park**, laid out by archbishops in the 13th century. The **Botanical Gardens** are one of the few areas of green open to the public in the New Town.

Generally, the larger parks are situated further out of the city. **Stromovka** was a royal deer park, while **Letná Park** was developed in 1858 on the open space of Letná Plain.

The Royal Garden of Prague Castle, planted with spring flowers

Troja Palace (c1703)

Clam-Gallas Palace (c1714)

PRAGUE THROUGH THE YEAR

SPRINGTIME in Prague sees the city burst into colour as its gardens start to bloom. Celebrations begin with the Prague Spring Music Festival. In summer, visitors are entertained by street performers and the city's glorious gardens come into their own. When the weather begins to turn cooler, Prague hosts the International Jazz Festival.

Painted Easter egg

The year often draws to a close with snow on the streets. The ball season starts in December, and in the coldest months, most events are held indoors. At Prague Castle, an all-year-round attraction is the changing of the guard around midday. For details of activities, check the listings magazines *(see p219)* or the Prague Information Service *(see p218)*.

Concert at Wallenstein Palace during the Prague Spring Music Festival

SPRING

As PRAGUE SEES its first rays of spring sunshine, the city comes alive. A mass of colours, blooms and cultural events makes this one of the most exciting times of the year to visit. The city's blossoming parks and gardens open their gates again, after the colder months of winter. During April the temperatures rise and an entertainment programme begins – dominated by the Prague Spring Music Festival.

EASTER

Easter Monday *(dates vary)* is a public holiday. Easter is observed as a religious holiday but it is also associated with a bizarre pagan ritual in which Czech men beat their women with willow sticks in order to keep them fertile during the coming year. The women retaliate by throwing water over their male tormentors. Peace is finally restored when the women present the men with a painted egg. Church services are held during the entire Easter period *(see p227)*.

MARCH

The Prague-Prčice March *(third Saturday of March)*. Thousands of people set out to walk from the city centre to the small town of Prčice, to the southwest of the city, in celebration of spring.

APRIL

Boat trips *(1 April)*. A number of boats begin trips up and down the Vltava.
Witch-burning *(30 April)*, at

the Exhibition Ground *(see p176)*. Concerts accompany this 500-year-old tradition where old brooms are burnt on bonfires, in a symbolic act to rid nature of evil spirits.

MAY

Labour Day *(1 May)*. Public holiday celebrated with numerous cultural events.
Opening day of Prague's gardens *(1 May)*. Regular summer concerts are held in many parks and gardens.
Anniversary of Prague Uprising *(5 May)*. At noon sirens are sounded for one minute. Flowers are laid at the commemorative plaques of those who died *(see p34)*.
Day of Liberation from Fascism *(8 May)*. Public holiday for VE day. Wreaths are laid on the graves of soldiers at Olšany cemeteries.
Prague International Book Fair *(second week in May)*, Palace of Culture *(see p176)*. The best of Czech and international authors.

THE PRAGUE SPRING MUSIC FESTIVAL

This international festival presents a busy programme of concerts, ballet and opera from 12 May to 1 June. Music lovers can hear a huge selection of music played by some of the best musicians in the world. The main venue is the Rudolfinum *(see p84)* but others include churches and palaces – some of which are only open to the public on these occasions. The festival begins on the anniversary of Bedřich Smetana's death *(see p79)*. A service is held at his grave in Vyšehrad *(see p178)*, and in the evening there is a concert at the Municipal House *(see p64)* where musicians perform his most famous work, *Má Vlast* (My Country). The festival also ends here, with Beethoven's Ninth Symphony.

Bedřich Smetana

Average Daily Hours of Sunshine

Sunshine Chart
Prague's longest and hottest days fall between May and August. At the height of summer, daylight starts at 5am. The snow-covered city looks stunning on a sunny winter's day. But sunny days can be spoiled by thick smog (see p53).

Czechs and tourists enjoying the beauty of Vyšehrad Park on a sunny afternoon

Summer

SUMMER arrives with high temperatures, frequent, sometimes heavy, showers and thousands of visitors. This is a beautiful, if busy, time to visit. Every weekend, Czechs set out for the country to go hiking in the surrounding hills or stay in country cottages. Those remaining in Prague visit the reservoirs and lakes *(see p213)*, just outside the city to try and escape the heat. There is a wealth of entertainment on offer as culture moves into the open air taking over the squares, streets and gardens. Street performers, buskers and classical orchestras all help to keep visitors entertained. Many cafés have tables outside allowing you to quench your thirst while watching the fun.

June

Mayoral Boat Race *(first weekend in June)*. Rowing races are held on the river Vltava, just below Vyšehrad.

Summer Concerts *(throughout the summer)*. Prague's gardens *(see pp46–9)* are the attractive and popular setting for a large number of free classical and brass-band concerts. One of the most famous, and spectacular, outdoor classical concerts is held by Křižík Fountain at the Exhibition Ground *(see p162)*. Full orchestras play to the stunning backdrop of coloured lights and water, synchronized to the music by computer.

Anniversary of the Murder of Reinhard Heydrich's Assassins *(18 June)*. A mass is held in remembrance at the Church of St Cyril and St Methodius *(see p152)* for those who died there.

Golden Prague *(first week of June)*, Kaiserstein Palace. International TV festival of prize-winning programmes.

Battle Re-enactments *(throughout summer)*, held in Prague's palaces and gardens.

Mozart's Prague *(mid-June to first week in July)*. Celebration of Mozart. International orchestras perform his works at Bertramka *(see p160)* and Lichtenstein Palace.

Dance Prague *(last week in June)*. An international festival of contemporary dance at the National Theatre *(see p156)*.

July

Remembrance of the Slavonic Missionaries *(5 July)*. Public holiday in honour of St Cyril and St Methodius *(see p152)*.

Anniversary of Jan Hus's Death *(6 July)*. A public holiday when flowers are laid on his memorial *(see pp26–7)*.

August

Theatre Island *(all of August)*, Střelecký Island. Czech theatre and puppet festival.

Changing of the Guard at Prague Castle

AVERAGE MONTHLY RAINFALL

Rainfall Chart
Prague has plenty of rain throughout the year. The wettest months are October and November, but there are frequent light showers in the summer months as well. Winter snowfalls can be quite heavy, but they are rarely severe.

AUTUMN

WHEN THE GARDENS below Prague Castle take on the shades of red and gold, and visitors start to leave, the city gets ready for the cold winter months. This is also the traditional mushroom-gathering season when you encounter people with baskets full of freshly-picked mushrooms. Market places are flooded with fruit and vegetables. The tree-lined slopes above the Vltava take on the beautiful colours of autumn. September and October still have a fair number of warm and sunny days, although November often sees the first snowfalls. Football fans fill the stadiums and the popular steeplechase course at Pardubice reverberates to the cheers of fans.

A view of St Vitus's Cathedral through autumn trees

SEPTEMBER

Prague Autumn *(early September)*, at the Rudolfinum *(see p84)*. An international classical music festival.
The Autumn Fair *(dates vary)*, at the Exhibition Ground *(see p176)*. Fairground, stalls, food and drink, theatrical and puppet shows and musical performances of all kinds.
Kite competitions *(third Sunday in September)*, on Letná Plain in front of Sparta Stadium. Very popular competition for children but open to anyone with a kite.
Bohemia Championship *(last Sunday in September)*. A 10-km (6-mile) road race which has been run since 1887. Starts from Běchovice, a suburb of Prague and ends in Žižkov. Open to people of all ages and levels of experience.

Jazz musicians playing at the International Jazz Festival

OCTOBER

The Great Pardubice Steeplechase *(second Sunday in October)*, held at Pardubice, east of Prague. This horse race has been run since 1874 and is considered to be the most difficult in Europe.
Velká Kunratická *(second Sunday in October)*. Popular, but gruelling, cross-country race in Kunratice forest. Anyone can enter.
The Locking of the Vltava *(early October)*. Symbolic conclusion of the water sports season, during which the Vltava is locked with a key until the arrival of spring.
International Jazz Festival *(date varies)*, Lucerna Palace. A famous jazz festival, held since 1964, attracts musicians from around the world.
The Day of the Republic *(28 October)*. Despite the splitting up of Czechoslovakia into two separate republics, the founding of the country in 1918 is still a public holiday.

NOVEMBER

Celebration of the Velvet Revolution *(17 November)*. Peaceful demonstrations take place around Wenceslas Square *(see pp144–5)*.

AVERAGE MONTHLY TEMPERATURE

Temperature Chart
The chart shows the average minimum and maximum temperatures for each month in Prague. The summer usually remains comfortably warm, while the winter months can get bitterly cold and temperatures often drop below freezing.

WINTER

IF YOU ARE lucky enough to catch Prague the morning after a snowfall with the sun shining, the effect is magical. The view over the Little Quarter rooftops with their pristine white covering is a memorable sight. Unfortunately Prague is rarely at its best during the winter months. The weather is changeable. Foggy days with temperatures just above freezing can quickly go down to -5° C (23° F). Pollution and Prague's geographical position in the Vltava basin, lead to smog being trapped just above the city.

As if to try and make up for the winter weather's shortcomings, the theatre season reaches its climax and there are a number of premieres. Balls and dances are held in these cold months. Just before Christmas Eve large barrels containing live carp – which is the traditional Czech Christmas delicacy – appear on the streets. Christmas trees adorn the city, and carol singers can be heard on street

View of the Little Quarter rooftops covered in snow

corners. Christmas mass is held in most churches and New Year's Eve is celebrated, in time-honoured style, throughout the entire city.

DECEMBER

Christmas markets *(throughout December)*, Můstek metro station, 28. října, Na příkopě, Old Town Square. Stalls sell Christmas decorations, gifts, hot wine, punch and the traditional Czech carp *(see p207)*.
Christmas Eve, Christmas Day and Boxing Day *(24, 25 and 26 December)*. Public holidays. Mass is held in churches throughout the city.
Swimming competitions in the Vltava *(26 December)*. Hundreds of hardened and determined swimmers gather together at the Vltava to swim in temperatures of around 3° C (37° F).
New Year celebrations *(31 December)*. Thousands of people congregate around Wenceslas Square.

JANUARY

New Year's Day
(1 January). Public holiday.

FEBRUARY

Dances and Balls
(early February).
Matthew Fair *(end of February to beginning of April)*, the Exhibition Ground *(see p176)*. Fairground, stalls and various entertainments.

Barrels of the traditional Christmas delicacy, carp, on sale in Prague

---

PUBLIC HOLIDAYS

New Year's Day (1 January); **Easter Monday**; **Labour Day** (1 May); **Day of Liberation from Fascism** (8 May); **Remembrance of the Slavonic Missionaries** (5 July); **Anniversary of Jan Hus's death** (6 July); **Day of the Republic** (28 October); **Christmas Eve, Christmas Day and Boxing Day** (24–26 December).

A RIVER VIEW
OF PRAGUE

THE VLTAVA RIVER has played a vital part in the city's history *(see pp20–21)* and has provided inspiration for artists, poets and musicians throughout the centuries.

Up until the 19th century, parts of the city were exposed to the danger of heavy flooding. To try and alleviate the problem, the river's embankments have been strengthened and raised many times, in order to try to prevent the water penetrating too far (the foundations of today's embankments are made of stone or concrete). During the Middle Ages, year after year of disastrous flooding led to the decision to bury the areas affected under 2 m (6 ft) of earth to try to minimize the damage. Although this strategy was only partially effective, it meant that the ground floors of many Romanesque and Gothic buildings were preserved and can still be seen today *(see pp78–9)*. Despite its destructive side, the Vltava has provided a vital method of transport for the city, as well as a source of income. As technology improved, the river became increasingly important; water mills, weirs and water towers were built. In 1912 a large hydroelectric power plant was built on Štvanice Island, supplying almost a third of Prague's electricity. To make the river navigable, eight dams, a large canal and weirs were constructed along the Slapy-Prague-Mělník stretch, where the Vltava flows into the river Elbe. For the visitor, an excursion on one of the many boats, paddle steamers and even a Chinese junk that travel up and down the river, is well worth it. River trips run daily in the summer months. There are trips to Troja *(see pp166–7)* and as far as Slapy Lake. Catching a boat from one of the piers on the river is one of the best ways of seeing the city and its surrounding countryside.

Statues on the wrought-iron Čechův Bridge

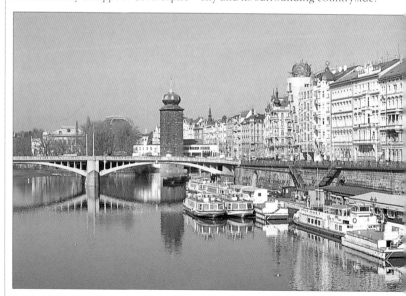

A view of the steamboat landing stage (přístaviště parníků) on Rašínovo nábřeží

Prague Castle dominates the view along the river. Here it is seen from the boarding point at Na Františku, on the right bank of the Vltava.

Stanice parníků Holešovice

Stanice parníků

See next page

Prague Castle and Hradčany

Little Quarter

Jewish Quarter

Old Town

New Town

Stanice parníků Kampa

Přístaviště parníků (Paroplavební)

0 kilometres 1

0 miles 0.5

KEY

■ Route

• • River boat boarding point

TOURS

There are frequent trips on the Vltava throughout the summer (April to the end of September). Tours range from trips to Troja Palace in the north of Prague and as far away as Slapy Lake in the south. Dining on board while slowly floating through the city centre is another popular option. These trips can be booked in advance at one of the tour companies. Alternatively, you can go directly to one of the river boat boarding points (see left) and buy tickets for one of the many private ships that land here. (Paroplavební pier is where most trips start.) The cost of each trip varies, depending on the vessel and the length of the excursion, but there are trips to suit almost every budget.

Akasi
Václavské náměstí 47..
Map 4 D5.
☎ 24 823 61 18.
FAX 24 23 72 35.

Thomas Cook
Národní 28.
Map 3 B5.
☎ 21 10 53 71.

Paroplavební (pier)
Rašínovo nábřeží přístaviště.
Map 5 A2.
☎ 29 83 09 /
29 38 03.
FAX 24 91 38 62.

The former municipal pool by Čechův most, on nábřeží Edvarda Beneše, is now the boarding point for the Chinese junk, Excess.

Prague River Trip

Taking a trip on the Vltava gives you a unique view of many of the city's historic monuments. Although the left bank was the site of the first Slavic settlement in the 9th century, it was the right bank, heavily populated by merchants and traders, that developed into a thriving and bustling commercial centre, and the tradition continues today. The left bank was never developed as intensively and much of it is still an oasis of parks and gardens. The river's beauty is enhanced by the numbers of swans which have made it their home.

Hanavský Pavilion
This flamboyant cast iron staircase is part of a pavilion built by Zdeněk Fiala for the Jubilee Exhibition of 1891.

Little Quarter Bridge Towers
The smaller tower was built in 1158 to guard the entrance to the original Judith Bridge, while the larger one was built on the site of an old Romanesque tower in 1464 (see p136).

Vltava Weir
The thickly-wooded slopes of Petřín Hill tower above one of several weirs on the Vltava. During the 19th century this weir, along with others on this stretch, were built to make the river navigable to ships.

The Vltava Statue on the northern tip of Children's Island is where, every year, wreaths are placed in memory of the drowned.

Little Quarter Water Tower
Built in 1560, the tower supplied river water to 57 fountains throughout the Little Quarter.

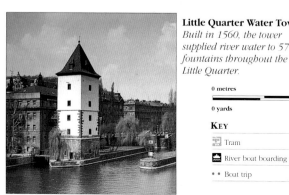

Map labels:
Karlův most
Kampa
stanice parníků Kampa
Grand Priory Mill
most Legií
Střelecký ostrov
Plavební Kanál
Jiráskův most
Palackého most
Apartment buildings of Art Nouveau design
Železniční most

0 metres		500
0 yards		500

Key

🚋 Tram

⚓ River boat boarding point

• • Boat trip

To Troja

stanice parníků

Rudolfinum
This allegorical statue of music by Antonín Wagner is one of two which decorate the imposing entrance to the Neo-Renaissance concert hall (see p84).

Cechův most

Iánesův most

The Clementinum, a former Jesuit college, is one of the largest buildings in the city *(see p79).*

The Old Town Bridge Tower was built as part of the city's 14th-century fortifications *(see p139).*

Smetana Museum

Weir

National Theatre
This symbol of the Czech revival, with its spectacularly-decorated roof, has dominated the skyline of the right bank since the 1860s (see pp156–7).

The Šítka Tower, with its late-18th-century Baroque roof, was originally built in 1495 and pumped water to the New Town.

Slovanský ostrov

"Ginger and Fred" Building
This charming, quirky office building is home to the stylish Perle de Prague restaurant (see p203).

The Memorial to František Palacký commemorates the life of this eminent 19th-century Czech historian and was built in 1905.

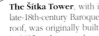

přístaviště parníků

Výtoň Excise House
The coat of arms on this 16th-century house – built to collect duty on timber transported along the river – is of the New Town from 1671.

The Na Slovanech Monastery was built in 1347 by Charles IV. Its two modern steeples are easily recognizable from the river.

Church of St Peter and St Paul
The Neo-Gothic steeples on this much-rebuilt church were designed by František Mikeš and erected in 1903. They are the dominant feature of Vyšehrad rock (see pp178–9).

PRAGUE AREA BY AREA

OLD TOWN

STARÉ MĚSTO

THE HEART OF the city is the Old Town and its central square. In the 11th century the settlements around the Castle spread to the right bank of the Vltava. A marketplace in what is now Old Town Square (Staroměstské náměstí) was mentioned for the first time in 1091. Houses and churches quickly sprang

Physician, Jan Marek (1595–1667)

up around the square, determining the random network of streets, many of which survive to this day. The area gained the privileges of a town in the 13th century, and, in 1338, a Town Hall. This and other great buildings, such as Clam-Gallas Palace and the importance of the Old Town.

SIGHTS AT A GLANCE

Churches
Church of St James ❹
Church of Our Lady before Týn ❽
Church of St Nicholas ⓫
Church of St Gall ⓮
Church of St Martin in the Wall ⓯
Church of St Giles ⓱
Bethlehem Chapel ⓲

Museums and Galleries
Náprstek Museum ⓰
Smetana Museum ㉔

Historic Streets and Squares
Celetná Street ❸
Old Town Square pp66–9 ❼
Mariánské Square ⓴
Charles Street ㉑
Knights of the Cross Square ㉕

Historic Monuments and Buildings
Powder Gate ❶
Municipal House ❷
Carolinum ❻
Jan Hus Monument ❿
Old Town Hall pp72–4 ⓬
House at the Two Golden Bears ⓭
Clementinum ㉓

Theatres
Estates Theatre ❺

Palaces
Golz-Kinský Palace ❾
Clam-Gallas Palace ⓳
Palace of the Lords of Kunštát ㉒

GETTING THERE
Můstek on metro lines A and B and Staroměstská on line A are both handy for the area. Trams do not cross the Old Town, but from Charles Bridge or Náměstí Republiky it is only a short walk to Old Town Square and the other sights.

KEY
Street-by-Street map
See pp62–3

Street-by-Street map
See pp76–7

Tram stop

P Parking

0 metres 250
0 yards 250

◁ **Café tables and strolling pedestrians in Old Town Square**

Street-by-Street: Old Town (East)

FREE OF TRAFFIC (except for a few horse-drawn carriages) and ringed with historic buildings, Prague's Old Town Square (Staroměstské náměstí) ranks among the finest public spaces in any city. Streets like Celetná and Ovocný trh are also pedestrianized. In summer, café tables spill out onto the cobbles, and though the area draws tourists by the thousands, the unique atmosphere has not yet been destroyed.

Golz-Kinský Palace
This stunning Rococo palace now serves as an art gallery **9**

Church of St Nicholas
The imposing façade of this Baroque church dominates one corner of Old Town Square **11**

STAROMĚSTSKÉ NÁMĚSTÍ

★ Old Town Square
This late-19th-century watercolour by Václav Jansa shows how little the Square has changed in 100 years **7**

MALÉ NÁMĚSTÍ

Jan Hus Monument
Religious reformer Hus is a symbol of integrity, and the monument brings together the highest and lowest points in Czech history **10**

U Rotta is a former iron-monger's shop, decorated with colourful paintings by the 19th-century artist Mikuláš Aleš.

House at the Two Golden Bears
The carved Renaissance portal is the finest of its kind in Prague **13**

★ Old Town Hall
The famous astronomical clock draws a crowd of visitors every hour **12**

The Štorch house has painted decoration based on designs by Mikuláš Aleš showing St Wenceslas on horseback.

0 metres	100
0 yards	100

KEY

– – – Suggested route

Church of Our Lady before Týn
The church's Gothic steeples are the Old Town's most distinctive landmark ❽

LOCATOR MAP
See Street Finder, maps 3–4

JEWISH QUARTER

OLD TOWN

NEW TOWN

Church of St James
This wooden Pietà, on the main altar, was made in the 15th century ❹

★ **Municipal House**
This Art Nouveau building is a popular concert venue ❷

Powder Gate
This much-restored Gothic gate is a relic of when there was a royal palace here at the entrance to the Old Town ❶

House at the Black Madonna

Estates Theatre
The theatre featured in director Miloš Forman's film Amadeus ❺

Ovocný trh was Prague's fruit market.

Celetná Street
This ornamental Baroque plaque is the sign of the House at the Black Sun ❸

Carolinum
A magnificently carved Oriel window projects from the oldest surviving part of the Carolinum university – founded by Charles IV in the 14th century ❻

STAR SIGHTS

★ **Old Town Square**

★ **Old Town Hall**

★ **Municipal House**

Powder Gate ❶
PRAŠNÁ BRÁNA

Náměstí Republiky. **Map** 4 D3.
Ⓜ *Náměstí Republiky.* 🚊 *5, 14,
26.* **Open** *Apr–Oct: 10am–6pm daily.*

Tʜᴇʀᴇ ʜᴀs ʙᴇᴇɴ a gate here
since the 11th century,
when it formed one of the 13
entrances to the Old Town.
In 1475, King Vladislav II laid
the foundation stone of the
New Tower, as it was to be
known. A coronation gift
from the city council, the
gate was modelled on Peter
Parler's Old Town bridge
tower built a century earlier.
The gate had little defensive
value; its rich sculptural
decoration was intended to
add prestige to the adjacent
palace of the Royal Court.
Building was halted eight
years later when the king
had to flee because of riots.
On his return in 1485 he
opted for the safety of the
Castle. Kings never again
occupied the Royal Court.

    The gate acquired its
present name when it was
used to store gunpowder in
the 17th century. The
sculptural decoration, badly
damaged during the Prussian
occupation in 1757 and mostly
removed soon afterwards,
was replaced in 1876.

**The Powder Gate viewed from
outside the Old Town**

Karel Špillar's mosaic *Homage to Prague* on Municipal House's façade

Municipal House ❷
OBECNÍ DŮM

Náměstí Republiky 5. **Map** 4 D3.
📞 22 00 21 00. Ⓜ *Náměstí
Republiky.* 🚊 *5, 14, 26.*
Gallery Open *10am–6pm daily.*

Pʀᴀɢᴜᴇ's ᴍᴏsᴛ prominent
Art Nouveau building
stands on the site of the
former Royal Court palace,
the King's residence between
1383 and 1485. Abandoned
for centuries, what remained
was used as a seminary and
later as a military college. It
was finally demolished in the
early 1900s to be replaced by
the present cultural centre
(1905–11) with its exhibition
halls and large auditorium,
designed by Antonín
Balšánek assisted by
Osvald Polívka.

    The exterior is embellished
with stucco and allegorical
statuary. Above the main
entrance there is a huge semicircular mosaic entitled
Homage to Prague by Karel
Špillar. Inside, topped by an
impressive glass dome, is
Prague's principal concert
venue and the core of the
entire building, the
Smetana Hall, sometimes

also used as a ballroom. The
interior of the building is
decorated with works by
leading Czech artists of the
first decade of the century,
including Alfons Mucha
(see p149).

    There are numerous smaller
halls, conference rooms and
offices, as well as cafés and
restaurants where visitors can
relax and enjoy the centre's
flamboyant Art Nouveau
decoration at
their leisure.
On 28 October,
1918, Prague's
Municipal
House was the
scene of the
momentous
proclamation
of the new
independent
state of
Czechoslovakia.

**Decorative detail
by Alfons Mucha**

Hollar
Hall

Foyer

Mayor's Salon
with paintings by
Alfons Mucha

Entrance hall

Entrance to Art
Nouveau café

Nightclubs

Celetná Street ❸

CELETNÁ ULICE

Map 3 C3. Ⓜ *Náměsti Republiky, Můstek.* **House of the Black Madonna** 〖 *24 21 17 32.* **Open** *10am–6pm Tue–Fri.*

O NE OF THE OLDEST streets in Prague, Celetná follows an old trading route from eastern Bohemia. Its name comes from the plaited bread rolls that were first baked here in the Middle Ages. It gained prestige in the 14th century as a section of the Royal Route *(see p172)* used for coronation processions. Foundations of Romanesque and Gothic buildings can be seen in some of the cellars, but most of the houses with their picturesque house signs are Baroque remodellings.

At No. 34, the House of the Black Madonna is home to a small but interesting collection of Czech Cubism, including paintings, sculpture, furniture, architectural plans and applied arts.

Church of St James ❹

KOSTEL SV. JAKUBA

Malá Štupartská. **Map** 3 C3. Ⓜ *Můstek, Náměstí Republiky.* **Open** *in the season, daily.* 🚻 📷

T HIS ATTRACTIVE Baroque church was originally the Gothic presbytery of a Minorite monastery. The order (a branch of the Franciscans) was invited to Prague by King Wenceslas I in 1232. It was

Baroque organ loft in the Church of St James

rebuilt in the Baroque style after a fire in 1689, allegedly started by agents of Louis XIV. Over 20 side altars were added, decorated with works by painters such as Jan Jiří Heinsch, Petr Brandl and Václav Vavřinec Reiner. The tomb of Count Vratislav of Mitrovice (1714–16), designed by Johann Bernhard Fischer von Erlach and executed by sculptor Ferdinand Brokof, is the most beautiful Baroque tomb in Bohemia. The count is said to have been accidentally buried alive – his corpse was later found sitting up in the tomb. Hanging on the right of the entrance is a mummified forearm. It has been there for over 400 years, ever since a thief tried to steal the jewels from the Madonna on the high altar. But the Virgin grabbed his arm and held on so tightly it had to be cut off.

Because of its long nave, the church's acoustics are excellent and many concerts and recitals are given here. There is also a magnificent organ built in 1702.

Estates Theatre ❺

STAVOVSKÉ DIVADLO

Ovocný Trh 1. **Map** 3 C4. 〖 *24 22 85 03.* Ⓜ *Můstek.* **Foyer open** *for performances only.*

B UILT BY COUNT NOSTITZ in 1783, the theatre is one of the finest examples of Neo-Classical elegance in Prague. It is a mecca for Mozart fans *(see p212).* On 29 October 1787, Mozart's opera, *Don Giovanni* had its debut here with Mozart at the piano conducting the orchestra. In 1834 a musical comedy called *Fidlovačka* had its premiere here. One of the songs, *Kde domov můj?* (Where is my Home?), became the Czech national anthem.

Carolinum ❻

KAROLINUM

Ovocný Trh 3. **Map** 3 C4. 〖 *24 49 11 11.* Ⓜ *Můstek.* **Closed** *to the public.* **Open** *for special exhibitions.*

A T THE CORE of the university founded by Charles IV in 1348 is the Carolinum. The chapel, arcade and walls still survive, together with a fine oriel window, but in 1945 the courtyard was reconstructed in Gothic style. In the 15th and 16th centuries the university played a leading role in the movement to reform the church. After the Battle of the White Mountain *(see pp30–31)*, the university was taken over by the Jesuits.

Old Town Square ❼

STAROMĚSTSKÉ NÁMĚSTÍ

See pp66–9.

Smetana Hall

Old Town Square: North and East Sides ❼
STAROMĚSTSKÉ NÁMĚSTÍ

SOME OF PRAGUE'S colourful history is preserved around the Old Town Square in the form of its buildings. The north side of the Square is dominated by the white façade of the Baroque church of St Nicholas. The east side boasts two superb examples of the architecture of their times: the House at the Stone Bell, restored to its former appearance as a Gothic town palace, and the Rococo Golz-Kinský Palace. An array of pastel-coloured buildings completes the Square.

★ House at the Stone Bell
At the corner of the building, the bell is the sign of this medieval town palace.

Statues by Ignaz Platzer from 1760–65

Golz-Kinský Palace
C G Bossi created the elaborate stucco decoration on the façade of this Rococo palace (see p70).

EAST SIDE

Rococo stucco work

NORTH SIDE

★ Church of St Nicholas
Besides its original purpose as a parish church and, later, a Benedictine monastery church, this has served as a garrison church and a concert hall (see p70).

STAR SIGHTS
★ **Church of Our Lady before Týn**
★ **House at the Stone Bell**
★ **Church of St Nicholas**

A solid gold effigy of the Virgin Mary

East and north side

Jan Hus Monument

★ **Church of Our Lady before Týn**
Astronomer and astrologer Tycho Brahe is buried in Týn Church (see p70).

Týn School
Gothic rib vaulting is a primary feature of this building, which was a school from the 14th to the mid-19th century.

Entrance to Týn Church

Romanesque arcaded house with 18th-century façade

Restaurant U Sv. Salvatora façade dates from 1696

Ministerstvo Hospodářství
Architect Osvald Polívka designed this Art Nouveau building for the Prague City Insurance Company in 1898, with figures of firefighters on the upper façade. It now houses the Ministry of Commerce.

Staroměstské náměstí, 1793
The engraving by Filip and František Heger shows the Old Town Square teeming with people and carriages. The Old Town Hall is on the left.

Old Town Square: South Side ❼
STAROMĚSTSKÉ NÁMĚSTÍ

A COLOURFUL ARRAY of houses of Romanesque or Gothic origin, with fascinating house signs, graces the south side of the Old Town Square. The block between Celetná Street and Železná Street is especially attractive. The Square has always been a busy focal point, and today offers visitors a tourist information centre, as well as a number of restaurants, cafés, shops, and galleries.

U Lazara (At the Poor Wretch's)
Romanesque barrel vaulting testifies to the house's early origins, though it was rebuilt during the Renaissance. The ground floor houses the Staroměstská restaurace.

FRANZ KAFKA (1883–1924)

The author of two of the most influential novels of the 20th century, *The Trial* and *The Castle*, Kafka spent most of his short life in the Old Town. From 1893 to 1901 he studied in the Golz-Kinský Palace *(see p70)*, where his father later had a shop. He worked as an insurance clerk, but frequented a literary salon in At the Golden Unicorn on Old Town Square, along with others who wrote in German. Hardly any of his work was published in his lifetime.

At the Stone Table

At the Golden Unicorn

Železná Street

SOUTH SIDE

★ **At the Stone Ram**
The early-16th-century house sign shows a young maiden with a ram. The house has been referred to as At the Unicorn due to the similarity between the one-horned ram and a unicorn.

★ **Štorch House**
The late-19th-century painting of St Wenceslas on horseback by Mikuláš Aleš appears on this ornate Neo-Renaissance building, also known as At the Stone Madonna.

STAR SIGHTS
★ Štorch House
★ At the Stone Ram

Melantrichova Passage
*Václav Jansa's painting (1898)
shows the narrow passageway
leading to the Old Town Square.*

At the Red Fox
*A golden Madonna and Child
look down from the Baroque
façade of an originally
Romanesque building.*

□ South side

Ⓐ Jan Hus Monument

At The Ox
*Named after its
15th-century owner,
the burgher Ochs,
this house features an
early-18th-century
stone statue of
St Anthony of Padua.*

At the
Blue Star

At the Storks

The arcade houses the
Franz Kafka Gallery.

U Orloje
restaurant

Melantrichova
Passage

TIMELINE

1338 Old Town
becomes
municipality

*Leopold II's Royal Procession through the
Old Town Square in 1791*

1735 Church of
St Nicholas completed

1948 Klement
Gottwald proclaims
Communist state
from balcony of
Golz-Kinský Palace

1300	1450	1600	1750	1900

1200 Square is
meeting point of
trade routes and
important market

1365
Building of
present Týn
Church

1621 Execution
of 27 anti-Habsburg
leaders in square
(see p31)

1689 Fire destroys
large part of Old Town

1784 Unification
of Prague towns

1915 Unveiling of
Jan Hus Monument

Hus Monument (detail)

Statue of the Madonna on Our Lady before Týn

Church of Our Lady before Týn **8**
KOSTEL PANNY MARIE PŘED TÝNEM

Týnská, Štupartská. **Map** 3 C3.
📞 231 81 86. Ⓜ Staroměstská, Můstek. **Open** only for services.
✝ 5:30pm Mon–Fri, 1pm Sat, 11:30am & 9pm Sun. 📷

D OMINATING THE Old Town Square are the magnificent multiple steeples of this historic church. The present Gothic church was started in 1365 and soon became associated with the reform movement in Bohemia. From the early 15th century until 1620 Týn was the main Hussite church in Prague. The Hussite king, George of Poděbrady, took Utraquist communion (see Church of St Martin in the Wall p73) here and had a gold chalice – the Utraquist symbol – mounted on the façade. After 1621 the chalice was melted down to become part of the statue of the Madonna that replaced it.

Kinský arms on Golz-Kinský Palace

On the northern side of the church is a beautiful entrance portal (1390) decorated with scenes of Christ's passion. The dark interior has some notable features, including Gothic sculptures of Calvary, a pewter font (1414) and a 15th-century Gothic pulpit. The Danish astronomer Tycho Brahe (1546–1601) is buried here.

Golz-Kinský Palace **9**
PALÁC GOLZ-KINSKÝCH

Staroměstské náměstí 12.
Map 3 C3. Ⓜ Staroměstská. **Closed** until spring 2001. 📷 🚫

T HIS LOVELY Rococo palace, designed by Kilian Ignaz Dientzenhofer, has a pretty pink and white stucco façade crowned with statues of the four elements by Ignaz Franz Platzer. It was bought from the Golz family in 1768 by Štěpán Kinský, an Imperial diplomat. In 1948 Communist leader, Klement Gottwald, used the balcony to address a huge crowd of party members – a key event in the crisis that led up to his coup d'état. The National Gallery now uses the Golz-Kinský Palace for temporary art exhibitions.

Jan Hus Monument **10**
POMNÍK JANA HUSA

Staroměstské náměstí. **Map** 3 B3.
Ⓜ Staroměstská.

A T ONE END of the Old Town Square stands the massive monument to the religious reformer and Czech hero, Jan Hus (see pp26–7). Hus was burnt at the stake after being pronounced a heretic by the Council of Constance in 1415. The monument by Ladislav Šaloun was unveiled in 1915 on the 500th anniversary of his death. It shows two groups of people, one of victorious Hussite warriors, the other of Protestants forced into exile 200 years later, and a young mother symbolizing national rebirth. The dominant figure of Hus emphasizes the moral authority of the man who gave up life rather than his beliefs.

Church of St Nicholas **11**
KOSTEL SV. MIKULÁŠE

Staroměstské náměstí. **Map** 3 B3. 📞 232 25 89. Ⓜ Staroměstská. **Open** 10am–4pm Tue, Thu–Sun, 10am–5pm Wed (and for evening concerts Apr–Nov). ✝ 10:30am Sun. 📷

T HERE HAS BEEN a church here since the 12th century. It was the Old Town's parish church and meeting place until Týn Church was completed in the 14th century. After the Battle of the White Mountain in 1620 (see pp30–31) the church became part of a Benedictine monastery. The present church by Kilian Ignaz Dientzenhofer, was completed in 1735. Its dramatic white façade is studded with statues by Antonín Braun.

Defiant Hussites on the Jan Hus Monument in Old Town Square

Church of St Nicholas in the Old Town

When in 1781 Emperor Joseph II closed all monasteries not engaged in socially useful activities, the church was stripped bare. In World War I the church was used by the troops of Prague's garrison. The colonel in charge took the opportunity to restore the church with the help of artists who might otherwise have been sent to the front. The dome has frescoes of the lives of St Nicholas and St Benedict by Kosmas Damian Asam. In the nave is a huge crown-shaped chandelier. At the end of the war, the church of St Nicholas was given to the Czechoslovak Hussite Church. Concerts are given now in the church during the summer.

Old Town Hall ⓬
STAROMĚSTSKÁ RADNICE

See pp72–3.

House at the Two Golden Bears ⓭
DŮM U DVOU ZLATÝCH MEDVĚDŮ

Kožná 1. **Map** 3 B4. ᵂ Můstek.
Closed to the public.

IF YOU LEAVE the Old Town Square by the narrow Melantrichova Street, make a point of turning into the first alleyway on the left to see the portal of the house called "At the Two Golden Bears". The present Renaissance building was constructed from two earlier houses in 1567. The portal was added in 1590, when a wealthy merchant, Lorenc Štork, secured the services of court architect Bonifaz Wohlmut, who had designed the spire on the tower of St Vitus's Cathedral (see pp100–3). His ornate portal with reliefs of two bears is one of the most beautiful Renaissance portals in Prague. Magnificent arcades, also dating from the 16th century, have been preserved in the inner courtyard. In 1885 Egon Erwin Kisch, known as the "Furious Reporter", was born here. He was a German-speaking Jewish writer and journalist, feared for the force of his left-wing rhetoric.

Church of St Gall ⓮
KOSTEL SV. HAVLA

Havelská. **Map** 3 C4. ᵂ Můstek.
231 81 86. **Open** only for services. 12:15pm Mon–Fri, 7:30am Sun.

DATING FROM around 1280, this church was built to serve an autonomous German community in the area known as Gall's Town (Havelské Město). In the 14th century this was merged with the Old Town. In the 18th century the church was given a Baroque facelift by Giovanni Santini-Aichel, who created a bold façade decorated with statues of saints by Ferdinand Brokof. Rich interior furnishings include paintings by the leading Baroque artist Karel Škréta, who is buried here. Prague's best-known market has been held in Havelská Street since the middle ages, selling flowers, vegetables, toys, and clothes.

One of nine statues on façade of St Gall's

Carved Renaissance portal of the House at the Two Golden Bears

Old Town Hall ⑫

STAROMĚSTSKÁ RADNICE

ONE OF THE most striking buildings in Prague is the Old Town Hall, established in 1338 after King John of Luxemburg agreed to set up a town council. Over the centuries a number of old houses were knocked together as the Old Town Hall expanded, and it now consists of a row of colourful Gothic and Renaissance buildings, most of which have been carefully restored after heavy damage inflicted by the Nazis in the 1945 Prague Uprising. The tower is 69.5 m (228 ft) high and offers a spectacular view of the city.

Old Council Hall
This 19th-century engraving features the well-preserved 15th-century ceiling.

Old Town Coat of Arms
Above the inscription, "Prague, Head of the Kingdom", is the coat of arms of the Old Town, which was adopted in 1784 for the whole city.

Tourist information and entrance to Tower

Temporary art exhibitions

EXECUTIONS IN THE OLD TOWN SQUARE

A bronze tablet below the Old Town Hall chapel records the names of the 27 Protestant leaders executed here by order of the Catholic Emperor Ferdinand on 21 June 1621. This was the humiliating aftermath of the Battle of the White Mountain *(see pp30–31)*. This defeat led to the emigration of Protestants unwilling to give up their faith, a Counter-Reformation drive and Germanization.

★ Old Town Hall Tower
In 1364 the tower was added to what was the private house of Volflin of Kamen. Its gallery provides a fine city view.

Viewing gallery

VISITORS' CHECKLIST

Staroměstské náměstí 1.
Map 3 C3. 24 22 84 56.
Staroměstská (line A),
Můstek (A & B). 17. **Open**
Apr–Oct: 9am–6pm daily; Nov–
Mar: 11am–5pm Mon, 9am–5pm
Tue–Sun.

Oriel Chapel
The original stained-glass windows on the five-sided chapel were destroyed in the last days of World War II, but were replaced in 1987.

Oriel Chapel Ceiling
The chapel, which was built on the first floor of the tower in 1381, has an ornate, recently restored ceiling.

Former house of Volflin of Kamen

Steps to gallery

★ Astronomical Clock
Mechanical figures perform above the zodiac signs in the upper section (see p74); the lower section is a calendar.

Calendar *(see pp32–3)*

Entrance hall decorated with mosaics

Gothic Door
This late Gothic main entrance to the Town Hall and Tower was carved by Matthias Rejsek. The entrance hall is filled with wall mosaics after designs by the Czech painter Mikuláš Aleš.

STAR FEATURES

★ Astronomical Clock

★ Old Town Hall Tower

Town Hall Clock

ORLOJ

Jan Táborský

THE TOWN HALL acquired its first clock at the beginning of the 15th century. In 1490, when it was rebuilt by a master clockmaker called Hanuš, the councillors are said to have been so anxious to prevent him from recreating his masterpiece elsewhere, that they blinded the poor man. Though it has been repaired many times since, the mechanism of the clock we see today was perfected by Jan Táborský between 1552 and 1572.

The Apostles

Vanity and Greed

Arabic numerals 1–24

Astronomical Clock with the sun in Libra

Death

APOSTLES

THE CENTREPIECE of the show that draws a crowd of spectators every time the clock strikes the hour is the procession of

Vojtěch Sucharda's Apostles, sculpted after the last set was burnt in 1945

Blue, representing the daylight hours

Calendar by Josef Mánes (see pp32–3)

The Turk, a symbol of lust

the 12 Apostles. First the figure of Death, the skeleton on the right of the clock, gives a pull on the rope that he holds in his right hand. In his left hand is an hourglass, which he raises and inverts. Two windows then open and the clockwork Apostles (or to be precise 11 of the Apostles plus St Paul) move slowly round, led by St Peter.

At the end of this part of the display, a cock crows and the clock chimes the hour. The other moving figures are a Turk, who shakes his head from side to side, Vanity, who looks at himself in a mirror and Greed, adapted from the original medieval stereotype of a Jewish moneylender.

ASTRONOMICAL CLOCK

THE CLOCKMAKER'S view of the universe had the Earth fixed firmly at the centre. The purpose of the clock was not to tell you the exact time but to imitate the supposed orbits of the sun and moon about the Earth. The hand with the sun, which points to the hour, in fact records three different kinds of time. The outer ring of medieval Arabic numerals measures Old Bohemian time, in which a day of 24 hours was reckoned from the setting of the sun. The ring of Roman numerals indicates time as we know it. The blue part of the dial represents the

visible part of the sky. This is divided into 12 parts. In so-called Babylonian time, the period of daylight was divided into 12 hours, which would vary in length from summer to winter.

The clock also shows the movement of the sun and moon through the 12 signs of the zodiac, which were of great importance in 16th-century Prague.

The figures of Death and the Turk

Church of St Martin in the Wall ❶
KOSTEL SV. MARTINA VE ZDI

Martinská. **Map** 3 B5. ᴹ *Národní třída, Můstek.* 6, 9, 18, 22. **Open** for concerts.

THIS 12TH-CENTURY church became part of the newly erected town wall during the fortification of the Old Town in the 13th century, hence its name. It was the first church where blessed wine, usually reserved for the clergy, was offered to the congregation as well as bread. This was a basic tenet of belief of the moderate Hussites *(see pp26–7)*, the Utraquists, who took their name from the Latin *sub utraque specie*, "in both kinds". In 1787 the church was converted into workshops, but rebuilt in its original form in the early years of this century.

Náprstek Museum ❶
NÁPRSTKOVO MUZEUM

Betlémské náměstí 1. **Map** 3 B4. 22 22 14 18. ᴹ *Národní třída.* 6, 9, 18, 22. **Open** 9am–noon, 12:45–5:30pm Tue–Sun.

VOJTA NÁPRSTEK, art patron and philanthropist, created this museum as a tribute to modern industry following a decade of exile in America after the 1848 revolution *(see pp32–3)*. On his return in 1862, inspired by London's Victorian museums, he began his collection. He created the Czech Industrial Museum by joining five older buildings together, and in the process virtually destroyed the family brewery and home – an 18th-century house called At the Haláneks (U Halánků). His interests later turned to ethnography and the collection now consists of artefacts from Asian, African and Native American cultures. There are weapons, hunting implements and ritual objects from the Aztecs, Toltecs and Mayas. The collection of statues and masks is particularly interesting. The Náprstek Museum is now part of the National Museum.

Ceiling fresco by Václav Vavřinec Reiner in Church of St Giles

Church of St Giles ❶
KOSTEL SV. JILJÍ

Husova. **Map** 3 B4. 24 22 02 35. ᴹ *Národní třída.* 6, 9, 18, 22. **Open** for services only. 7am & 6:30pm Mon–Fri, 6:30pm Sat, 8:30am, 10:30am, noon, 6:30pm Sun.

DESPITE A beautiful Gothic portal on the southern side, the inside of this church is essentially Baroque. Founded in 1371 on the site of an old Romanesque church, it became a Hussite parish church in 1420. Following the Protestant defeat in 1620 *(see pp30–31)*, Ferdinand II presented the church to the Dominicans, who built a huge friary on its southern side. It has now been returned to the Dominicans, religious orders having been abolished under the Communists.

The vaults of the church are decorated with frescoes by the painter Václav Vavřinec Reiner, who is buried in the nave before the altar of St Vincent. The main fresco, a glorification of the Dominicans, shows St Dominic and his friars helping the pope defend the Catholic Church from non-believers.

Bethlehem Chapel ❶
BETLÉMSKÁ KAPLE

Betlémské náměstí. **Map** 3 B4. ᴹ *Národní třída.* 6, 9, 18, 22. **Open** Apr–Oct: 9am–6pm daily; Nov–Mar: 9am–5pm daily.

THE PRESENT "chapel" is a faithful reconstruction of a hall built by the followers of the radical preacher Jan Milíč z Kroměříže in 1391–4. The hall was used for preaching in Czech. Between 1402 and 1413 Jan Hus *(see pp26–7)* preached in the Chapel. Strongly influenced by the teachings of the English religious reformer, John Wycliffe, Hus condemned the corrupt practices of the Church, arguing that the Scriptures should be the sole source of doctrine. After the Battle of the White Mountain in 1620 *(see pp30–31)*, when Protestant worship was outlawed, the building was handed over to the Jesuits, who completely rebuilt it with six naves. In 1786 it was almost demolished and an apartment house built on the site. After World War II the chapel was reconstructed following old illustrations.

16th-century illustration showing Jan Hus preaching in Bethlehem Chapel

Street-by-Street: Old Town (West)

THE NARROW STREETS near Charles Bridge follow
Prague's medieval street plan. For centuries Charles
Street (Karlova) was the main route across the Old
Town. The picturesque, twisting street is lined with
shops and houses displaying Renaissance and Baroque
façades. In the 17th century the Jesuits bought up a
vast area of land to the north of the street to house
the complex of the Clementinum university.

★ Clementinum
*This plaque records the
founding in 1783 of a state-
supervised seminary in place
of the old Jesuit university* ㉓

**Knights of the
Cross Square**
*From the façade of
the Church of the
Holy Saviour, black-
ened statues overlook
the small square* ㉕

Church of
St Francis

★ Smetana Museum
*A museum devoted to the life
and work of composer Bedřich
Smetana is housed in this Neo-
Renaissance building set on the
riverfront, which was once
an old waterworks* ㉔

A N E N S K Á

St Anne's Convent
was abolished in 1782.
Some of its buildings
are now used by the
National Theatre
(see pp156–7).

The Old Town Bridge Tower
dates from 1380. The Gothic sculptural
decoration on the eastern façade was
from Peter Parler's workshop. The
kingfisher was the favourite personal
symbol of Wenceslas IV (son of
Charles IV) in whose reign the tower
was completed *(see p139).*

Charles Street
*Among the many decorated houses
along the ancient street, be sure to
look out for this Art Nouveau
statue of the legendary Princess
Libuše (see p21) surrounded by
roses at No. 22/24* ㉑

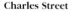

Mariánské Square

The square used to be flooded so often, it was called "the puddle". The Art Nouveau sculptures on the balcony of the New Town Hall, built here in 1911, are by Stanislav Sucharda **20**

LOCATOR MAP
See Street Finder, map 3

Observatory tower

MARIÁNSKÉ
NÁMĚSTÍ

Clam-Gallas Palace

One of Prague's grandest Baroque palaces and full of wonderful statuary, the Clam-Gallas is sadly in need of repair **19**

KARLOVA

LILIOVÁ

To Old Town Square

HUSOVA

ŘETĚZOVÁ

Church of St Giles

Much of the Baroque sculpture, like this angel on the altar (1738), is by František Weiss **17**

Palace of the Lords of Kunštát

George of Poděbrady lived here before he became King in 1458 **22**

Bethlehem Chapel

In this spacious chapel, rebuilt in the 1950s, Hus and other reformers preached to huge congregations **18**

| 0 metres | 100 |
| 0 yards | 100 |

KEY

– – – Suggested route

STAR SIGHTS

★ **Clementinum**

★ **Smetana Museum**

Clam-Gallas Palace ⑲

CLAM-GALLASŮV PALÁC

Husova 20. **Map** 3 B4.
☎ 26 21 00, 24 48 31 57.
Ⓜ *Staroměstská.* **Open** for concerts only.

THE INTERIOR of this magnificent Baroque palace had suffered during its use as a store for the city archives, but has now been lovingly restored. The palace, designed by Viennese court architect Johann Bernhard Fischer von Erlach, was built in 1713–30 for the Supreme Marshal of Bohemia, Jan Gallas de Campo. Its grand portals, each flanked by two pairs of Hercules sculpted by Matthias Braun, give a taste of what lies within. The main staircase is also decorated with Braun statues, set off by a ceiling

fresco, *The Triumph of Apollo* by Carlo Carlone. The palace has a theatre, where Beethoven performed some of his works.

Mariánské Square ⑳

MARIÁNSKÉ NÁMĚSTÍ

Map 3 B3. Ⓜ *Staroměstská, Můstek.*

TWO STATUES dominate the square from the corners of the forbidding Town Hall, built in 1912. One illustrates the story of the long-lived Rabbi Löw *(see p88)* finally being caught by the Angel of Death. The other is the Iron Man, a local ghost condemned to roam the Old Town after murdering his mistress. A niche in the garden wall of the Clam-Gallas Palace houses a statue of the River Vltava, depicted as a nymph pouring water from a jug. There is a story that an old soldier once made the nymph sole beneficiary of his will.

Charles Street ㉑

KARLOVA ULICE

Map 3 A4. Ⓜ *Staroměstská.*

A 19th-century sign on the House at the Golden Snake

DATING BACK to the 12th century, this narrow, winding street was part of the Royal Route *(see pp174–5)*, along which coronation processions passed on the way to Prague Castle. Many original Gothic and Renaissance houses remain, most converted into shops to attract the procession of tourists between Old Town Square and Charles Bridge.

A café at the House at the Golden Snake (No. 18) was established in 1714 by an Armenian, Deodatus Damajan, who handed out slanderous pamphlets from here. It is now a restaurant. Look out for At the Golden Well (No. 3), which has a magnificent Baroque façade and stucco reliefs of saints including St Roch and St Sebastian, who are believed to offer protection against plagues.

Palace of the Lords of Kunštát ㉒

DŮM PÁNŮ Z KUNŠTÁTU

Řetězová 3. **Map** 3 B4. ☎ 22 22 12 40. Ⓜ *Národní třída, Staroměstská.* 🚊 6, 9, 18, 22. **Open** May–Sep: 10am–6pm Tue–Sun.

THE BASEMENT of the palace, dating from around 1200, contains three of the best-preserved Romanesque rooms in Prague. It was originally the ground floor, but over the years the surrounding ground level was raised by 3m (10 ft) to prevent flooding. In the 15th century the house was enlarged in Gothic style by its

Matthias Braun's statues on a portal of the Clam-Gallas Palace (c.1714)

owners, the Lords of Kunštát and Poděbrady. The palace houses a historical exhibition devoted to Bohemia's only Hussite king, George of Poděbrady (see pp26–7), who lived here for a time.

Clementinum 🅮
KLEMENTINUM

Křižovnické náměstí 4, Mariánské náměstí 5, Seminářská 1. **Map** 3 A4. 📞 21 66 31 11. ⓜ *Staroměstská.* 🚊 17, 18. **Library open** 8am–7pm Mon–Fri, 8am–2pm Sat. **Church open** only for services. 🕑 7pm Tue, 8pm Thu, 2pm & 8pm Sun. 🚫 ♿

Former Jesuit Church of the Holy Saviour in the Clementinum

In 1556 EMPEROR Ferdinand I invited the Jesuits to Prague to help bring the Czechs back into the Catholic fold. They established their headquarters in the former Dominican monastery of St Clement, hence the name Clementinum. This soon became an effective rival to the Carolinum (see p65), the Utraquist university. Prague's first Jesuit church, the Church of the Holy Saviour (Kostel sv. Salvátora) was built here in 1601. Its façade, with seven large statues of saints by Jan Bendl (1659), is dramatically lit up at night.

Expelled in 1618, the Jesuits were back two years later more determined than ever to stamp out heresy. In 1622 the two universities were merged, resulting in the Jesuits gaining a virtual monopoly on higher education in Prague. They believed two-thirds of the population were secret heretics,

searched for books in Czech and then burnt them by the thousand. Between 1653 and 1723 the Clementinum expanded eastwards. Over 30 houses and three churches were pulled down to make way for the new complex.

When in 1773 the pope dissolved their order, the Jesuits had to leave Prague and education was secularized. The Clementinum became the Prague University library, today the National Library. Look out for any classical concerts performed in the beautiful Chapel of Mirrors (Zrcadlová kaple).

Smetana Museum 🅯
MUZEUM BEDŘICHA SMETANY

Novotného lávka 1. **Map** 3 A4. 📞 24 22 90 75. ⓜ *Staroměstská.* 🚊 17, 18. **Open** 10am–5pm Wed–Mon. 📷 🚫

On a spit of land beside the Vltava, a former Neo-Renaissance waterworks has been turned into a memorial to Bedřich Smetana, the father of Czech music. The museum contains documents, letters, scores and musical instruments detailing the composer's life and work. Smetana was a fervent patriot and his music helped inspire the Czech national revival. Deaf towards the end of his life, he never heard his cycle of symphonic poems *Má Vlast* (My Country), being performed.

Statue of Charles IV (1848) in Knights of the Cross Square

Knights of the Cross Square 🅱
KŘIŽOVNICKÉ NÁMĚSTÍ

Map 3 A4. 📞 21 10 82 37. ⓜ *Staroměstská.* 🚊 17, 18. 🚌 135, 207. **Church of St Francis open** only for services. 🕑 7am Mon–Fri, 9am Sun. 🚫 ♿ **Gallery Křižov open** 10am–5pm daily.

This small square in front of the Old Town Bridge Tower offers fine views across the Vltava. On the north side is the Church of St Francis (kostel sv. Františka), once part of the monastery of the crusading Knights of the Cross with the Red Star. To the east is the Church of the Holy Saviour, part of the huge Clementinum complex. On the western side is the Gallery Křižov, holding the art collection and Treasury of the Knights of the Cross. In the centre of the square stands a large bronze Neo-Gothic statue of Charles IV.

Sgraffitoed façade of the Smetana Museum

JEWISH QUARTER

JOSEFOV

IN THE MIDDLE AGES there were two distinct Jewish communities in Prague's Old Town: Jews from the west had settled around the Old-New Synagogue, Jews from the Byzantine Empire around the Old Shul (on the site of today's Spanish Synagogue). The two settlements gradually merged and were confined in an enclosed ghetto. For centuries Prague's Jews suffered from oppressive laws – in the 16th century they had to wear a yellow circle as a mark of shame. Christians

Art Nouveau detail on house in Kaprova

often accused them of starting fires and poisoning wells – any pretext for a pogrom. Discrimination was partially relaxed in 1784 by Joseph II, and the Jewish Quarter was named Josefov after him. In 1850 the area was officially incorporated as part of Prague. In the 1890s the city authorities decided to raze the ghetto slums because the area's complete lack of sanitation made it a health hazard. However, the Town Hall, a number of synagogues and the Old Jewish Cemetery were saved.

SIGHTS AT A GLANCE

Synagogues and Churches
Pinkas Synagogue **4**
Klausen Synagogue **5**
Old-New Synagogue pp88–9 **6**
High Synagogue **7**
Maisel Synagogue **9**
Church of the Holy Ghost **10**
Spanish Synagogue **11**
Church of St Simon and St Jude **13**
Church of St Castullus **14**

Concert Hall
Rudolfinum **1**

Museums and Galleries
Museum of Decorative Arts **2**
St Agnes's Convent pp92–3 **15**

Historic Buildings
Jewish Town Hall **8**
Cubist Houses **12**

Cemeteries
Old Jewish Cemetery pp86–7 **3**

GETTING THERE

Staroměstská station on metro line A is close to all the major sights in the Jewish Quarter. The alternative is to take tram 17 or 18 to Náměstí Jana Palacha. For St Agnes's Convent, buses 126, 135 and 207 are convenient.

| 0 metres | 250 |
| 0 yards | 250 |

KEY

Street-by-Street map
See pp82–83

Metro station

Tram stop

Parking

River boat boarding point

◁ **Densely-packed gravestones in the Old Jewish Cemetery**

Street-by-Street: Jewish Quarter

T HOUGH THE OLD GHETTO has disappeared, much of the area's fascinating history is preserved in the synagogues around the Old Jewish Cemetery, while the newer streets are lined with many delightful Art Nouveau buildings. The old lanes to the east of the former ghetto lead to the quiet haven of St Agnes's Convent, beautifully restored as a branch of the National Gallery.

Cubist Houses
One of the new architectural styles used in the rebuilding of the old Jewish Quarter was based on the ideas of Cubism ⓬

★ **Old Jewish Cemetery**
Thousands of gravestones are crammed into the ancient cemetery ❸

★ **Old-New Synagogue**
The Gothic hall with its distinctive crenellated gable has been a house of prayer for over 700 years ❻

High Synagogue
The interior has splendid Renaissance vaulting ❼

Klausen Synagogue
The exhibits of the State Jewish Museum include this alms box, dating from about 1800 ❺

★ **Museum of Decorative Arts**
Stained glass panels on the staircase depict the crafts represented in the museum's wide-ranging collection ❷

Pinkas Synagogue
The walls are now a moving memorial to the Czech Jews killed in the Holocaust ❹

To Metro
Staroměstská

Jewish Town Hall
The 16th-century building still serves the Czech Jewish community ❽

Maisel Synagogue
The original synagogue was built as a tribute to Mayor Mordechai Maisel in 1591 ❾

★ **St Agnes's Convent**
Antonín Chittussi's
Parisian Embankment *is
one of the 19th-century
Czech works on show in
the converted
convent* ⑮

LOCATOR MAP
See Street Finder, map 3

Na Františku
Hospital

Former
Charnel
House

**Church of
St Castullus**
*Some fine mid-
14th-century
Gothic vaulting
has been pre-
served in this
restored parish
church* ⑭

Parsonage of
St Castullus

**Church of St Simon
and St Jude**
*After the Merciful
Brethren had taken
over the church in the
17th century, it became
part of the new Na
Františku Hospital* ⑬

Spanish Synagogue
*The newest of the
synagogues in this
part of Prague, it was
built in flamboyant
imitation Moorish
style in 1868* ⑪

Church of the Holy Ghost
*This Baroque statue of St John
Nepomuk by Ferdinand
Brokof (1727) stands in
front of the church* ⑩

| 0 metres | 50 |
| 0 yards | 50 |

KEY

– – – Suggested route

STAR SIGHTS

★ **Museum of
Decorative Arts**

★ **Old Jewish Cemetery**

★ **Old-New Synagogue**

★ **St Agnes's Convent**

Stage of the Dvořák Hall in the Rudolfinum

Rudolfinum **❶**

Alšovo Nábřeží 12. **Map** 3 A3.
🚇 *Staroměstská.* 🚊 *17, 18.*
🚌 *135, 207. Philharmonic* 🕿 *24
89 31 11. Galerie Rudolphinum*
🕿 *24 89 32 05.* **Open** 10am–6pm
Tue–Sun. 🚫 🎫 ♿ 🔲

Now the home of the Czech
Philharmonic Orchestra,
the Rudolfinum is one of the
most impressive landmarks
on the Old Town bank of the
Vltava. Many of the major
concerts of the Prague Spring
music festival *(see p50)* are
held here. There are several
concert halls, the sumptuous
Dvořák Hall ranking among
the finest creations of 19th-
century Czech architecture.

The Rudolfinum was built
between 1876 and 1884 to a
design by Josef Zítek and Josef
Schulz and named in honour
of Crown Prince Rudolph of
Habsburg. Like the National
Theatre *(see pp156–7)*, it is an
outstanding example of Czech
Neo-Renaissance style. The
curving balustrade is decorated
with statues of distinguished
Czech, Austrian and German
composers and artists.

Also known as the House of
Artists (Dům umělců), the
building houses the Gallerie

Rudolphinum, a collection of
modern art. Between 1918
and 1939, and for a brief
period after World War II, the
Rudolfinum was the seat of
the Czechoslovak parliament.

Museum of Decorative Arts **❷**
UMĚLECKOPRŮMYSLOVÉ MUZEUM

17. listopadu 2. **Map** 3 B3.
🕿 *51 09 31 11.* 🚇 *Staroměstská.*
🚊 *17, 18.* 🚌 *135, 207.* **Open**
10am–6pm Tue–Sun. 🎫 🚫 🔲

For some years after its
foundation in 1885, the
museum's collections were
housed in the Rudolfinum.
The present building, designed
by Josef Schulz in French
Neo-Renaissance style, was
completed in 1901.

The museum's glass collection
is one of the largest in the
world, but only a fraction
of it is ever on display.
Pride of place goes to the
Bohemian glass, of which
there are many fine Baroque
and 19th- and 20th-century
pieces. Medieval and Venetian
Renaissance glass are also
well represented.

Among the permanent
exhibitions of other crafts are
Meissen porcelain, the Gobelin
tapestries and the intricate
timepieces made by Erasmus
Habermel, clockmaker to
Rudolph II. The furniture
collection has exquisitely
carved escritoires and bureaux
from the Renaissance. On the
mezzanine floor are halls for
temporary exhibitions and
an art library housing over
100,000 publications.

Old Jewish Cemetery **❸**
STARÝ ŽIDOVSKÝ HŘBITOV

See pp86–7.

Pinkas Synagogue **❹**
PINKASOVA SYNAGÓGA

Široká 3. **Map** 3 B3. 🚇 *Staroměstská.*
🚊 *17, 18.* 🚌 *135, 207.*
Open Apr–Oct: 9am–6pm Sun–Fri;
Nov–Mar: 9am–4:30pm. 🎫 🚫 ♿

The synagogue was
founded in 1479 by Rabbi
Pinkas and enlarged in 1535
by his great nephew Aaron
Meshulam Horowitz. It has
been rebuilt many times over
the centuries. Excavations
have turned up fascinating
relics of life in the medieval
ghetto, including a *mikva* or
ritual bath. The core of the
present building is a
hall with

Names of Holocaust victims on Pinkas Synagogue wall

Gothic vaulting. The gallery for women was added in the early 17th century.

The synagogue now serves as a memorial to all the Jewish Czechoslovak citizens who were imprisoned in Terezín concentration camp and later deported to various Nazi extermination camps. The names of the 77,297 who did not return are inscribed on the synagogue walls.

Klausen Synagogue ❺
KLAUSOVÁ SYNAGÓGA

U starého hřbitova 3a. **Map** 3 B3. Staroměstská. 17, 18. 135, 207. **Open** Apr–Oct: 9am–6pm daily; Nov–Mar: 9am–4:30pm.

BEFORE THE FIRE of 1689, this site was occupied by a number of small Jewish schools and prayer houses known as *klausen*. The name was preserved in the Klausen Synagogue, built on the ruins and completed in 1694. The High Baroque structure has a fine barrel-vaulted interior with rich stucco decorations. It now houses Hebrew prints and manuscripts and an exhibition of Jewish traditions and customs, tracing the history of the Jews in Central Europe back to the early Middle Ages. Many exhibits relate to famous figures in the city's Jewish community including the 16th-century Rabbi Löw *(see p88)*, who, according to legend, created an artificial man or *golem* out of clay.

19th-century Torah pointer in Klausen Synagogue

Adjoining the synagogue is a building which looks like a tiny medieval castle. It was built in 1906 as the ceremonial hall of the Jewish Burial Society. In 1944 an exhibition was put on here detailing the history of the Prague ghetto. The building now houses a permanent exhibition of children's drawings from the Terezín concentration camp.

18th-century silver-gilt Torah shield in the High Synagogue

Old-New Synagogue ❻
STARONOVÁ SYNAGÓGA

See pp88–9.

High Synagogue ❼
VYSOKÁ SYNAGÓGA

Červená 4. **Map** 3 B3. Staroměstská. 17, 18. 135, 207. **Open** Apr–Oct: 9am–6pm daily; Nov–Mar: 9am–4:30pm.

LIKE THE Jewish Town Hall, the building of the High Synagogue was financed by Mordechai Maisel, mayor of the Jewish Town, in the 1570s. Originally the two buildings formed a single complex and to facilitate communication with the Town Hall, the main hall of the synagogue was on the first floor. It was not until the 19th century that the two buildings were separated and the synagogue was given a staircase and street entrance. You can still see the original Renaissance vaulting and stucco decoration.

The exhibition in the synagogue includes richly embroidered Torah mantles, curtains and other religious textiles. There are also silver ornaments,

such as shields and finials, used to decorate the Ark, where the Torah scrolls are kept. These date from the 16th to the 19th centuries.

Jewish Town Hall ❽
ŽIDOVSKÁ RADNICE

Maislova 18. **Map** 3 B3. 23 18 664. Staroměstská. 17, 18. 135, 207. **Closed** to the public.

THE CORE of this attractive pink and white building is the original Jewish Town Hall, built in 1570–77 by the immensely rich mayor, Mordechai Maisel. In 1763 it acquired a new appearance in the flowery style of the Late Baroque. The last alterations date from 1908, when the southern wing was enlarged.

On the roof stands a small wooden clock tower with a distinctive green steeple. The right to build the tower was originally granted to the Jewish community after their part in the defence of Charles Bridge against the Swedes in 1648 *(see pp30–31)*. On one of the gables there is another clock. This one has Hebrew figures and, because Hebrew reads from right to left, hands that turn in an anti-clockwise direction. The Town Hall is now the seat of the Council of Jewish Religious Communities in the Czech Republic.

Façade and clock tower of the Jewish Town Hall

Old Jewish Cemetery ❸

STARÝ ŽIDOVSKÝ HŘBITOV

This remarkable site was, for over 300 years, the only burial ground permitted to Jews. Founded in 1478, it was slightly enlarged over the years but still basically corresponds to its medieval size. Because of the lack of space people had to be buried on top of each other, up to 12 layers deep. Today you can see over 12,000 gravestones crammed into the tiny space, but an estimated 100,000 people are thought to have been buried here. The last burial was of Moses Beck in 1787.

View across the cemetery towards the western wall of the Klausen Synagogue

Jewish printers, Mordechai Zemach (d 1592) and his son Bezalel (d 1589), are buried under this square gravestone.

The Pinkas Synagogue is the second-oldest in Prague *(see p84)*.

David Gans' Tombstone
The tomb of the writer and astronomer (1541–1613) is decorated with the symbols of his name – a star of David and a goose (Gans in German).

The oldest tomb is that of the writer Rabbi Avigdor Kara (1439).

Rabbi David Oppenheim (1664–1736)
The chief rabbi of Prague owned the largest collection of old Hebrew manuscripts and prints in the city.

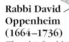

Klausen Synagogue *(see p85)*

The Nephele Mound was where infants who died under a year old were buried.

The gravestone of Moses Beck

Main entrance

STAR SIGHTS

★ Tombstone of Rabbi Löw

★ Tombstone of Hendela Bassevi

★ 14th-Century Tombstones

★ 14th-Century Tombstones
Embedded in the wall are fragments of Gothic tombstones brought here from an older Jewish cemetery discovered in 1866 in Vladislavova Street in the New Town.

Prague Burial Society
Founded in 1564, the group carried out ritual burials and performed charitable work in the community. Members of the society wash their hands after leaving the cemetery.

VISITORS' CHECKLIST

Široká 3 (main entrance). **Map** 3 B3. 22 17 191 (reservations), 24 81 00 99 (Jewish Museum). *Staroměstská.* 17, 18 to Staroměstská. **Open** Apr–Oct: 9am–6pm Sun–Fri; Nov–Mar: 9am–4:30pm Sun–Fri (last admission 30 minutes before closing). as part of Jewish Museum.

The Museum of Decorative Arts
(see p84)

★ **Tombstone of Rabbi Löw**
The most visited grave in the cemetery is that of Rabbi Löw (1520–1609). Visitors place hundreds of pebbles and wishes on his grave as a mark of respect.

The Neo-Romanesque Ceremonial Hall

Mordechai Maisel (1528–1601) was Mayor of Prague's Jewish Town and a philanthropist.

★ **Tombstone of Hendela Bassevi**
The highly-decorated tomb (1628) was built for the beautiful wife of Prague's first Jewish nobleman.

UNDERSTANDING THE GRAVESTONES

From the late 16th century onwards, tombstones in the Jewish cemetery were decorated with symbols denoting the background, family name or profession of the deceased person.

Blessing hands: Cohen family

A pair of scissors: tailor

A stag: Hirsch or Zvi family

Grapes: blessing or abundance

Old-New Synagogue

STARONOVÁ SYNAGOGA

Star of David in Červená Street

BUILT AROUND 1270, this is the oldest synagogue in Europe and one of the earliest Gothic buildings in Prague. The synagogue has survived fires, the slum clearances of the 19th century and many Jewish pogroms. Residents of the Jewish Quarter have often had to seek refuge within its walls and today it is still the religious centre for Prague's Jews. It was originally called the New Synagogue until another synagogue was built nearby – this was later destroyed.

The synagogue's eastern side

The 14th-century stepped brick gable

★ **Jewish Standard**
The historic banner of Prague's Jews is decorated with a Star of David and within it the hat that had to be worn by Jews in the 14th century.

These windows formed part of the 18th-century extensions built to allow women a view of the service.

RABBI LÖW AND THE GOLEM

The scholar and philosophical writer Rabbi Löw, director of the Talmudic school (which studied the Torah) in the late 16th century, was also thought to possess magical powers. He was supposed to have created a figure, the Golem, from clay and then brought it to life by placing a magic stone tablet in its mouth. The Golem went berserk and the Rabbi had to remove the tablet. He hid the creature among the Old-New Synagogue's rafters.

Rabbi Löw and the Golem

Candlestick holder

★ **Five-rib Vaulting**
Two massive octagonal pillars inside the hall support the five-rib vaults.

Right-hand Nave
The glow from the bronze chandeliers provides light for worshippers using the seats lining the walls.

The tympanum above the Ark is decorated with 13th-century leaf carvings.

★ Rabbi Löw's Chair
A star of David marks the chair of the Chief Rabbi, placed where the distinguished 16th-century scholar used to sit.

The cantor's platform and its lectern is surrounded by a wrought-iron Gothic grille.

Entrance to the Synagogue in Červená Street

The Ark
This shrine is the holiest place in the synagogue and holds the sacred scrolls of the Torah.

Entrance Portal
The tympanum above the door in the south vestibule is decorated with clusters of grapes and vine leaves growing on twisted branches.

STAR FEATURES

★ Rabbi Löw's Chair

★ Five-rib Vaulting

★ Jewish Standard

18th-century silver Torah crown in the Maisel Synagogue

Maisel Synagogue ⑨
MAISELOVA SYNAGÓGA

Maiselova 10. **Map** 3 B3.
'M' Staroměstská. 🚋 17, 18.
🚌 135, 207. **Open** Apr–Oct:
9am–6pm Sun–Fri; Nov–Mar
9am–4.30pm Sun–Fri. 📷 🚫 ♿

W HEN IT WAS FIRST built at
the end of the 16th
century, this was a private
house of prayer for the use of
mayor Mordechai Maisel and
his family. Maisel had made a
fortune lending money to
Emperor Rudolph II to
finance wars against the
Turks, and his synagogue was
the most richly decorated in
the city. The original building
was a victim of the fire that
devastated the Jewish Town
in 1689 and a new synagogue
was built in its place. Its
present crenellated, Gothic
appearance dates from the
start of the 20th century.
Since the 1960s the Maisel
Synagogue has housed a
fascinating collection
of Jewish silver and
other metalwork
dating from
Renaissance times
to the 20th century.
It includes many Torah
crowns, shields and finials.
Crowns and finials were
used to decorate the
rollers on which the text of
the Torah (the five books of
Moses) was kept. The shields
were hung over the mantle
that was draped over the
Torah and the pointers were

used to follow the text so that
it was not touched by
readers' hands. There are also
objects such as wedding
plates, lamps and candlesticks.
By a tragic irony, nearly all
these Jewish treasures were
brought to Prague by the
Nazis from synagogues
throughout Bohemia and
Moravia with the intention of
founding a museum of a
vanished people.

Church of the Holy Ghost ⑩
KOSTEL SV. DUCHA

Dušní, Široká. **Map** 3 B3. 📞 69 76
474. 'M' Staroměstská. 🚋 17. 🚌
135, 207. **Open** only for services. ⛪
8am Mon–Sat, 9:30am Sun. 📷 ♿

T HIS CHURCH stands on the
narrow strip of Christian
soil which once separated the
two Jewish communities of
the Middle Ages – the Jews of
the eastern and western rites.
Built in the mid-14th century,
the single-naved Gothic church
was originally part of a convent
of Benedictine nuns. The
convent was destroyed in
1420 during the Hussite Wars
(see pp26–7) and not rebuilt.
The church was badly
damaged in the Old Town
fire of 1689. The exterior
preserves the original Gothic
buttresses and high windows,
but the vault of the nave was
rebuilt in Baroque style after
the fire. The furnishings too

are mainly Baroque. The high
altar dates from 1760, and
there is an altar painting of
St Joseph by Jan Jiří Heintsch
(c1647–1712). In front of the
church stands a stone statue
of St John Nepomuk (see p137)
distributing alms (1727) by
the prolific sculptor of the
Czech Baroque Ferdinand
Maximilian Brokof. Inside the
church there are a few earlier
statues, including a 14th-
century Pietà (the heads of
the figures are later, dating
from 1628), a Late Gothic
statue of St Ann and busts of
St Wenceslas and St Adalbert
from the early 16th century.

Church of the Holy Ghost

Spanish Synagogue ⑪
ŠPANĚLSKÁ SYNAGÓGA

Vězeňská 1. **Map** 3 B2.
'M' Staroměstská. 🚋 17.
Open Apr–Oct: 9am–6pm Sun–Fri;
Nov–Mar 9am–4.30pm Sun–Fri. ♿

P RAGUE'S first syna-
gogue, known as the
Old School (Stará
Škola), once stood on
this site. In the 11th
century the Old
School was the
centre of the
community of
Jews of the
eastern rite, who
lived strictly apart
from the Jews of the
western rite, who were
concentrated round the
Old-New Synagogue.
The present building
dates from the second half
of the 19th century. The
exterior and interior are
both pseudo-Moorish in

**Motif of the Ten Commandments
on the Spanish Synagogue's façade**

appearance. The rich stucco decorations on the walls and vaults are reminiscent of the Alhambra in Spain, hence the name of the synagogue. Once closed to the public, it now houses a permanent exhibition dedicated to the history of the Jews of Bohemia.

Cubist Houses ⑫
KUBISTICKÉ DOMY

Elišky Krásnohorské, 10–14. **Map** 3 B2. Ⓜ *Staroměstská.* 🚋 *17.* **Closed** *to the public.*

THE REBUILDING of the old Jewish Quarter at the turn of the 20th century gave Prague's architects scope to experiment with many new styles. Most of the blocks in this area are covered with flowing Art Nouveau decoration, but on the corner of Bílkova and Elišky Krásnohorské there is a plain façade with a few simple repeated geometric shapes. This is an example of Cubist architecture, a fashion that did not really catch on in the rest of Europe, but was very popular with the avant-garde in Bohemia and Austria before and after World War I. This block was built for a cooperative of teachers in 1919–21.

At No. 7 Elišky Krásnohorské you can see the influence of Cubism in the curiously flattened atlantes supporting the windows. Another interesting Cubist building is the House of the Black Mother of God in Celetná *(see pp172–3).*

Church of St Simon and St Jude ⑬
KOSTEL SV. ŠIMONA A JUDY

U milosrdných. **Map** 3 B2. Ⓜ *Staroměstská.* 🚋 *17.* 🚌 *135, 207.* **Open** *for concerts.*

MEMBERS OF THE Bohemian Brethren built this church with high Late Gothic windows in 1615–20. The Brethren, founded in the mid-15th century, agreed with the Utraquists *(see p75)* in directing the congregation to receive both bread and wine

Cubist-style atlantes framing a window in Elišky Krásnohorské Street

at Holy Communion. In other respects they were more conservative than other Protestant sects, continuing to practise celibacy and Catholic sacraments such as confession. After the Battle of the White Mountain *(see pp30–31),* the Brethren were expelled from the Empire.

The church was then given to a Catholic order, the Brothers of Mercy, becoming part of a monastery and hospital. Tradition has it that the monastery's wooden steps were built from the scaffold on which 27 Czechs were executed in 1621 *(see p72).* In the 18th century the city's first anatomy lecture hall was established here and the complex continues to serve as a hospital – the Na Františku. It has not been decided what use should be made of the church.

Detail of Baroque façade of Church of St Simon and St Jude

Church of St Castullus ⑭
KOSTEL SV. HAŠTALA

Haštalské náměstí. **Map** 3 C2. 📞 *69 76 474.* 🚋 *5, 14, 26.* 🚌 *135, 125, 207.* **Open** *irregularly.* ⛪ *5pm Sun.* 🚫 ♿

THIS PEACEFUL little corner of Prague takes its name – Haštal – from the parish church of St Castullus. One of the finest Gothic buildings in Prague, the church was erected on the site of an older Romanesque structure in the second quarter of the 14th century. Much of the church had to be rebuilt after the fire of 1689, but fortunately the double nave on the north side survived. It has beautiful slender pillars supporting a delicate ribbed vault.

The interior furnishings are mainly Baroque, though there are remains of wall paintings of about 1375 in the sacristy and a metal font decorated with figures dating from about 1550. Standing in the Gothic nave is an impressive sculptural group depicting *Calvary* (1716) from the workshop of Ferdinand Maximilian Brokof.

St Agnes's Convent ⑮
KLÁŠTER SV. ANEŽKY

See pp92–3.

St Agnes's Convent ⓯
KLÁŠTER SV. ANEŽKY

Head of statue of St Agnes by Josef Myslbek

IN 1234 A CONVENT of the Poor Clares was founded here by Agnes, sister of King Wenceslas I. She was not canonized until 1989. The convent, one of the very first Gothic buildings in Bohemia, was abolished in 1782 and fell into disrepair. Following painstaking restoration in the 1960s, it has recovered much of its original appearance and is now used by the National Gallery to display a collection of 19th-century Czech art. The paintings include depictions of incidents from Czech myth and history, and Romantic landscapes.

★ Josefina
This is one of the finest portraits by Czech artist Josef Mánes (1820–71).

First floor

★ Winter Evening in Town
Jakub Schikaneder (1855–1924) painted scenes of life in Prague. Many have a mysterious, melancholy quality, but this depiction of a woman and child trudging through the snow is lighter in tone.

Ground floor

Steps to first-floor gallery

★ George of Poděbrady and Matthias Corvinus
Mikuláš Aleš (1852–1913) painted many patriotic historical scenes. Corvinus, King of Hungary, was forced to sign a treaty with King George in 1469.

Terrace café

STAR EXHIBITS

- **★ Josefina by Josef Mánes**

- **★ George of Poděbrady and Matthias Corvinus by Mikuláš Aleš**

- **★ Winter Evening in Town by Jakub Schikaneder**

Cloister
The Gothic vaulting around the cloister of the convent dates from the 14th century.

GALLERY GUIDE

The permanent exhibition is housed on the first floor of the old convent in a long gallery and smaller rooms around the cloister. One displays a model and plans for the National Theatre (see pp156–7).

Steps down to cloister

Upper part of Church of the Holy Saviour

Upper part of concert hall

VISITORS' CHECKLIST

U milosrdných 17. **Map** 3 C2.
24 81 06 28. Náměstí Republiky, Staroměstská. 17 to Law Faculty (Právnická fakulta), 5, 14, 26 to Dlouhá třída. **Open** 10am–6pm Tue–Sun (last guided tour: 5pm).

The Engraver Vorlíček and his Family

This realistic group portrait is by Karel Purkyně (1834–68), son of the great physiologist Jan Purkyně (see p151).

Oldřich and Božena

František Ženíšek painted many episodes from Czech legend and history. Here Prince Oldřich, who lived in the 11th century, spots his future bride, the beautiful Božena, in a group of village girls.

Church of the Holy Saviour

This capital decorated with heads of five Bohemian queens is matched by one with five Přemyslid kings.

Chapel of St Mary Magdalene

Church of St Francis

Entrance to Convent from Anežská

KEY

- 19th-century Czech Art
- Cloister
- Churches
- Concert hall
- Special exhibitions
- Non-exhibition space

PRAGUE CASTLE AND HRADČANY

PRAŽSKÝ HRAD A HRADČANY

THE HISTORY of Prague begins with the Castle, founded in the 9th century by Prince Bořivoj. Its commanding position high above the river Vltava soon made it the centre of the lands ruled by the Přemyslids. The buildings enclosed by the Castle walls included a palace, three churches and a monastery. In about 1320 a town called Hradčany was founded in part of the Castle's

Stained-glass window in St Vitus's Cathedral

outer bailey. The Castle has been rebuilt many times, most notably in the reigns of Charles IV and Vladislav Jagiello. After a disastrous fire in 1541, the badly-damaged buildings were rebuilt in Renaissance style and the Castle enjoyed its cultural heyday under Rudolph II. Later Habsburgs resided in Vienna, using the Castle only occasionally. Since 1918 it has been the seat of the president of the Republic.

SIGHTS AT A GLANCE

Churches and Monasteries
St Vitus's Cathedral pp100–3 ❷
St George's Basilica ❺
Capuchin Monastery ⓲
The Loreto pp116–17 ⓳
Strahov Monastery pp120–21 ㉒

Palaces
Royal Palace pp104–5 ❹
Lobkowicz Palace ❽
Belvedere ⓫
Archbishop's Palace ⓭
Martinic Palace ⓯
Černín Palace ⓴

Historic Buildings
Powder Tower ❸
Dalibor Tower ❾

Museums and Galleries
Picture Gallery of Prague Castle ❶
St George's Convent pp106–9 ❻
Sternberg Palace pp112–15 ⓮
Schwarzenberg Palace ⓰

Historic Streets
Golden Lane ❼
New World ⓱
Pohořelec ㉑

Parks and Gardens
South Gardens ⓾
Royal Garden ⓬

KEY

Street-by-Street map
See pp96–7

Tram stop

P Parking

Castle wall

GETTING THERE

Take the 22 tram to Pražský hrad (Prague Castle) or to Pohořelec. If you feel energetic, take the 12 or 22 tram to Malostranské náměstí in the Little Quarter, then walk up Nerudova or go to Malostranská metro and walk up Staré zámecké schody (Old Castle Steps). To avoid steep steps, take metro line A to Hradčanská (see Street Finder map 2).

0 metres 500
0 yards 500

◁ **The main entrance to Prague Castle**

Street-by-Street: Prague Castle

DESPITE PERIODIC FIRES and invasions, Prague Castle has retained churches, chapels, halls and towers from every period of its history, from the the Gothic splendour of St Vitus's Cathedral to the Renaissance additions of Rudolph II, the last Habsburg to use the Castle as his principal residence. The courtyards date from 1753–75 when the whole area was rebuilt in Late Baroque and Neo-Classical styles. The Castle became the seat of the Czechoslovak president in 1918 and Václav Havel, president of the Czech Republic, has an office here.

Powder Tower
Used in the past for storing gunpowder and as a bell foundry, the tower is now a museum ❸

Gothic reliquary of St George's arm in St Vitus's Cathedral

★ St Vitus's Cathedral
This relief decorates St Vitus's Golden Portal ❷

Picture Gallery of Prague Castle
Renaissance and Baroque paintings hang in the restored stables of the castle ❶

President's office

To Royal Garden

Second courtyard

Matthias Gate (1614)

First courtyard

To Hradčanské náměstí

Steps down to Little Quarter

Church of the Holy Rood

The Castle gates are crowned by copies of 18th-century statues of Fighting Giants by Ignaz Platzer.

South Gardens
18th-century statues decorate the gardens laid out in the old ramparts ❿

★ Golden Lane
The picturesque artisans' cottages along the inside of the castle wall were built in the late 16th century for the Castle's guards and gunners ⑦

LOCATOR MAP
See Street Finder, map 2

White Tower

Dalibor Tower
This grim tower takes its name from the first man to be imprisoned in it ⑨

Old Castle steps to Malostranská Metro

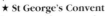

Lobkowicz Palace
The historical collection of the National Museum is housed here ⑧

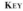

★ St George's Basilica
The vaulted chapel of the royal Bohemian martyr St Ludmilla is decorated with 16th-century paintings ⑤

★ St George's Convent
The convent houses early Bohemian art. This detail is from The Resurrection of Christ *by the 14th-century Master of the Třeboň Altar* ⑥

KEY

– – – Suggested route

0 metres	60
0 yards	60

STAR SIGHTS

★ St Vitus's Cathedral

★ Royal Palace

★ St George's Basilica and Convent

★ Golden Lane

★ Royal Palace
The uniform exterior of the palace conceals many fine Gothic and Renaissance halls. Coats of arms cover the walls and ceiling of the Room of the New Land Rolls ④

Picture Gallery of Prague Castle ❶

OBRAZÁRNA PRAŽSKÉHO HRADU

Prague Castle, the second courtyard.
Map 2 D2. 📞 24 37 33 68.
🚋 Malostranská, Hradčanská.
🚊 22, 23 **Open** 10am–6pm daily
📷 ♿

THE GALLERY was created in
1965 to hold works of art
collected since the reign of
Rudolph II *(see pp28–9)*.
Though most of the collection
was looted by the Swedes in
1648, many interesting paintings remain. Paintings from
the 16th–18th centuries form
the bulk of the collection, but
there are also sculptures,
among them a copy of a bust
of Rudolph by Adriaen de
Vries. Highlights include
Titian's *The Toilet of a Young
Lady*, Rubens' *The Assembly of
the Olympic Gods* and Guido
Reni's *The Centaur Nessus
Abducting Deianeira*. Master
Theodoric, Paolo Veronese,
Tintoretto and the Czech
Baroque artists Jan Kupecký
and Petr Brandl are among
other artists represented. The
Picture Gallery houses many
of Rudolph's best paintings.
  You can also see the
remains of the Castle's first
church, the 9th-century Church
of our Lady, thought to have

been built by Prince Bořivoj,
the first Přemyslid prince
to be baptized a Christian
(see pp20–21). The historic
site was discovered during
reconstruction.

St Vitus's Cathedral ❷

CHRÁM SV. VÍTA

See pp100–3.

Powder Tower ❸

PRAŠNÁ VĚŽ

Prague Castle, Vikářská. **Map** 2 D2.
📞 24 37 33 68. 🚋 Malostranská,
Hradčanská. 🚊 22, 23. **Open**
Apr–Oct: 9am–5pm Nov–Mar:
9am–4pm daily. 📷 🚫 🔲

A TOWER WAS BUILT here in
about 1496 by the King
Vladislav II's architect Benedikt
Ried as a cannon bastion overlooking the Stag Moat. The
original was destroyed in the
fire of 1541, but it was rebuilt
as the home and workshop of
gunsmith and bell founder
Tomáš Jaroš. In 1549 he made
Prague's largest bell, the 18-
tonne Sigismund, for the bell
tower of St Vitus's Cathedral.
  During Rudolph II's reign
(1576–1612), the tower
became a laboratory for
alchemists. It was here that

**View of the Powder Tower from
across the Stag Moat**

adventurers such as Edward
Kelley performed experiments
that convinced the emperor
they could turn lead into gold.
  In 1649, when the Swedish
army was occupying the
Castle, gunpowder exploded in
the tower, causing serious
damage. Nevertheless it was
used as a gunpowder store
until 1754, when it was
converted into flats for the
sacristans of St Vitus's
Cathedral. In the 1960s it
became a museum with
exhibits relating to Jaroš's bell
foundry and alchemy practised
in the reign of Rudolph II.

Royal Palace ❹

KRÁLOVSKÝ PALÁC

See pp104–5.

St George's Basilica ❺

BAZILICA SV. JIŘÍ

Jiřské náměstí. **Map** 2 E2. 📞 24 37 33
68. 🚋 Malostranská, Hradčanská. 🚊
22, 23. **Open** Apr–Oct: 9am–5pm daily;
Nov–Mar: 9am–4pm daily. 📷 🚫

FOUNDED by Prince Vratislav
(915–21), the basilica
predates St Vitus's Cathedral
and is the best-preserved

Titian's *The Toilet of a Young Lady* in the Castle Picture Gallery

Romanesque church in Prague. It was enlarged in 973 when the adjoining St George's Convent was established here, and rebuilt following a fire in 1142. The massive twin towers and austere interior have been scrupulously restored to give a good idea of the church's original appearance. However, the rusty red façade was a 17th-century Baroque addition.

Buried in the church is St Ludmilla, widow of the 9th-century ruler Prince Bořivoj *(see pp20–21)*. She became Bohemia's first female Christian martyr when she was strangled as she knelt at prayer on the orders of Drahomíra, her daughter-in-law. Other members of the Přemyslid dynasty buried here include Vratislav. His simple, austere tomb stands on the right-hand side of the nave at the foot of the curving steps that lead up to the choir. The impressive Baroque grille opposite encloses the tomb of Boleslav II (973–99).

St George's Convent **6**
KLÁŠTER SV. JIŘÍ

See pp106–9.

Golden Lane **7**
ZLATÁ ULIČKA

Map 2 E2. Malostranská, Hradčanská. 22, 23.

NAMED AFTER the goldsmiths who lived here in the 17th century, this short, narrow street is one of the most picturesque in Prague. One side of the lane is lined with

Façade and towers of St George's Basilica

tiny, brightly painted houses which were built right into the arches of the Castle walls. They were constructed in the late 1500s for Rudolph II's 24 Castle guards. A century later the goldsmiths moved in and modified the buildings. But by the 19th century the area had degenerated into a slum and was populated by Prague's poor and the criminal community. In the 1950s all the remaining tenants were moved and the area restored to something like its original state. Most of the houses were converted into shops selling books, Bohemian glass and other souvenirs for tourists, who flock to the narrow lane.

Golden Lane has been home to some well-known writers, including the Nobel prize-winning poet, Jaroslav Seifert, and Franz Kafka *(see p68)* who stayed at No. 22 with his sister for a few months in 1916–17.

Detail of 16th-century sgraffito on façade of Lobkowicz Palace

Because of its name, legends have spread about the street being filled with alchemists huddled over their bubbling alembics trying to produce gold for Rudolph II. In fact the alchemists had laboratories in Vikářská, the lane between St Vitus's Cathedral and the Powder Tower.

Lobkowicz Palace **8**
LOBKOVICKÝ PALÁC

Jiřská 3. **Map** 2 E2. 53 73 06. Hradčanská. 22, 23. **Open** 9am–5pm Tue–Sun. **Toy Museum** 24 37 22 94. **Open** 9:30am–5:30pm daily.

THIS IS ONE of the palaces that sprang up after the fire of 1541, when Hradčany was almost totally destroyed. It dates from 1570, and some original *sgraffito* on the façade has been preserved, but most of the present palace is Carlo Lurago's 17th-century reconstruction for the Lobkowicz family, who had inherited it in 1627. The most splendid room is the 17th-century banqueting hall with mythological frescoes by Fabian Harovník.

The palace is part of the National Museum. Its superb permanent exhibition traces Czech history from the first settlement of the Czech lands to the revolution of 1848 by means of documents, paintings, engravings, jewellery, glass, sculpture and weapons. Copies of the Czech Coronation Jewels, kept in St Vitus's Cathedral, are also on display.

Opposite the palace at No. 6 is a delightful toy museum claiming to be the world's second largest, with toys from ancient Greece to the present.

One of the tiny houses in Golden Lane

St Vitus's Cathedral ❷

CHRÁM SV. VÍTA

WORK BEGAN ON the city's most distinctive landmark in 1344 on the orders of John of Luxembourg. The first architect was the French Matthew of Arras. After his death, Swabian Peter Parler took over. His masons' lodge continued to work on the building until the Hussite Wars. Finally completed by 19th- and 20th-century architects and artists, the cathedral houses the crown jewels and the tomb of "Good King" Wenceslas *(pp20–21)*.

St Vitus's Cathedral
This 19th-century engraving shows how the cathedral looked before the additions made in 1872–1929.

Twin west spires

Triforium

Rose Window
Designed by František Kysela in 1925–7, the window above the portals depicts scenes from the biblical story of the creation.

Gargoyles
On the ornate west front, gutter spouts are given their traditional disguise.

West front

Main entrance

Nave

TIMELINE

c925 Rotunda of St Vitus built by St Wenceslas	**1359** Masterbuilder Peter Parler summoned to continue work on the cathedral	*Bust of Peter Parler on triforium*	**1619** Calvinists take over cathedral as house of prayer	**1929** Consecration of completed cathedral, nearly 1,000 years after death of St Wenceslas

1000	1200	1400	1600	1800

| **1060** Building of triple-naved basilica begins on orders of Prince Spytihněv | *Tomb of Přemysl Otakar II* | **1421** Hussites occupy St Vitus's | **1589** Royal tomb completed | **1872** Joseph Mocker begins work on west nave |
| | | **1344** King John of Luxembourg founds Gothic cathedral. French architect Matthew of Arras begins work | | **1770** New steeple added to tower after fire |

★ Flying Buttresses
The slender buttresses that surround the exterior of the nave and chancel, supporting the vaulted interior, are richly decorated like the rest of the cathedral.

Chancel

The Renaissance bell tower is capped with a Baroque "helmet".

VISITORS' CHECKLIST

Prague Castle, third courtyard.
Map 2 D2. Ⓜ *Hradčanská,
Malostranská*. 🚃 *22, 23 to
Prague Castle (Pražský hrad)
or to U Prašného mostu.*
Cathedral open *Apr–Oct:
9am–5pm daily (except during
services)*. 🚻 📷 ♿ **Steeple
open** *10am–4pm daily*. **Closed**
in bad weather. 📷

★ Chapel of St Wenceslas
The bronze ring on the chapel's north portal was thought to be the one to which St Wenceslas clung as he was murdered by his brother Boleslav (see pp20–21).

To Royal Palace
(See pp104–5)

The tomb of St Wenceslas is connected to an altar, decorated with semi-precious stones.

★ Golden Portal
Until the 19th century this was the main cathedral entrance, and it is still used on special occasions. Above it is a mosaic of The Last Judgment by 14th-century Venetian craftsmen.

Gothic Vaulting
The skills of architect Peter Parler are never more clearly seen than in the delicate fans of ribbing that support the three Gothic arches of the Golden Portal.

STAR FEATURES

★ **Chapel of St Wenceslas**

★ **Golden Portal**

★ **Flying Buttresses**

A Guided Tour of St Vitus's Cathedral

West door: St Wenceslas' murder

A WALK AROUND St Vitus's takes you back through a thousand years of history. Go in through the west portal to see some of the best elements of the modern, Neo-Gothic style and continue past a succession of side chapels to catch glimpses of religious artefacts such as saintly relics, and works of art from Renaissance paintings to modern statuary. Allow plenty of time to gaze at the richly decorated, jewel-encrusted St Wenceslas Chapel before you leave.

② Chancel
The chancel was built by Peter Parler from 1372. It is remarkable for the soaring height of its vault, counter-pointed by the intricacy of the webbed Gothic tracery.

Cathedral organ (1757)

New sacristy

① Alfons Mucha Window
The cathedral contains many superb examples of 20th-century Czech stained glass, notably St Cyril and St Methodius.

Main entrance (West Portal)

Thun Chapel

Chapel of St Ludmilla

THE FOUR ERAS OF ST VITUS'S

Excavations have revealed sections of the northern apse of St Wenceslas's original rotunda, and architectural and sculptural remains of the later basilica, beneath the existing cathedral. The western, Neo-Gothic end is a faithful completion of the 14th-century plan.

KEY

☐	Rotunda, 10th century
▨	Basilica, 11th century
☐	Gothic cathedral, 14th century
☐	19th- and 20th-century additions to cathedral

Leopold II is shown in a contemporary engraving being crowned King of Bohemia at the cathedral in September 1791. Mozart composed an opera, *La Clemenza di Tito*, in honour of the occasion.

③ Flight of Frederick of the Palatinate

In depicting the sad aftermath of the Battle of the White Mountain in 1620 (see p31), this carved wooden panel shows 17th-century Prague in fascinating detail.

Chapel of St John the Baptist

Pulpit (1618)

③

②

④

⑦

⑤

Chapel of the Holy Relics

Chapel of the Holy Rood

⑥

⑧

Stairs to crypt

Exit from crypt

Golden Portal

④ Tomb of St John Nepomuk

Crafted from solid silver in 1736, this elaborate tomb honours the saint who became the focus of a Counter-Reformation cult (see p137).

⑤ Royal Oratory

The vault of the 15th-century Late-Gothic oratory is carved with branches instead of ribs.

⑥ Crypt

Steps lead down to the royal tombs, including those of Charles IV and his four wives, as well as vestiges of the early rotunda and basilica.

⑧ St Wenceslas Chapel

Gothic frescoes with scenes from the Bible and the life of the saint cover the walls, interspersed with a patchwork of polished gemstones and fine gilding. Every object is a work of art – this golden steeple held the wafers and wine for Holy Communion.

⑦ Royal Mausoleum

Ferdinand I died in 1564. His beloved wife and son, Maximilian II, are buried alongside him in the mausoleum.

KEY

 — Tour route

Royal Palace ❹

KRÁLOVSKÝ PALÁC

FROM THE TIME Prague Castle was first fortified in the 11th century *(see pp22–3)*, the palace was the seat of Bohemian princes. The building consists of three different architectural layers. A Romanesque palace built by Soběslav I around 1135 forms the cellars of the present building. Přemysl Otakar II and Charles IV then added their own palaces above this, while the top floor, built for Vladislav Jagiello, contains the massive Gothic Vladislav Hall. During the period of Habsburg rule the palace housed government offices, courts and the old Bohemian Diet (parliament). In 1924 it was extensively restored.

Riders' Staircase

These wide and gently sloping steps, with their Gothic rib vault, were used by knights on horseback to get to Vladislav Hall for indoor jousting competitions.

The Diet, the medieval parliament, was also the throne room. Destroyed by fire in 1541, it was rebuilt by Bonifaz Wohlmut in 1563.

An overhead passage from the palace leads to the Royal Oratory in St Vitus's Cathedral *(see p103)*.

14

4

3

2

5

Entrance

Vladislav Hall

The 17th-century painting by Aegidius Sadeler shows that the Royal Court was very like a public market. The hall's magnificent rib vaulting was designed by Benedikt Ried in the 1490s.

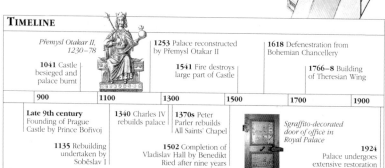

TIMELINE

Přemysl Otakar II, 1230–78

1041 Castle besieged and palace burnt

1253 Palace reconstructed by Přemysl Otakar II

1541 Fire destroys large part of Castle

1618 Defenestration from Bohemian Chancellery

1766–8 Building of Theresian Wing

900	1100	1300	1500	1700	1900

Late 9th century Founding of Prague Castle by Prince Bořivoj

1135 Rebuilding undertaken by Soběslav I

1340 Charles IV rebuilds palace

1370s Peter Parler rebuilds All Saints' Chapel

1502 Completion of Vladislav Hall by Benedikt Ried after nine years

Sgraffito-decorated door of office in Royal Palace

1924 Palace undergoes extensive restoration

PLAN AND CROSS SECTION OF ROYAL PALACE

The cross section of the palace shows the three distinct levels of the building, all constructed at different times. The plan shows how Vladislav Hall dominates the entire palace structure.

Upper floor

Ground level

Lower floor

VISITORS' CHECKLIST

Prague Castle, third courtyard.
Map 2 D2. **[** 24 37 33 68.
M Hradčanská, up K Brusce, then through the Royal Garden; Malostranská, left up Klárov, then up Old Castle Steps. **[** 22 to Prague Castle (Pražský hrad). **Open** Apr–Oct: 9am–5pm; Nov– Mar: 9am–4pm Tue–Sun (last adm: 1hr before closing).

All Saints' Chapel was built by Peter Parler for Charles IV. After the 1541 fire, its vault had to be rebuilt and it was redecorated in the Baroque style.

KEY TO ROYAL PALACE

☐ Romanesque and Early Gothic

☐ Late Gothic

☐ Rebuilt after 1541 fire

☐ Baroque and later

1 Eagle Fountain	**10** All Saints' Chapel
2 Vestibule	**11** Diet Hall
3 Green Chamber	**12** Riders' Staircase
4 King's Bedchamber	**13** Court of Appeal
5 Romanesque tower	**14** Palace courtyard
6 Vladislav Hall	**15** Hall of the
7 Bohemian	Romanesque palace
Chancellery	**16** Old Land Rolls
8 Imperial Council	**17** Palace of
Room steps	Charles IV
9 Terrace	**18** New Land Rolls

The Theresian Way was built to house the office registers.

Bohemian Chancellery
This 17th-century Dutch-style stove decorates the former royal offices of the Habsburgs. The chancellery is the site of the 1618 defenestration.

DEFENESTRATION OF 1618

Painting by Václav Brožík, 1889

On 23 May, 1618, more than 100 Protestant nobles, led by Count Thurn, marched into the palace to protest against the succession to the throne of the intolerant Habsburg Archduke Ferdinand. The two Catholic Governors appointed by Ferdinand, Jaroslav Martinic and Vilém Slavata, were confronted and, after a row, the Protestants threw both the Governors and their secretary, Philipp Fabricius, out of the eastern window. Falling some 15 m (50 ft), they survived by landing in a dung heap. This event signalled the beginning of the Thirty Years' War. The Catholics attributed the survival of the Governors to the intervention of angels.

The New Land Rolls
These rooms are decorated with the crests of clerks who worked here from 1561 to 1774.

St George's Convent ●

KLÁŠTER SV. JIŘÍ

THE FIRST CONVENT in Bohemia was founded here close to the Royal Palace in 973 by Prince Boleslav II. His sister Mlada was its first abbess. Rebuilt over the centuries, the convent was finally abolished in 1782 and converted into barracks. In 1962–74 it was reconstructed to house the National Gallery's Czech art of the Gothic, Renaissance and Baroque periods. It includes magnificent religious paintings from the 14th century, when Bohemia was one of the most cultured kingdoms in Europe.

★ St Elizabeth
Master Theodoric painted 127 such panels for the Chapel of the Holy Cross at Karlstein in 1360–65 (see p168). His art is remarkable for the realism in the faces of his saints.

Lower floor

★ Christ on the Mount of Olives
This coloured panel (c1350) is by the Master of the Vyšší Brod (Hohenfurth) Altar, and is one of a series of Scenes from the Life of Christ.

Stairs down from ground floor

GALLERY GUIDE

The exhibits are arranged in chronological order, beginning with sculpture and paintings of the 14th century, which means you must begin your tour on the lower floor. You have to follow a more or less fixed route, which takes you back up to the ground floor for later Gothic art, then up to the first floor to the Renaissance and Baroque collections.

Stairs to upper and lower floors

Ground floor

KEY

☐	14th-century Czech art
☐	15th-century Czech art
☐	16th-century Czech art
☐	Rudolphian Mannerism (c1600)
☐	Czech art of the Baroque
☐	Chapel of St Anne
☐	St George's Basilica
☐	Special exhibitions
☐	Non-exhibition space

Entrance to Gallery from Jiřské náměstí

Assumption of the Virgin Mary

In 15th-century Bohemia the Church encouraged the cult of the Virgin. This painting (1450) by an unknown master used to hang in a chapel in Deštná in southern Bohemia.

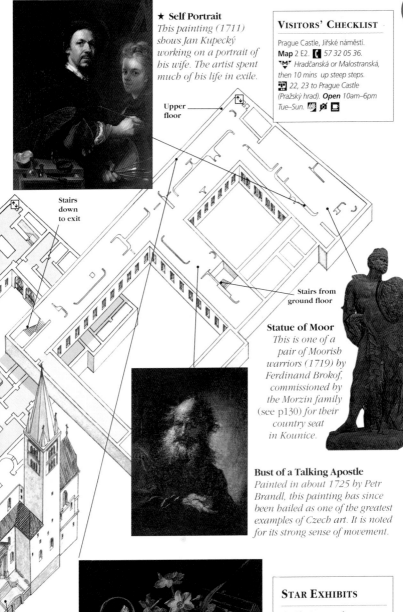

★ **Self Portrait**
This painting (1711) shows Jan Kupecký working on a portrait of his wife. The artist spent much of his life in exile.

Upper floor

Stairs down to exit

Stairs from ground floor

St George's Basilica *(see pp98–9)*

Statue of Moor
This is one of a pair of Moorish warriors (1719) by Ferdinand Brokof, commissioned by the Morzin family (see p130) for their country seat in Kounice.

Bust of a Talking Apostle
Painted in about 1725 by Petr Brandl, this painting has since been hailed as one of the greatest examples of Czech art. It is noted for its strong sense of movement.

Still Life with Watch
Johann-Adalbert Angermayer (1674–1740) filled his delicate still lifes with symbols of the transience and vanity of human life.

VISITORS' CHECKLIST

Prague Castle, Jiřské náměstí.
Map 2 E2. 57 32 05 36.
Hradčanská or Malostranská, then 10 mins up steep steps.
22, 23 to Prague Castle (Pražský hrad). **Open** 10am–6pm Tue–Sun.

STAR EXHIBITS

★ **Christ on the Mount of Olives by the Master of the Vyšší Brod Altar**

★ **St Elizabeth by Master Theodoric**

★ **Self Portrait by Jan Kupecký**

Exploring the St George's Collection

THIS WONDERFUL COLLECTION gives a fascinating insight into the art and sculpture of the two periods of Prague's history that are so conspicuous in the city's architecture – the Gothic from the age of Charles IV and the Baroque. The earlier period is represented by many naive, but expressive woodcarvings and panel paintings, while the Baroque has dramatic biblical paintings and statues of saints and angels in flamboyant poses. Some exhibits are occasionally on loan to museums in other parts of the country.

Wooden statue of *Suckling Madonna* from Konopiště (c1380)

14TH-CENTURY CZECH ART

BOHEMIA'S great period of political and economic power under the Emperor Charles IV was also a golden age for painting and sculpture. The first section of the gallery contains works by the two greatest painters of Charles's reign, the anonymous Master of the Vyšší Brod Altar and the only painter of the time whose name we know – Master Theodoric. The latter is justly famous for his panels of saints from Karlstein *(see p166).* It is the humanity of his portraits of *St Elizabeth, St Jerome, St Matthew* and *St Vitus* that makes them so appealing. The influence of Theodoric is evident in the large *Votive Panel of Bishop*

Jan Očko of Vlašim, which shows Charles IV kneeling before the Virgin in heaven *(see p24).* The Master of the Vyšší Brod Altar, who like Theodoric was active in the middle of the 14th century, painted a magnificent series of brilliantly coloured *Scenes from the Life of Christ.*

The wood carvings from various churches in Bohemia are mainly of Madonnas and the Crucifixion. Originally they would all have been painted and gilded, but few traces of their bright colours remain. There are also sights you may recognize from the streets of Prague, including the tympanum of the Gothic gateway to the Church of Our Lady of the Snows *(see p146)* and the statue of *St George Slaying the Dragon* that stands in the courtyard right outside St Vitus's Cathedral.

The ones in situ are copies; these are the originals, on display here for safekeeping.

On the ground floor make sure you go into the room containing the works of the Master of the Třeboň Altar to see his *Resurrection* and *The Madonna of Roudnice.*

15TH-CENTURY CZECH ART

AFTER 1400 Bohemia never recovered the prosperity of the preceding century and art, especially in the period of the Hussite Wars *(see pp26–7),* was generally of lesser quality. Nevertheless look out for the delightful *Assumption of the Virgin Mary* from Deštná and the triptych from St George's Basilica with a central panel depicting the death of the Virgin. In the many grim and gory paintings of the Cruci-fixion in this section, notice the souls of the two thieves crucified with Christ. Angels carry the good thief's soul up to heaven, while demons drag the other's down to hell.

EARLY 16TH-CENTURY CZECH ART

LATER WORKS in the gallery's collection of Gothic art show greater similarity with contemporary German and

Altarpiece of *The Holy Trinity* by Master of the Litoměřice Altar (c1515)

Stag Hunt (c1610) by Roelant Savery, artist at the court of Rudolph II

Italian paintings. The finest Bohemian painter of this period is the Master of the Litoměřice Altar, active at the beginning of the 16th century. His most impressive works are an altar triptych showing *The Holy Trinity* and *The Visitation of the Virgin Mary*. The last room in this section is devoted to reliefs by a woodcarver who signed his works with the initials I P. His style is that of the so-called Danube school and his figures are clearly influenced by Dürer. Dating from about 1520, the *Votive Altarpiece of Zlíchov* shows a kneeling knight with the Virgin Mary, St Andrew, Christ and Death.

RUDOLPHIAN MANNERISM (c1600)

Mannerism is the rather disparaging term used to describe a style that evolved in Italy after the Renaissance. Many 16th-century painters and sculptors strove to outdo the exaggerated poses of Michelangelo's later works just for the sake of creating a startling effect. A typical example of this is *The Last Judgment* by Josef Heintz. A more successful exponent of this style was Bartholomaeus Spranger from Antwerp. He died in Prague in 1611 while in the employment of the Emperor Rudolph II *(see p28–9)*. With his passion for the unusual and the artificial, Rudolph loved Mannerist artists and invited many to work at his court in Prague.

Rudolph's great collection was dispersed when Prague Castle was looted in 1648, but the few works on show here give an idea of his tastes. The best are probably the paintings of the German-born Hans von Aachen and the sculptures of the Dutch-born Adriaen de Vries. Not all the works here are typically Mannerist. The landscapes of Roelant Savery, for example, show a genuine feeling for the beauty of the Bohemian forests gained during his stay in Prague (1604–12).

CZECH ART OF THE BAROQUE

There are many agreeable surprises in the collection of Baroque art. Of the paintings of religious subjects, the finest are undoubtedly those by Petr Brandl. The old men who feature in many of his works are beautifully painted. Particularly moving is the painting known as *Simeon and the Infant Jesus*. Then there are several masterly portraits by the 17th-century Karel Škréta and by Jan Kupecký. On a smaller scale, look out for the delightful still lifes by the Swiss painter Johann Rudolf Bys and his pupil Johann-Adalbert Angermayer.

The sculptures are chiefly by the 18th-century artists whose works decorate so many of the city's Baroque churches: Ferdinand Brokof, Matthias Braun and Ignaz Platzer. Several of the more flamboyant saints and angels are in painted wood, an unexpected link with the early polychrome wood carvings of the Gothic period.

Hedvika Francesca Wussin by Jan Kupecký (1710)

Old prison in the Dalibor Tower

Dalibor Tower ❾
DALIBORKA

Prague Castle, Zlatá ulička. **Map** 2 E2.
🚇 *Malostranská.* 🚋 *22, 23.*
Closed for renovation. 🈺 🚫

THIS 15TH-CENTURY tower with a conical roof was part of the fortifications built by King Vladislav Jagiello *(see p26–7)*. His coat of arms can be seen on the outer wall. The tower also served as a prison and is named after its first inmate, Dalibor of Kozojedy, a young knight sentenced to death for harbouring some outlawed serfs. While awaiting execution, he was kept in an underground dungeon, into which he had to be lowered through a hole in the floor.

According to legend, while in prison he learnt to play the violin. People sympathetic to his plight came to listen to his playing and provided him with food and drink, which

they lowered on a rope from a window – prisoners were often left to starve to death. The story was used by Bedřich Smetana in his opera *Dalibor*. The tower ceased to serve as a prison in 1781. Visitors can see part of the old prison.

South Gardens ❿
JIŽNÍ ZAHRADY

Prague Castle (access from Hradčanské náměstí). **Map** 2 D3.
🚇 *Malostranská, Hradčanská.* 🚋 *22, 23.* **Open** Apr–Oct: 10am–6pm daily. 📷

THE GARDENS occupy the long narrow band of land below the Castle overlooking the Little Quarter. Several small gardens have been linked to form what is now known as the South Gardens. The oldest, the Paradise Garden (Rajská zahrada), laid out in 1562, contains a circular pavilion built for Emperor Matthias in 1617. Its carved wooden ceiling shows the coloured emblems of the 39 countries of the Habsburg Empire. The Garden on the Ramparts (Zahrada Na valech) dates from the 19th century. It occupies a former vegetable patch and is famous as the site of the defenestration of 1618 *(see p105)*, when two Imperial governors were thrown from a first-floor window. Two obelisks were subsequently erected by Ferdinand II to mark the spots where they

landed. Extensive modifications were carried out in the 1920s by Josip Plečnik, who built the Bull Staircase leading to the Paradise Garden and the observation terrace. Below the terrace, in the former Hartig Garden, is a Baroque music pavilion designed by Giovanni Battista Alliprandi. Beside it stand four statues of Classical gods by Antonín Braun.

Alliprandi's music pavilion in the South Gardens

Belvedere ⓫
BELVEDÉR

Prague Castle, Royal Garden. **Map** 2 E1.
🚇 *Malostranská, Hradčanská.* 🚋 *22, 23.* **Open** only for exhibitions. 🈺

BUILT BY FERDINAND I for his beloved wife Anne, the Belvedere is one of the finest Italian Renaissance buildings north of the Alps. Also known as the Royal Summer Palace (Královský letohrádek), it is an arcaded summerhouse

The Belvedere, Emperor Ferdinand I's summer palace in the Royal Garden beside Prague Castle

Antonín Braun's statue of *The Allegory of Night* in front of the *sgraffito* decoration of the Ball Game Hall in the Royal Garden

The Royal Garden is the best-kept garden in Prague and a beautiful place for a stroll, especially in spring when thousands of tulips bloom in its immaculate beds. This is where tulips, bought from Turkey by Ferdinand I's ambassador, were first acclimatized to Europe before being taken to Holland.

At the entrance to the garden is the Lion Court where Rudolph II had his zoo (now a restaurant). As well as lions, Rudolph kept bears, leopards, panthers and many other wild animals. Some roamed free in the Stag Moat, which separates the garden from the Castle.

Archbishop's Palace ⑬
ARCIBISKUPSKÝ PALÁC

Hradčanské náměstí 16. **Map** 2 D3. ☎ 20 39 21 11. ⛔ *Malostranská, Hradčanská.* 🚊 22, 23. **Not open** to the public.

Ferdinand I bought this sumptuous palace in 1562 for the first Catholic Archbishop since the Hussite Wars *(see pp26–7)*. It replaced the old Archbishop's Palace in the Little Quarter, which had been destroyed during the wars, and has remained the Archbishop's seat in Prague ever since. In the period after the Battle of the White Mountain *(see p30–31)*, the presence of the Archbishop's Palace right beside the castle was a powerful symbol of Catholic domination of the city and the Czech lands. Its spectacular cream-coloured Rococo façade was designed by Johann Joseph Wirch in the 1760s for Archbishop Antonín Příchovský, whose coat of arms sits proudly above the earlier 17th-century portal.

with slender Ionic columns topped by a roof shaped like an inverted ship's hull clad in blue-green copper. The main architect was Paolo della Stella, who was also responsible for the ornate reliefs inside the arcade. Work began in 1538, but was interrupted by the great Castle fire of 1541. The Belvedere was eventually completed in 1564.

In the middle of the small geometrical garden in front of the palace stands the Singing Fountain. Dating from 1568, it owes its name to the musical sound the water makes as it hits the bronze bowl, though you have to place your head very close to appreciate the effect. The fountain was cast by Tomáš Jaroš, the famous bell founder, who lived and worked in the Powder Tower *(see p98)*.

Many of the Belvedere's works of art were plundered by the occupying Swedish army in 1648. The statues stolen included Adriaen de Vries's 16th-century bronze of *Mercury and Psyche*, which is now in the Louvre in Paris. The Belvedere is now used as an art gallery.

Royal Garden ⑫
KRÁLOVSKÁ ZAHRADA

Prague Castle, U Prašného mostu. **Map** 2 D2. ⛔ *Malostranská, Hradčanská.* 🚊 22, 23. **Open** May–Oct: 10am–6pm daily. 🅿️ 📷 ♿

The garden was created in 1535 for Ferdinand I. Its appearance has been altered over time, but nevertheless some excellent examples of 16th-century garden architecture have survived, notably the Belvedere and the Ball Game Hall (Míčovna), built by Bonifaz Wohlmut in 1569. The building is covered in beautiful, though much re-stored, Renaissance *sgraffito*, a form of decoration created by cutting a design through the wet top layer of plaster onto a contrasting undercoat. The Ball Game Hall was used primarily for playing a form of real tennis, but the game gradually went out of fashion and in 1723 the building was converted into stables.

Příchovský coat of arms

Sternberg Palace ⑭
ŠTERNBERSKÝ PALÁC

See pp112–15.

Sternberg Palace **⑭**

ŠTERNBERSKÝ PALÁC

F RANZ JOSEF STERNBERG founded the Society of
Patriotic Friends of the Arts in Bohemia in 1796.
Fellow noblemen would lend their finest pictures and
sculpture to the society, which had its headquarters
in the early-18th-century Sternberg Palace. Since
1949, the fine Baroque building has been used to
house the National Gallery's collection of European
art, with its superb range of Old Masters.

★ Scholar in his Study
*In this painting from 1634
Rembrandt used keenly ob-
served detail to convey
wisdom in the face of
the old scholar.*

Cardinal Cesi's Garden
*Henrick van Cleve's paint-
ing (1548) provides
a valuable image of a
Renaissance collec-
tions of antiquities.
The garden was
later destroyed.*

First floor

Ground floor

Garden Room

Stairs to second floor

Stairs to first floor

STAR SIGHTS

★ **Head of Christ
by El Greco**

★ **Scholar in his Study
by Rembrandt**

★ **Adam and Eve
by Cranach the Elder**

Ticket office

**Passageway
to Hradčanské
náměstí**

KEY

- ☐ Icons, Classical and ancient art
- ☐ German and Austrian art
(1400–1800)
- ☐ Italian art (1300–1550)
- ☐ Flemish and Dutch art (1400–1600)
- ☐ Flemish and Dutch art (1600–1800)
- ☐ Italian, French and Spanish art
(1600–1800)
- ☐ Special exhibition space
- ☐ Non-exhibition space

Concerning the Eden (1618)
Roelandt Savery studied models of exotic animals, brought to Prague by Persian nobles, at the court of Emperor Rudolf II. He was then able to paint real animals.

Second floor

Chinese Cabinet

★ **Head of Christ**
Painted by El Greco in the 1590s, this portrait emphasizes the humanity of Christ. At the same time the curious square halo framing the head gives the painting the qualities of an ancient icon.

Stairs down to other floors and exit

GALLERY GUIDE
The gallery is arranged on three floors around the central courtyard of the palace. The ground floor, reached from the courtyard, houses temporary exhibitions. The stairs to the collections on the upper floors are opposite the ticket office at the main entrance. With a few exceptions, the earlier works are on the first floor, the later ones on the second.

★ **Adam and Eve** (c1538)
The nudes in Lucas Cranach the Elder's painting show the spirit of the Renaissance, tempered by Lutheran reform.

The Lamentation of Christ
The frozen, sculptural figures make this one of the finest paintings by Lorenzo Monaco (1408).

Exploring the Sternberg Collections

T HE NATIONAL GALLERY'S collection of European art ranks among the best collections of comparable size. Since the transfer of the outstanding 19th- and 20th-century exhibits to Veletržní Palace in 1996 *(see pp164–5)* the Sternberg has been expanding its permanent exhibition, with especially strong representations from Italian medieval art, Neapolitan artists of the 17th and 18th centuries, Dutch and Flemish works, and German art of the 15th to 17th centuries. There is also a fine collection of Renaissance bronzes, and the fascinating Chinese Cabinet is on display again after a restoration lasting several years.

St John the Baptist by Rodin

ICONS, CLASSICAL AND ANCIENT ART

A SMALL ROOM on the first floor contains an odd assortment of paintings that do not quite fit in with the rest of the collection. These include a *Portrait of a Young Woman* dating from the 2nd century AD, discovered during excavations at Fayoum in Egypt in the 19th century.

The majority of the exhibits, however, are icons of the Orthodox church. These come from a variety of Eastern European countries – some are Byzantine, some Italo-Greek and some Russian. The finest examples are two of the later 16th-century works, *The Lamentation of Christ* from Crete and *Christ's Entry Into Jerusalem* from Russia.

Christ's Entry into Jerusalem, a **16th-century Russian icon**

GERMAN AND AUSTRIAN ART (1400–1800)

O NE OF THE most celebrated paintings in the Sternberg is Albrecht Dürer's *The Feast of the Rosary*, painted during the artist's stay in Venice in 1506. It has special significance for Prague since it was bought by Emperor Rudolph II. The two figures seen in front of the Virgin and Child are Maximilian I (Rudolph's great-great-grandfather) and Pope Julius II.

There are works by several other important German painters of the Renaissance, including Hans Holbein the Elder and the Younger and Lucas Cranach the Elder. Cranach is represented by four works including a striking *Adam and Eve* and a wooden panel depicting St Christine, a rare relic from a destroyed altarpiece that once stood in St Vitus's Cathedral.

ITALIAN ART (1300–1550)

W HEN YOU ENTER the rooms on the first floor, you are greeted by a splendid array of early diptychs, triptychs and other richly gilded panel paintings from the churches of Tuscany and northern Italy. Most came originally from the d'Este collection at Konopiště Castle *(see p169)*. Of particularly high quality are the two triangular panels of saints by the 14th-century Sienese painter Pietro Lorenzetti and a moving *Lamentation of Christ* by Lorenzo Monaco.

A fascinating element of the collection is the display of Renaissance bronze statuettes. Fashionable amongst Italian nobility of the 15th century, these little bronzes were at first cast from famous or newly-discovered works of antiquity. Later, sculptors began to use the medium more freely – Padua, for example, specialized in the depiction of small animals – and producers also adapted items for use as decorative household goods such as oil lamps, ink pots and door knockers. This small collection has representative works from all the major Italian producers except Mantua and, while many variations can be found in other museums throughout the world, there are some pieces here that are both unique and outstanding examples of the craft.

The Feast of the Rosary by Dürer (1506)

Don Miguel de Lardizábal (1815), by Francisco Goya

ITALIAN, FRENCH AND SPANISH ART (1600–1800)

Painters are grouped in a slightly arbitrary way in this part of the gallery, called the "piano nobile", but there are several delightful surprises here. Italian paintings include *St Jerome* by Tintoretto and *The Flagellation of Christ* and *Portrait of an Elderly Man* by Jacopo Bassano. There is also an expressive portrait by Bronzino of *Eleanor of Toledo*, wife of Cosimo de' Medici.

French art is represented chiefly by the 17th-century painters Simon Vouet (*The Suicide of Lucretia*), Sébastien Bourdon and Charles Le Brun, but there are also bronzes by Rodin. Spanish painting is even less well represented, but two of the collection's finest works are a haunting *Head of Christ* by El Greco – the only work by the artist on display in the Czech Republic – and a noble half-length portrait of the politician *Don Miguel de Lardizábal* by Goya.

FLEMISH AND DUTCH ART (1400–1600)

There are two rich and varied collections of Flemish and Dutch art, ranging from rural scenes by Pieter Brueghel the Elder to portraits by Rubens and Rembrandt.

Highlights of the former include an altarpiece showing the *Adoration of the Magi* by Geertgen tot Sint Jans. Other early works of great interest include *St Luke Drawing the Virgin* by Jan Gossaert (c1515), one of the first works of art from the Netherlands to show the clear influence of the Italian Renaissance.

FLEMISH AND DUTCH ART (1600–1700)

The collection from the 17th century includes several major works, notably by Peter Paul Rubens who, in 1639, sent two paintings to the Augustinians of the Church of St Thomas *(see p127)* in the Little Quarter. The originals were lent to the gallery in 1896 and replaced by copies.

The violence and drama of *The Martyrdom of St Thomas* is in complete contrast to the spiritual calm of *St Augustine*. Two other fine portraits are those of Rembrandt's *Scholar in His Study* and Frans Hals' *Portrait of Jasper Schade*.

Also on display is a wide assortment of paintings by other, less-prominent, artists who nonetheless represent the range and quality of the so-called "golden century".

Eleanor of Toledo (1540s) by the Florentine Mannerist painter Agnolo Bronzino

THE CHINESE CABINET

After several years of difficult restoration work, this curiosity is once again open to the public. The richly-decorated little chamber was part of the original furnishings of the Sternberg Palace, and was designed as an intimate withdrawing room away from the bustle of the grand state rooms. In its plethora of decorative styles, Baroque mingles with Far Eastern motifs and techniques, which were fashionable at the turn of the 18th century. The vaulted ceiling features the Star of the Sternbergs among its geometric decorations. Black lacquered walls are embellished with cobalt blue and white medallions in golden frames, while gilded shelves once held rare Oriental porcelain.

The Loreto ⓳

LORETA

EVER SINCE ITS CONSTRUCTION in 1626, the Loreto has been an important place of pilgrimage. It was commissioned by Kateřina of Lobkowicz, a Czech aristocrat who was very keen to promote the legend of the Santa Casa of Loreto *(see opposite)*. The heart of the complex is a copy of the house believed to be the Virgin Mary's. The Santa Casa was enclosed by cloisters in 1661, and a Baroque façade 60 years later by Christoph and Kilian Ignaz Dientzenhofer. The grandiose design and miraculous stories about the Loreto were part of Ferdinand II's campaign to re-catholicize the Czechs *(see pp30–31)*.

Katerina Lobkowicz, founder of the Santa Casa

Bell Tower
Enclosed in this large Baroque tower, is a set of 27 bells cast in 1694 by the Danish engineer Petr Naumann.

Chapel of St Joseph

Fountain decorated with a sculpture of the Resurrection

Chapel of St Francis Seraphim

Chapel of St Ann

Entrance from Loretánské náměstí

★ Loreto Treasury
This gold-plated, diamond-encrusted monstrance, for displaying the host, is one of the valuable liturgical items in the Loreto treasury, most of which originated in the 16th–18th centuries.

Baroque Entrance
The balustrade above the Loreto's front entrance is decorated with statues of St Joseph and St John the Baptist by Ondřej Quitainer.

STAR SIGHTS

★ **Loreto Treasury**

★ **Santa Casa**

★ **Church of the Nativity**

★ **Santa Casa**
Stucco figures of many of the Old Testament prophets and reliefs from the life of the Virgin Mary by Italian artists decorate the chapel.

VISITORS' CHECKLIST

Loretánské náměstí, Hradčany.
Map 1C3 | 20 51 67 40.
🚃 22 to Pohořelec. **Open**
9am–12:15pm, 1–4:30pm
Tue–Sun. 🎫 📷

★ **Church of the Nativity**
Gruesome relics, including fully-clothed skeletons with death masks made of wax, line the walls of this 18th-century church. The frescoes are by Václav Vavřinec Reiner.

Chapel of the Holy Rood

17th-Century Cloister
Built originally as a shelter for the many pilgrims who visited the shrine, the cloister is covered with frescoes.

Chapel of St Anthony of Padua

Chapel of Our Lady of Sorrows

Fountain Sculpture
This copy of The Ascension of the Virgin Mary *is taken from Jan Brüderle's 1739 sandstone statue, now in the Lapidarium (see pp176–7).*

LEGEND OF THE SANTA CASA

The original house, said to be where the Archangel Gabriel told Mary about the future birth of Jesus, is in the small Italian town of Loreto. It was believed that angels transported the house from Nazareth to Loreto in 1278 following threats by infidels. After the Protestants' defeat in 1620 *(see pp30–31)*, Catholics promoted the legend, and 50 replicas of the Loreto were built in Bohemia and Moravia. This, the grandest, became the most important in Bohemia, and received many visitors.

The stuccoed Santa Casa

Martinic Palace **⑮**
MARTINICKÝ PALÁC

Hradčanské náměstí 8. **Map** 1 C2.
📞 24 30 81 11, 53 64 16.
🚇 Malostranská, Hradčanská.
🚋 22, 23. **Closed** to the public.

IN THE COURSE of the palace's restoration in the early 1970s, workmen uncovered the original 16th-century façade decorated with ornate cream and brown *sgraffito* (*see p111*). It depicts Old Testament scenes, including the story of Joseph and Potiphar's wife. More *sgraffito* came to light in the courtyard, showing the story of Samson and the Labours of Hercules.

Martinic Palace was enlarged by Jaroslav Bořita of Martinice, who was one of the imperial governors thrown from a window of the Royal Palace in 1618 (*see p105*).

According to an old legend, between 11pm and midnight the ghost of a fiery black dog appears at the palace and accompanies walkers as far as the Loreto (*see pp116–17*), where it disappears again. Today the palace houses the city architecture department.

Schwarzenberg Palace **⑯**
SCHWARZENBERSKÝ PALÁC

Hradčanské náměstí 2. **Map** 2 D3.
📞 20 20 20 23. 🚇 Malostranská, Hradčanská. 🚋 22, 23. **Open** May–Oct: 10am–5:30pm Tue–Sun.
🎥 📷

FROM A DISTANCE, the façade of this grand Renaissance palace appears to be clad in projecting pyramid-shaped stonework. On closer inspection, this turns out to be an illusion created by *sgraffito* patterns

incised on a flat wall. Built originally for the Lobkowicz family by the Italian architect Agostino Galli in 1545–76, the gabled palace is Florentine rather than Bohemian in style. It passed through several hands before the Schwarzenbergs, a leading family in the Habsburg Empire, bought it in 1719. Much of the interior decoration has survived, including four painted ceilings on the second floor dating from 1580. Since 1945 the palace has housed the Museum of Military History, a collection of arms and uniforms from the wars that in Bohemia from the time of the first Slavs up to 1918. Look out for the section illustrating the tactics adopted by the Hussites in the 15th century.

New World **⑰**
NOVÝ SVĚT

Map 1 B2. 🚋 22, 23.

NOW A CHARMING STREET of small cottages, Nový Svět (New World) used to be the name of this area of Hradčany. Developed in the mid-14th century to provide houses for the castle workers, the area was twice destroyed by fire, the last time being in 1541. Most of the cottages date from the 17th century. They have been spruced up, but are otherwise unspoilt and very different in character from the

Tycho Brahe, Rudolph II's astronomer

rest of Hradčany. In defiance of their poverty, the inhabitants chose golden house signs to identify their modest houses – you will see a Golden Pear, a Grape, a Foot, a Bush and an Acorn. Plaques identify No. 1 as the former home of Rudolph II's brilliant court astronomer, Tycho Brahe, and No. 25 as the 1857 birthplace of the great Czech violinist František Ondříček.

Capuchin Monastery **⑱**
KAPUCÍNSKÝ KLÁŠTER

Loretánské náměstí 6. **Map** 1 B3.
🚋 22, 23. **Closed** to the public except the church.

BOHEMIA'S FIRST Capuchin monastery was founded here in 1600. It is connected to the neighbouring Loreto (*see pp116–17*) by an overhead roofed passage. Attached to the monastery is the Church of Our Lady Queen of Angels, a single-naved building with plain furnishings, typical of the ascetic Capuchin order.

The church is famous for its miraculous statue of the Madonna and Child. Emperor Rudolph II liked the statue so much he asked the Capuchins to give it to him to place in his private chapel. The monks agreed, but then the statue somehow found its way back to the church. Three times Rudolph had the Madonna brought back but each time

Schwarzenberg Palace, showing the loggia and the sgraffitoed façade

she returned to her original position. The Emperor eventually gave up, left her where she was and presented her with a gold crown and a robe. Each year at Christmas the church attracts crowds of visitors to see its delightful Baroque nativity scene of life-sized figures dressed in costumes from the period.

Church of the Capuchin Monastery

The Loreto ⑲
LORETA

See pp116–17.

Černín Palace ⑳
ČERNÍNSKÝ PALÁC

Loretánské náměstí 5. **Map** 1 B3. 🕻 24 18 11 11. 🚋 22, 23. **Closed to** *the public.*

B UILT IN 1668 for Count Černín of Chudenice, the Imperial Ambassador to Venice, the Černín Palace is 150 m (500 ft) long with a row of 30 massive Corinthian half-columns running the length of its upper storeys. The palace towers over the attractive, small, grassy square that lies between it and the Loreto.

The huge building suffered as a result of its prominent position on one of Prague's highest hills. It was looted by the French in 1742 and badly damaged in the Prussian bombardment of the city in 1757. In 1851 the impoverished Černín family sold the palace to the state and it became a

barracks. After the creation of Czecho-slovakia in 1918 the palace was restored to its original design and became the Ministry of Foreign Affairs. A few days after the Communist Coup in 1948 the Foreign Minister, Jan Masaryk, the popular son of Czechoslovakia's first President, Tomáš Masaryk, died as the result of a fall from a top-floor window of the Palace. He was the only non-Communist in the government that had just been formed. No-one really knows whether he was pushed or jumped, but he is still widely mourned.

Capital on
Černín Palace

Pohořelec ㉑

Map 1 B3. 🚋 22, 23.

F IRST SETTLED IN 1375, this is one of the oldest parts of Prague. The name is of more recent origin: Pohořelec means "place destroyed by fire", a fate the area has suffered three times in the course of its history – the last time being in 1741. It is now a large open square on a hill high over the city and part of the main access route to Prague Castle. In the centre stands a large monument to St John Nepomuk (1752) *(see p137)*, thought to be by Johann Anton Quitainer. The houses around the square are mainly Baroque and Rococo. In front of the Jan Kepler grammar school stands a monument to Kepler and his predecessor as astronomer at the court of Rudolph II, Tycho Brahe, who died in a house on the school site in 1601.

Strahov Monastery ㉒
STRAHOVSKÝ KLÁŠTER

See pp120–21.

Kučera Palace, a Rococo building in Pohořelec

Strahov Monastery ②

STRAHOVSKÝ KLÁŠTER

The bust of Joseph II over entrance gate

WHEN IT WAS FOUNDED in 1140 by an austere religious order, the Premonstratensians, Strahov rivalled the seat of the Czech sovereign in size. Destroyed by fire in 1258, it was rebuilt in the Gothic style, with later Baroque additions. Its famous library, in the theological and philosophical halls, is over 800 years old and despite being ransacked by many invading armies, is one of the finest in Bohemia. Strahov also escaped Joseph II's 1783 dissolution of the monasteries by changing its library into a research institute. It is now a working monastery and museum.

Statue of St John
A Late-Gothic, painted statue of St John the Evangelist situated in the Theological Hall, has the saint's prayer book held in a small pouch.

Baroque tower

The Museum of National Literature is devoted to Czech literature.

Refectory

Entrance to main courtyard of the monastery

Baroque organ on which Mozart played

★ Church of Our Lady
The interior of this Baroque church is highly decorated. Above the arcades of the side naves, there are 12 paintings with scenes from the life of St Norbert, founder of the Premonstratensian order, by Jiří Neunhertz.

Entrance to Church of Our Lady

STAR FEATURES

★ **Church of Our Lady**

★ **Philosophical Hall**

★ **Theological Hall**

Church Façade
The elaborate statues, by Johann Anton Quitainer, were added to the western façade of the church when it was remodelled by the architect Anselmo Lurago in the 1750s.

View from Petřín Hill
A gate at the eastern end of the first courtyard leads to Petřín Hill, part of which was once the monastery's orchards.

★ Theological Hall
One of the 17th-century astronomical globes by William Blaeu that line the hall. The stucco and wall paintings relate to librarianship.

The façade of the Philosophical Hall is decorated with vases and a gilded medallion of Joseph II by Ignaz Platzer.

★ Philosophical Hall
The ceiling fresco depicts the Struggle of Mankind to Know Real History by Franz Maulbertsch. It was built in 1782 to hold the Baroque bookcases and their valuable books from a dissolved monastery near Louka, in Moravia.

Entrance to libraries

Strahov Gospel Book
A facsimile of this superb and precious 9th-century volume, is now on display in the Theological Hall.

LITTLE QUARTER
MALÁ STRANA

THE LITTLE QUARTER is the part of Prague least affected by recent history. Hardly any new building has taken place here since the late 18th century and the quarter is rich in splendid Baroque palaces and old houses with attractive signs. Founded in 1257, it is built on the slopes below the Castle hill with magnificent views across the river to the Old Town.

Sign from At the Golden Horseshoe in Nerudova

The centre of the Little Quarter has always been Little Quarter Square (Malostranské náměstí), dominated by the Church of St Nicholas. The Grand Prior's millwheel still turns, pilgrims still kneel before the Holy Infant of Prague in the Church of Our Lady Victorious, and music rings out from churches and palaces as it did when Mozart stayed here.

SIGHTS AT A GLANCE

Churches
Church of St Thomas **3**
Church of St Nicholas pp128–9 **5**
Church of Our Lady Victorious **9**
Church of Our Lady beneath the Chain **13**
Church of St Lawrence **21**

Parks and Gardens
Vrtba Garden **8**
Vojan Park **17**
Ledebour Garden **18**
Observation Tower **19**
Mirror Maze **20**
Observatory **22**
Petřín Park **24**
Funicular Railway **25**

Historic Monuments
Hunger Wall **23**

Historic Restaurants and Beer Halls
At St Thomas's **2**
At the Three Ostriches **15**

Historic Streets and Squares
Little Quarter Square **4**
Nerudova Street **6**
Italian Street **7**
Maltese Square **10**
Grand Priory Square **12**
Bridge Street **16**

Bridges and Islands
Kampa Island **11**
Charles Bridge pp136–9 **14**

Palaces
Wallenstein Palace and Garden **1**
Michna Palace **26**

0 metres   250
0 yards   250

GETTING THERE
The area has little public transport, but Malostranská metro on line A is close to most of the sights. Trams 12 and 22 go to Malostranské náměstí and along Újezd to the funicular railway that takes you up Petřín Hill.

◁ **Charles Bridge and the Little Quarter Bridge Towers**

Street-by-Street: Around Little Quarter Square

THE LITTLE QUARTER, most of whose grand Baroque palaces
now house embassies, has preserved much of its
traditional character. The steep, narrow streets and
steps have an air of romantic mystery and you will
find fascinating buildings decorated
with statues and house signs at every
turn. Some smart new
restaurants have
been established
in the old
buildings.

**At the Three Little
Fiddles**, now a restaurant,
acquired its house sign
when it was the home
of a family of violin
makers around 1700.

Thun-Hohenstein Palace
(1721–6) has a doorway
crowned with two sculpted
eagles by Matthias Braun.
The palace is now the seat
of the Italian embassy.

★ **Nerudova Street**
*This historic street
leading up to Prague
Castle is named after
the 19th-century writer
Jan Neruda* ❻

Morzin Palace has a striking Baroque
façade with a pair of sculpted moors.

Italian Street
*From the 16th to the 18th century, houses in
the street, like the House at the Golden Scales,
were occupied by Italian craftsmen* ❼

STAR SIGHTS

★ **Wallenstein Palace**

★ **Church of
St Nicholas**

★ **Nerudova Street**

Vrtba Garden
*Laid out in about 1725 by
František Maximilián Kaňka,
these fine Baroque terraces
(currently closed) provide
good views over the rooftops
of the Little Quarter* ❽

★ Wallenstein Palace
On the main hall ceiling, Albrecht von Wallenstein, the great general of the 30 Years' War, appears as the god Mars ❶

Czech National Assembly

Plague Column

To Malostranská Metro

Wallenstein Gardens

LOCATOR MAP
See Street Finder, map 2

PRAGUE CASTLE & HRADČANY

LITTLE QUARTER

Vltava

Little Quarter Town Hall

At St Thomas's
This traditional beer hall occupies the cellars of a medieval monastery brewery ❷

Church of St Thomas
A statue of St Augustine by Hieronymus Kohl (1684) decorates the church's dramatic Baroque façade ❸

Little Quarter Square
This 18th-century view shows the lower half of the square between the church of St Nicholas and the Town Hall ❹

★ Church of St Nicholas
The cupola and bell tower of this Baroque church are the best-known landmarks of the Little Quarter ❺

Schönborn Palace, now the American Embassy, is decorated with caryatids from the work-shop of Matthias Braun.

0 metres   100
0 yards   100

KEY

‑ ‑ ‑ Suggested route

Wallenstein Palace and Garden ❶

VALDŠTEJNSKÝ PALÁC

Valdštejnské náměsti 4. **Map** 2 E3.
🚇 *Malostranská.* ☎ 57 07 11 11.
🚊 *12, 22, 23.* **Riding school open**
10am–6pm Tue–Sun. 🚫 ♿ *from
Valdštejnská.* **Garden open** *May–
Sep: 9am–7pm daily; Apr, Oct 10am–
6pm.* 📷 ♿ *from Valdštejnské
náměsti.*

The main hall of Wallenstein Palace

THE FIRST LARGE secular
building of the Baroque
era in Prague, the palace
stands as a monument to the
fatal ambition of imperial
military commander Albrecht
von Wallenstein (1581–1634).
His string of victories over the
Protestants in the 30 Years'
War *(see pp30–31)* made him
vital to Emperor Ferdinand II.
Already showered with titles,
Wallenstein started to covet
the crown of Bohemia. In
1630 he was relieved of com-
mand, but was
reinstated the
following year. He
began to negotiate
independently
with the enemy
and in 1634 was
killed on the
Emperor's orders
by mercenaries.

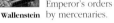

Wallenstein

Wallenstein's intention was to
overshadow even Prague
Castle with his palace, built
between 1624 and 1630. To
obtain a suitable site, he had
to purchase 23 houses, three
gardens and the municipal
brick kiln. The magnificent
main hall rises to a height of
two storeys with a ceiling
fresco of Wallenstein himself
portrayed as Mars, the god of
war, riding in a triumphal
chariot. The architect,
Andrea Spezza, and
nearly all the artists
employed in the
decoration of the
palace were Italians.
   Today the palace
is used as the home
of the Czech Senate,
and will be open to
the public when
restoration work is
complete. The gardens

are laid out as they were when
Wallenstein dined in the huge
sala terrena (garden pavilion)
that looks out over a fountain
and rows of bronze statues.
These are copies of works by
Adriaen de Vries that were
stolen by the Swedes in 1648
(see pp30–31). There is also a
pavilion with fine frescoes
showing scenes from the
legend of the Argonauts and
the Golden Fleece.
Wallenstein was a holder
of the Order of the
Golden Fleece, the
highest order of
chivalry of the Holy
Roman Empire. At the
far end of the garden
is a large ornamental
pond with a central
statue. Behind this
stands the old Riding
School, now used
to house special
exhibitions by the
National Gallery.
Both gardens and
riding school have
undergone sub-
stantial restoration.

Palace

Sala terrena

**Copy of a bronze statue of
Eros by Adriaen de Vries**

Avenue of sculptures

Riding School

**Valdštejnská
Street
entrance**

The grotesquery is a curious
imitation of the walls of a limestone
cave, covered in stalactites.

**Letenská
Street
entrance**

**Statue of
Hercules**

Klárov entrance

At St Thomas's ❷

U SV. TOMÁŠE

Letenská 12. **Map** 2 E3. ☎ *57 32 01 01.* Ⓜ *Malostranská.* ⬛ *12, 22.* **Open** *11:30am–11pm daily.* 📷

NO OTHER BEER HALL in Prague can match the antiquity of At St Thomas's. Beer was first brewed here in 1352 by Augustinian monks. The brewery gained such renown that it was appointed sole purveyor of beer to Prague Castle. It remained in operation until 1951. Since then a special dark beer from the Braník brewery has been sold here. The basement of the old brewery has three beer halls, the most spectacular being the so-called "Cave", furnished in mock medieval style.

Church of St Thomas ❸

KOSTEL SV. TOMÁŠE

Josephská 8. **Map** 2 E3. ☎ *57 31 31 42.* Ⓜ *Malostranská.* ⬛ *12, 22, 23.* **Open** *for services.* ☎ *6:45am, 12:15pm Mon–Fri; 12:15pm, 6pm (in English) Sat; 9:30am, 11am (in English), 5pm Sun.* 🚫 ♿

FOUNDED by Wenceslas II in 1285 as the monastery church of the Augustinians, the original Gothic church was completed in 1379. In the Hussite period *(see pp26–7)* this was one of the few churches to remain Catholic. As a result it suffered serious fire damage. During the reign of Rudolph II *(see pp28–9)*, St Thomas's developed strong links with the Imperial court. Several prominent members of Rudolph's entourage were buried here, including court architect Ottavio Aostalli and the sculptor Adriaen de Vries.

In 1723 the church was struck by lightning and Kilian Ignaz Dientzenhofer was called in to rebuild it. The shape of the original church was preserved in the Baroque reconstruction but, apart from the prominent spire, the church today betrays little of its Gothic origins. The interior of the dome and the curving ceiling frescoes in the nave were painted by Dientzen-hofer's collaborator Václav Vavřinec Reiner. Above the altar are copies of paintings by Rubens – *The Martyrdom of St Thomas* and a picture of St Augustine. The originals are in the Sternberg Palace *(see pp112–15).*

Baroque ceiling in the nave of the Church of St Thomas

Little Quarter Square ❹

MALOSTRANSKÉ NÁMĚSTÍ

Map 2 E3. Ⓜ *Malostranská.* ⬛ *12, 22.*

THE SQUARE HAS BEEN the centre of life in the Little Quarter since its foundation in 1257. It had started life as a large marketplace in the outer bailey of Prague Castle. Buildings sprang up in the middle of the square dividing it in half – a gallows and pillory stood in its lower part.

Most of the houses around the square have a medieval core, but all were rebuilt in the Renaissance and Baroque periods. The centre of the square is dominated by the splendid Baroque church of St Nicholas. The large building beside it was a Jesuit college. Along the upper side of the square, facing the church, runs the vast Neo-Classical façade of Lichtenstein Palace. In front of it stands a column raised in honour of the Holy Trinity to mark the end of a plague epidemic in 1713.

Other important buildings include the Little Quarter Town Hall with its splendid Renaissance façade and the Sternberg Palace, built on the site of the outbreak of the fire of 1541, which destroyed most of the Little Quarter. Beside it stands the Smiřický Palace. Its turrets and hexagonal towers make it an unmistakable landmark on the northern side of the lower square. The Baroque Kaiserstein Palace is situated at the eastern side. On the façade is a bust of the great Czech soprano Emmy Destinn, who lived there between 1908 and 1914. She often sang with the famous Italian tenor Enrico Caruso.

Church of St Nicholas ❺

KOSTEL SV. MIKULÁŠE

See pp128–9.

Arcade in front of buildings on the north side of Little Quarter Square

Church of St Nicholas ❺

KOSTEL SV. MIKULÁŠE

THE CHURCH OF ST NICHOLAS divides and dominates the two sections of Little Quarter Square. Building began in 1703, and the last touches were put to the glorious frescoed nave in 1761. It is the acknowledged masterpiece of father-and-son architects Christoph and Kilian Ignaz Dientzenhofer, Prague's greatest exponents of High Baroque *(see opposite)*, although neither lived to see the completion of the church. The statues, frescoes and paintings inside the church are by leading artists of the day, and include a fine *Crucifixion* of 1646 by Karel Škréta. Extensive renovation in the 1950s reversed the damage caused by 200 years of leaky cladding and condensation.

★ Pulpit
Dating from 1765, the ornate pulpit is by Richard and Peter Prachner. It is lavishly adorned with golden cherubs.

Altar Paintings
The side chapels hold many works of art. This painting of St Michael is by Francesco Solimena.

Baroque Organ
A fresco of St Cecilia, patron saint of music, watches over the superb organ. Built in 1746, the instrument was played by Mozart in 1787.

Entrance
from west side of Little Quarter Square

Chapel of St Ann

Chapel of St Catherine

STAR FEATURES

★ Dome Fresco

★ Pulpit

★ Statues of the Church Fathers

Façade
St Paul, by John Frederick Kohl, is one of the statues that grace the curving façade. It was completed in 1710 by Christoph Dientzenhofer, who was influenced by Italian architects Borromini and Guarini.

The dome was completed by Kilian Ignaz Dientzenhofer in 1751, shortly before his death.

The belfry was the last part to be built. It was added in 1751–6 by Anselmo Lurago.

★ **Dome Fresco**
Franz Palko's fresco, The Celebration of the Holy Trinity *(1752–3), fills the 70 m (230 ft) high dome.*

High Altar
A copper statue of St Nicholas by Ignaz Platzer surmounts the high altar. Below it, the painting of St Joseph is by Johann Lukas Kracker, who also painted the nave fresco.

★ **Statues of the Church Fathers**
The great teachers by Ignaz Platzer stand at the four corners of the crossing. St Cyril dispatches the devil with his crozier.

Chapel of St Francis Xavier

THE DIENTZENHOFER FAMILY
Christoph Dientzenhofer (1655–1722) came from a family of Bavarian master builders. His son Kilian Ignaz (1689–1751) was born in Prague and educated at the Jesuit Clementinum *(see p79).* They were responsible for the greatest treasures of Jesuit-influenced Prague Baroque architecture. The Church of St Nicholas, their last work, was completed by Kilian's son-in-law, Anselmo Lurago.

Kilian Ignaz Dientzenhofer

Nerudova Street ⑥
NERUDOVA ULICE

Map 2 D3. ☽ *Malostranská.*
🚊 *12, 22, 23.*

A PICTURESQUE narrow street leading up to Prague Castle, Nerudova is named after the poet and journalist Jan Neruda, who wrote many short stories set in this part of Prague. He lived in the house called At the Two Suns (No. 47) between 1845 and 1857.

Up until the introduction of numbers in 1770, Prague's houses were distinguished by signs. Nerudova's houses have a splendid selection of heraldic beasts and emblems. As you make your way up Nerudova's steep slope, look out in particular for the Red Eagle (No. 6), the Three Fiddles (No. 12), the Golden Horseshoe (No. 34), the Green Lobster (No. 43) and the White Swan (No. 49) as well as the Old Pharmacy museum (No. 32).

There are also a number of grand Baroque buildings in the street, including the Thun-Hohenstein Palace (No. 20, now the Italian embassy) and the Morzin Palace (No. 5, the Rumanian embassy). The latter has a façade with two massive statues of moors (a pun on the name Morzin) supporting the semicircular balcony on the first floor. Another impressive façade is that of the Church of Our Lady of Unceasing Succour, the church of the Theatines, an order founded during the Counter-Reformation.

Italian Street, heart of the former colony of Italian craftsmen

Italian Street ⑦
VLAŠSKÁ ULICE

Map 1 C4. ☽ *Malostranská.*
🚊 *12, 22.*

I TALIAN IMMIGRANTS started to settle here in the 16th century. Many were artists or craftsmen employed to rebuild and redecorate the Castle. If you approach the street from Petřín, on the left you will see the former Italian Hospital, a Baroque building with an arcaded courtyard. Today it maintains its traditional allegiance as the cultural section of the Italian embassy.

The grandest building in the street is the former Lobkowicz Palace, now the German embassy. One of the finest Baroque palaces in Prague, it has a large oval hall on the ground floor leading out onto a magnificent garden. Look out too for the pretty stucco sign on the house called At the Three Red Roses, dating from the early 18th century.

Vrtba Garden ⑧
VRTBOVSKÁ ZAHRADA

Karmelitská 25. **Map** 2 D4.
☽ *Malostranská.* 🚊 *12, 22, 23.*
Open Apr-Oct: 10am-6pm daily. 📷

B EHIND VRTBA PALACE lies a beautiful Baroque garden with steep flights of steps and balustraded terraces. From the highest part of the garden there are magnificent views of Prague Castle and the Little Quarter. The Vrtba Garden was designed by František Maximilián Kaňka in about 1720. The statues of Classical gods and stone vases are the work of Matthias Braun and the paintings in the *sala terrena* (garden pavilion) in the lower part of the garden are by Václav Vavřinec Reiner.

View of the Little Quarter from the terrace of the Vrtba Garden

Church of Our Lady Victorious ⑨
KOSTEL PANNY MARIE VÍTĚZNÉ

Karmelitská. **Map** 2 E4. 📞 *57 31 67 80.* 🚊 *12, 22.* **Open** 9am-7pm daily. ✝ *5:45pm Mon-Fri, 7:45am, 7pm Sat, 10am, noon (English), 8pm (Oct–May: 7pm) Sun.*

T HE FIRST BAROQUE building in Prague was the Church of the Holy Trinity, built for the German Lutherans by Giovanni Maria Filippi. It was finished in 1613 but after the Battle of the White Mountain *(see p31)* the Catholic authorities gave the church to the Carmelites, who rebuilt it and renamed it in honour of the victory.

Sign of Jan Neruda's house, At the Two Suns, 47 Nerudova Street

The fabric has survived including the portal. Enshrined on a marble altar in the right aisle is a glass case containing the Holy Infant of Prague (better-known by its Italian name – *il Bambino di Praga*). This wax effigy has a record of miracle cures and is one of the most revered images in the Catholic world. It was brought from Spain and presented to the Carmelites in 1628 by Polyxena of Lobkowicz. A small museum adjacent to the church traces its history.

Maltese Square ⓿
MALTÉZSKÉ NÁMĚSTÍ

Map 2 E4. 🚈 *12, 22, 23.*

THE SQUARE TAKES its name from the Priory of the Knights of Malta, which used to occupy this part of the Little Quarter. At the northern end stands a group of sculptures featuring St John the Baptist by Ferdinand Brokof – part of a fountain erected in 1715 to mark the end of a plague epidemic.

Most of the buildings were originally Renaissance houses belonging to prosperous townspeople, but in the 17th and 18th centuries the Little Quarter was taken over by the Catholic nobility and many were converted to flamboyant Baroque palaces. The largest, Nostitz Palace, stands on the southern side. Part of the palace now houses the Dutch embassy. It was built in the mid-17th century, then in about 1720 a balustrade was added with Classical vases and statues of emperors. In summer, concerts are given at the Palace. The Japanese embassy is housed in the Turba Palace (1767), an attractive pink Rococo building designed by Joseph Jäger.

Čertovka (the Devil's Stream) with Kampa Island on the right

Kampa Island ⓫
KAMPA

Map 2 F4. 🚈 *6, 9, 12, 22, 23.*

KAMPA, AN ISLAND formed by a branch of the Vltava known as the Devil's Stream (Čertovka), is a delightfully peaceful corner of the Little Quarter. The stream got its name in the 19th century, allegedly after the diabolical temper of a lady who owned a house nearby in Maltese Square. For centuries the stream was used as a millrace and from Kampa you can see the remains of three old mills. The wheel of the Grand Prior's Mill has been totally restored. Beyond it, the stream disappears under a small bridge below the piers of Charles Bridge. From here it flows between rows of houses. Predictably, the area has become known as "the Venice of Prague", but instead of gondolas you will see canoes.

For most of the Middle Ages there were only gardens on Kampa, though the island was also used for washing clothes and bleaching linen. After the Little Quarter fire of 1541, rubble from the

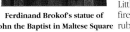
Ferdinand Brokof's statue of John the Baptist in Maltese Square

ruins was used to reinforce the banks, making building on Kampa safer. In the 17th century the island became well-known for its pottery markets. There are some enchanting houses from this period around Na Kampě Square. Most of the land from here to the southern tip of the island is a quiet park, created from several old palace gardens.

Grand Priory Square ⓬
VELKOPŘEVORSKÉ NÁMĚSTÍ

Map 2 F4. 🚇 *Malostranská.* 🚈 *12, 22, 23.*

ON THE NORTHERN SIDE of this small leafy square stands the former seat of the Grand Prior of the Knights of Malta. In its present form the palace dates from the 1720s. The doorways, windows and decorative vases were made at the workshop of Matthias Braun. On the opposite side of the square is the Buquoy Palace, now the French embassy, a delightful Baroque building roughly contemporary with the Grand Prior's Palace.

The only incongruous features are a painting of John Lennon and graffiti exhorting the world to "give peace a chance". These have decorated the wall of the Grand Prior's garden since Lennon's death.

Street-by-Street: Little Quarter Riverside

O N EITHER SIDE of Bridge Street lies a delightful
half-hidden world of gently decaying squares,
picturesque palaces, churches and gardens.
When you have run the gauntlet of the trinket-
sellers on Charles Bridge, escape to Kampa
Island to enjoy a stroll in its informal park, the
views across the Vltava weir to the Old Town
and the flocks of swans
gliding along the river.

**The Church of
St Joseph** dates
from the late
17th century.
The painting
of *The Holy
Family* (1702)
on the gilded
high altar is
by the leading
Baroque artist
Petr Brandl.

**The House at the Golden
Unicorn** in Lázeňská Street
has a plaque commemorating
the fact that Beethoven
stayed here in 1796.

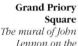

Bridge Street
*A major thoroughfare for
750 years, the narrow street
leads to Little Quarter Square* **16**

**To Little
Quarter Square**

**Grand Priory
Square**
*The mural of John
Lennon, on the
wall of the Grand
Priory of the
Knights of Malta
is now crumbling
and obscured by
fans' graffitti* **12**

Church of Our Lady beneath the Chain
*Two massive towers survive from when
this was a fortified priory* **13**

**Church of Our Lady
Victorious**
*This Baroque church houses
the famous effigy, the Holy
Infant of Prague* **9**

Maltese Square
*Grand palaces surround the
oddly-shaped square. This
coat of arms decorates the
17th-century Nostitz Palace, a
popular venue for concerts* **10**

0 metres   100

0 yards   100

KEY

 Suggested route

Vojan Park
Quiet shady paths have been laid out under the apple trees of this former monastery garden **17**

At the Three Ostriches
A restaurant and hotel have kept the sign of a seller of ostrich plumes **15**

U LUŽICKÉHO SEMINÁŘE

★ Charles Bridge
The approach to this magnificent 14th-century bridge, with its files of Baroque statues, passes under an arch below a Gothic tower **14**

Čertovka (the Devil's Stream)

The Grand Priory Mill has had its wheel meticulously restored, though it now turns very slowly in the sluggish water of the Čertovka, the former millrace.

NA KAMPĚ

Lichtenstein Palace

★ Kampa Island
This 19th-century painting by Soběslav Pinkas shows boys playing on Kampa. The island's park is still a popular place for children **11**

STAR SIGHTS
★ Charles Bridge
★ Kampa Island

Church of Our Lady beneath the Chain ⑬
KOSTEL PANNY MARIE POD ŘETĚZEM

Lázeňská. **Map** 2 E4. 【 53 29 76.
Ⓜ Malostranská. 🚋 12, 22, 23
Open for concerts and services.
🕆 5pm (4pm in winter) Mon–Sat,
8am, 9:30am, 11am Sun.

THIS CHURCH, the oldest in the Little Quarter, was founded in the 12th century. King Vladislav II presented it to the Knights of St John, the order which later became known as the Knights of Malta. It stood in the centre of the Knights' heavily fortified monastery that guarded the approach to the old Judith Bridge. The church's name refers to the chain used in the Middle Ages to close the monastery gatehouse.

A Gothic presbytery was added in the 13th century, but in the following century the original Romanesque church was demolished. A new portico was built with a pair of massive square towers, but work was then abandoned and the old nave became a courtyard between the towers and the church. This was given a Baroque facelift in 1640 by Carlo Lurago. The painting by Karel Škréta on the high altar shows the Virgin Mary and John the Baptist coming to the aid of the Knights of Malta in the famous naval victory over the Turks at Lepanto in 1571.

Charles Bridge ⑭
KARLŮV MOST

See pp136–9.

Fresco that gave At the Three Ostriches its name

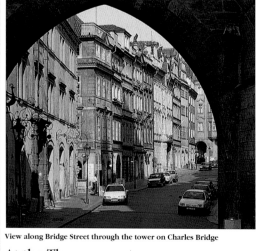
View along Bridge Street through the tower on Charles Bridge

At the Three Ostriches ⑮
U TŘÍ PŠTROSŮ

Dražického náměstí 12. **Map** 2 F3.
【 57 32 05 65. Ⓜ Malostranská.
🚋 12, 22, 23. See **Where to Stay**
pp182–9, **Restaurants** pp198–209.

MANY OF PRAGUE'S colourful house signs indicated the trade carried on in the premises. In 1597 Jan Fux, a merchant dealing in ostrich feathers, bought this house beside Charles Bridge. At the time ostrich plumes were very fashionable as decoration for hats among the courtiers and officers at Prague Castle. Fux even supplied feathers to foreign armies. So successful was his business, that in 1606 he had the house rebuilt and decorated with a large fresco of ostriches. He could afford to employ a respected artist to paint his sign rather than the usual journeymen.

The first floor of the house was added in 1657 and some beamed ceilings painted with vine motifs have been preserved from that time. In 1714 Prague's first coffee house opened here. The building is now an expensive hotel and restaurant.

Bridge Street ⑯
MOSTECKÁ ULICE

Map 2 E3. Ⓜ Malostranská.
🚋 12, 22, 23.

SINCE THE MIDDLE AGES this street has linked Charles Bridge with the Little Quarter Square. Crossing the bridge from the Old Town you can see the doorway of the old customs house built in 1591 in front of the Judith Tower. On the first floor of the tower there is a 12th-century relief of a king and a kneeling man.

Throughout the 13th and 14th centuries the area to the north of the street was the Court of the Bishop of Prague. This was destroyed during the Hussite Wars (see pp26–7), but one of its Gothic towers is preserved in the courtyard of the house called At the Three Golden Bells. It can be seen from the higher of the two bridge towers. The street is lined with a mixture of Renaissance and Baroque houses. As you walk up to Little Quarter Square, look out for the house called At the Black Eagle on the left. It has rich sculptural decoration and a splendid Baroque wrought-iron grille. Kaunic Palace, also on the left, was built in the 1770s. Its Rococo façade has striking stucco decoration and sculptures by Ignaz Platzer.

Vojan Park ⑰
VOJANOVY SADY

U lužického semináře. **Map** 2 F3. Ⓜ *Malostranská.* 🚊 *12, 18, 22, 23* **Open** *9am–6pm daily.*

A TRANQUIL SPOT hidden behind high white walls, the park dates back to the 17th century, when it was the garden of the Convent of Barefooted Carmelites. Two chapels erected by the Order have survived among the park's lawns and fruit trees. One is the Chapel of Elijah, who, because of his Old Testament associations with Mount Carmel, is regarded as the founder of the Order. His chapel takes the form of a stalagmite and stalactite cave. The other chapel, dedicated to St Theresa, was built in the 18th century as an expression of gratitude for the convent's preservation during the Prussian siege of Prague in 1757. In a niche to the left of the entrance to the park, there is an 18th-century statue of St John Nepomuk *(see p137)* by Ignaz Platzer. The saint is depicted standing on a fish – a reference to his martyrdom by drowning in the Vltava.

Ledebour Garden ⑱
LEDEBURSKÁ ZAHRADA

Valdštejnské náměstí 3. **Map** 2 F2. ☎ 57 01 04 01 Ⓜ *Malostranská.* 🚊 *12, 18, 22, 23.* **Open** Apr–Oct: 10am–6pm (Jul–Aug: 7:30pm) daily. 📷 ♿ ▣

T HE STEEP SOUTHERN slope below Prague Castle was covered with vineyards and gardens during the Middle Ages. But in the 16th century, when nobles started building palaces here, they laid out larger formal terraced gardens based on Italian Renaissance models. Most of these were then rebuilt during the 18th century and decorated with Baroque garden statuary and fountains. Three of the gardens – those belonging to the former Ledebour, Černín and Pálffy Palaces – have been linked together and are normally open to the public. Recently, however, a much-needed programme of restoration work has been taking place, and entry to the gardens can be restricted due to work in progress.

The refined and pleasantly atmospheric old-world elegance of the gardens is enhanced by magnificent views of Prague from their terraces. The Ledebour Garden, designed in the early 18th century, has a fine *sala terrena* (garden pavilion) by Giovanni Battista Alliprandi. The Pálffy Garden was laid out in the mid-18th century with terraces (the second still has its original sundial) and loggias. The most beautiful of the three

18th-century statue of Hercules located in the Ledebour Garden

and architecturally the richest is the Kolowrat-Černín Garden, created in 1784 by Ignaz Palliardi. The highest terrace has a *sala terrena* decorated with statues and Classical urns. Below this there is a wonderful assortment of staircases, archways and balustrades, and the remains of Classical statuary and old fountains.

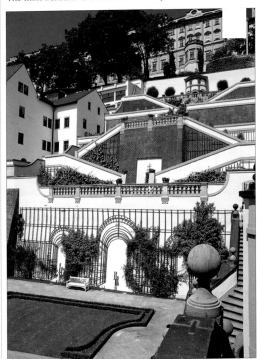

The foot of the Ledebour Garden

Charles Bridge (Little Quarter Side) ⑭

KARLŮV MOST

Pᴿᴬɢᴜᴇ'ꜱ ᴍᴏꜱᴛ ꜰᴀᴍɪʟɪᴀʀ monument, connects the Old Town with the Little Quarter. Although it is now pedestrianized, at one time it could take four carriages abreast. Today, due to wear and tear, many of the statues on the bridge are copies; the originals are kept in the Lapidarium of the National Museum *(see p162)* and at Vyšehrad *(see p179)*. The Gothic Old Town Bridge Tower *(see p139)* is one of the finest buildings of its kind in existence.

Little Quarter Bridge Tower

Tower entrance

★ View from Little Quarter Bridge Tower
The tall pinnacled wedge tower, gives a superb view of the city of 100 spires. The shorter tower is the remains of Judith Bridge.

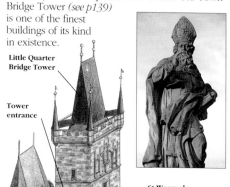

St Adalbert, 1709
Adalbert, Bishop of Prague, founded the Church of St Lawrence (see p141) on Petřín Hill in 991. He is known to the Czechs as Vojtěch.

St Philip Benizi, 17▶

St Wenceslas, 1858

Judith Bridge Tower, 1158

Steps to Saská Street

Christ between St Cosmas and St Damian, 1709

St John de Matha, St Felix de Valois and the Blessed Ivan, 1714
These saints, sculpted by Ferdinand Brokof, founded the Trinitarian Order of mendicants to collect money to buy the freedom of Christians enslaved by the infidels (represented at the foot of the sculpture).

St Vitus, 1714
This engraving of the statue shows the 3rd-century martyr with the lions which were supposed to maul him, but licked him instead. St Vitus is the patron saint of dancers and often invoked against convulsive disorders.

Sᴛᴀʀ Fᴇᴀᴛᴜʀᴇꜱ

★ **Little Quarter Bridge Tower and View**

★ **St John Nepomuk**

★ **St Luitgard**

★ **St Luitgard, 1710**
This statue, regarded as the most artistically remarkable on the bridge, was sculpted by Matthias Braun when he was only 26. It is based on the blind Cistercian nun's celebrated vision when Christ appeared and she kissed his wounds.

VISITORS' CHECKLIST

Map 2 F4. 🚋 12, 22, 23 to Malostranské náměstí, then walk down Mostecká. **Little Quarter Bridge Towers open** Apr–Oct: 10am–6pm daily. 🚻 📷

★ **St John Nepomuk, 1683**
Reliefs on the bridge depict the martyrdom of St John Nepomuk. Here the saint is polished bright from people touching it for good luck.

St Cajetan, 1709

St Augustine, 1708

St Jude Thaddaeus, 1708

St Anthony of Padua, 1707

Steps to Kampa Island

St Nicholas Tolentino, 1708

St Francis of Assisi, with two angels, 1855

St Ludmilla, 1710

St Vincent Ferrer and St Procopius, 1712
This detail shows a rabbi saddened by St Vincent's success in converting many Jews to Christianity. St Procopius is one of Bohemia's patron saints.

ST JOHN NEPOMUK

The cult of St John Nepomuk, canonized in 1729, was promoted by the Jesuits to rival the revered Jan Hus *(see p27)*. Jan Nepomucký, vicar-general of the Archdiocese of Prague, was arrested in 1393 by Wenceslas IV along with the archbishop and others who had displeased the king over the election of an abbot. The archbishop escaped, but John died under torture. The body was bound and thrown off Charles Bridge. Statues modelled on the one placed here in 1683 can be seen throughout central Europe, especially on bridges.

Charles Bridge (Old Town Side) ⓮

KARLŮV MOST

UNTIL 1741, CHARLES BRIDGE was the only crossing over the Vltava. It is 520 m (1,706 ft) long and is built of sandstone blocks, rumoured to be strengthened by mixing mortar with eggs. The bridge was commissioned by Charles IV in 1357 to replace the Judith Bridge and built by Peter Parler. The bridge's original decoration was a simple cross. The first statue – of St John Nepomuk – was added in 1683, inspired by Bernini's sculptures on Rome's Ponte Sant'Angelo.

★ 17th-Century Crucifixion
For 200 years, the wooden crucifix stood alone on the bridge. The gilded Christ dates from 1629 and the Hebrew words "Holy, Holy, Holy Lord", were paid for by a Jew as punishment for blasphemy.

St Francis Xavier, 1711
The Jesuit missionary is supported by three Moorish and two Oriental converts. The sculptor Brokof is seated on the saint's left.

St Norbert, St Wenceslas and St Sigismund, 1853

St Francis Borgia, 1710

St John the Baptist, 1857

St Cyril and St Methodius, 1938

St Christopher, 1857

St Ann, 1707

St Joseph, 1854

Thirty Years' War
In the last hours of this war, the Old Town was saved from the Swedish army. The truce was signed in the middle of the bridge in 1648.

STAR FEATURES

★ **Old Town Bridge Tower**

★ **17th-Century Crucifixion**

TIMELINE

1100	1300	1500	1700	1900
	1357 Charles IV commissions new bridge	**1621** Heads of ten Protestant nobles exhibited on the Old Town Bridge Tower	**1648** Swedes damage part of the bridge and Old Town Bridge Tower	
	1342 Judith Bridge destroyed by floods			*1890 flood damage*
1158 Europe's second medieval stone bridge, Judith Bridge, is built	**1393** St John Nepomuk thrown off Bridge on the orders of Wenceslas IV		**1890** Three arches destroyed by flood	**1938** Karel Dvořák's sculpture of St Cyril and St Methodius
	Sculptor Matthias Braun (1684–1738)		**1713** Bridge decorated with 21 statues by Braun, Brokof and others	

1890 flood damage

Sculptor Matthias Braun (1684–1738)

**The Madonna,
St Dominic and
St Thomas, 1708**
*The Dominicans,
(known in a Latin pun
as* Domini canes, *the
dogs of God), are shown
with the Madonna and
their emblem, a dog.*

VISITORS' CHECKLIST

Map 3 A4. 🚇 *17, 18 to
Křižovnické náměstí.* **Old Town
Bridge Tower open** *Apr–Oct:
10am–6pm daily; Nov–Mar
10am–5pm daily.* 🎫 📷

**Madonna and
St Bernard, 1709**
*Cherubs and symbols of the
Passion, including the dice,
the cock and the centurion's
gauntlet, form part of the statue.*

Old Town
Bridge Tower

Tower
entrance

Pietà,
1859

St Barbara,
St Margaret and St
Elizabeth, 1707

★ OLD TOWN BRIDGE TOWER

This magnificent Gothic tower,
designed by Peter Parler, was built at
the end of the 14th century. A fitting
ornament to the new Charles Bridge,
it was also an integral part of the
Old Town's fortifications.

Pinnacled
wedge spire

Roof viewing point

The viewing gallery is a
rib-vaulted room, on the
tower's first floor. It
provides a wonderful
view of Prague Castle
and the Little Quarter.

Bridge Tower sculptures
by Peter Parler include
St Vitus, the bridge's patron saint,
Charles IV (left) and Wenceslas IV.

Observation Tower ⑲

ROZHLEDNA

Petřín. **Map** 1 C4. 🚋 *22, then take funicular railway.* 🚌 *132, 143, 149, 217.* **Closed** *for reconstruction until 2002.* 📷 📷

THE MOST conspicuous landmark in Petřín Park is an imitation Eiffel Tower, built for the Jubilee Exhibition of 1891. The octagonal Petřín tower is only 60 m (200 ft), a quarter the height of the Eiffel Tower. The only way to the viewing platform is to climb up the 299 steps of its spiral staircase. You will be rewarded by the views. On a clear day, you can see as far as Bohemia's highest peak, Sněžka in the Krkonoše (Giant) Mountains, 150 km (100 miles) to the northeast. The tower is currently undergoing major renovation work.

Mirror Maze ⑳

ZRCADLOVÉ BLUDIŠTĚ

Petřín. **Map** 1 C4. 📞 *53 13 62.* 🚋 *22, then take funicular railway.* 🚌 *132, 143, 149, 217.* **Open** *Mar–Aug: 10am–7pm daily; Sep & Oct: 10am–5pm Mon–Fri, 10am–6pm Sat & Sun; Nov–Feb: 10am–5pm Sat & Sun.* 📷 📷 ♿

LIKE THE Observation Tower, the maze, which has walls lined with distorting mirrors, is a relic of the Exhibition of 1891. It is in a wooden pavilion in the shape of the old Špička Gate, part of the Gothic

The 100-year-old Observation Tower overlooking the city

fortifications of Vyšehrad *(see pp178–9)*. This amusement house moved to Petřín at the end of the exhibition and has stood here ever since.

When you have navigated your way through the maze and laughed at your reflection, your reward is to view the vivid diorama of *The Defence of Prague against the Swedes,* which took place on Charles Bridge *(see p138)* in 1648.

Church of St Lawrence ㉑

KOSTEL SV. VAVŘINCE

Petřín. **Map** 1 C5. 🚋 *22, then take funicular railway.* 🚌 *132, 143, 149, 217.* **Closed** *to the public.*

ACCORDING TO LEGEND, the church was initially founded in the 10th century by the pious Prince Boleslav II

and St Adalbert on the site of a pagan shrine. The ceiling of the sacristy is decorated with a painting illustrating this legend. The painting dates from the 18th century when the Romanesque church was swallowed up by a large new Baroque structure, featuring a cupola flanked by two onion-domed towers.

The small Calvary Chapel, which dates from 1735, is situated just to the left of the entrance to the church. Its façade has been decorated with modern graffito that portrays *The Resurrection of Christ.*

Observatory ㉒

HVĚZDÁRNA

Petřín 205. **Map** 2 D5. 📞 *57 72 05 40.* 🚋 *22, then funicular.* **Open** *Apr–Oct: 6am–8pm Tue–Thu, 10am–noon, 2pm–8pm Sat, Sun. Nov–Mar: 4pm–7pm Mon, 2pm–6pm Tue–Thu.* 📷 🚫

One of the telescopes in the Observatory on Petřín Hill

SINCE 1930, PRAGUE'S amateur astronomers have been able to enjoy the facilities of this observatory on Petřín Hill. You can use its telescopes to view anything from the craters of the moon to unfamiliar distant galaxies. There is an exhibition of old astronomical instruments and special events for children are held on Saturdays and Sundays.

Hunger Wall ㉓

HLADOVÁ ZEĎ

Újezd, Petřín, Strahovská. **Map** 2 D5. 🚋 *6, 9, 12, 22, then take funicular railway.* 🚌 *132, 143, 149, 217.*

THE FORTIFICATIONS built around the southern edge of the Little Quarter on the orders of Charles IV in

Diorama of *The Defence of Prague against the Swedes* in the Mirror Maze

1360–62 have been known for centuries as the Hunger Wall. Nearly 1,200 m (1,300 yards) of the wall have survived, complete with crenellated battlements and a platform for marksmen on its inner side. It runs from Újezd across Petřín Park to Strahov. The story behind the name is that Charles commissioned its construction with the aim of giving employment to the poor during a period of famine. It is true that a great famine did break out in Bohemia in the 1360s and the two events, the famine and the building of the wall, became permanently linked in the people's memory.

Petřín Park 24
PETŘÍNSKÉ SADY

Map 2 D5. 🚇 6, 9, 12, 22, then take funicular railway. See **Three Guided Walks** pp176–7.

To the west of the Little Quarter, the wooded slopes of Petřín hill rise above the city to a height of 318 m (960 ft). The name derives either from the Slavonic god Perun, to whom sacrifices were made on the hill or from the Latin name Mons Petrinus, meaning "rocky hill". A forest used to stretch from here as far as the White Mountain *(see p31).* In the 12th century the southern side of the hill was planted with vineyards, but by the 18th century most of these had been transformed into gardens and orchards. The lower slopes are still covered with old apple and pear trees.

Today a path winds up the slopes of Petřín, offering magnificent panoramas of Prague. The park is especially popular in the spring when the fruit trees are in blossom and young lovers lay flowers on the monument to Karel Hynek Mácha, the most famous Czech Romantic poet, who died aged 26 in 1836.

Nebozízek, the station halfway up Petřín's funicular railway

Statue of Karel Hynek Mácha in Petřín Park

Funicular Railway 25
LANOVÁ DRÁHA

Újezd. **Map** 2 D5. 🚇 6, 9. 12, 22.
In operation 5am–midnight daily.
📷 🅿️ ♿

Built to carry visitors to the 1891 Jubilee Exhibition up to the Observation Tower at the top of Petřín hill, the funicular was originally powered by water. In this form, it remained in operation until 1914, then between the wars was converted to electricity. In 1965 it had to be shut down because part of the hillside collapsed – coal had been mined here during the 19th century. Shoring up the slope and rebuilding the railway took 20 years, but since its reopening in 1985 it has proved a reliable way of getting up Petřín Hill. At the halfway station, Nebozízek, there is a restaurant *(see p202)* with fine views of the Castle and the city across the river.

Michna Palace 26
MICHNŮV PALÁC

Újezd 40. **Map** 2 E4. 📞 53 21 93.
🚇 12, 22. **Open** 9am–5pm Thu, Sat, Sun. 📷 Ø ♿

In about 1580 Ottavio Aostalli built a summer palace here for the Kinský family on the site of an old Dominican convent. In 1623 the building was bought by Pavel Michna of Vacínov, a supply officer in the Imperial Army, who had grown rich after the Battle of the White Mountain. He commissioned a new Baroque building that he hoped would rival the palace of his late commander, Wallenstein *(see p126).*

In 1767 the Michna Palace was sold to the army and over the years it became a crumbling ruin. After 1918 it was bought by Sokol (a physical culture association) and converted into a gym and sports centre with a training ground in the old palace garden. The restored palace was renamed Tyrš House in honour of Sokol's founder. The ground floor now houses the Museum of Physical Culture and Sport.

Restored Baroque façade of the Michna Palace (Tyrš House)

NEW TOWN
NOVÉ MĚSTO

THE NEW TOWN, founded in 1348 by Charles IV, was carefully planned and laid out around three large central market-places: the Hay Market (Senovážné Square), the Cattle Market (Charles Square) and the Horse Market (Wenceslas Square). Twice as large as the

Art Nouveau decoration on No. 12 Wenceslas Square

Old Town, the area was mainly inhabited by tradesmen and craftsmen such as blacksmiths, wheelwrights and brewers. During the late 19th century, much of the New Town was demolished and completely redeveloped, giving it the appearance it has today.

SIGHTS AT A GLANCE

Churches and Monasteries
Church of Our Lady of the Snows ❷
Church of St Ignatius ❽
Church of St Cyril and St Methodius ⓫
Church of St John on the Rock ⓭
Slavonic Monastery ⓮
Church of St Catherine ⓰
Church of St Stephen ⓳
Church of St Ursula ㉒

Historic Buildings
Hotel Europa ❹
Jesuit College ❾
Faust House ⓬
New Town Hall ⓴

Theatres and Opera Houses
State Opera ❻
National Theatre pp156–7 ㉓

Historic Squares
Wenceslas Square ❶
Charles Square ❿

Museums and Galleries
National Museum ❺
Mucha Museum ❼
Dvořák Museum ⓲

Historic Restaurants and Beer Halls
Chalice Restaurant ⓱
U Fleků ㉑

Parks and Gardens
Franciscan Garden ❸
Botanical Gardens ⓯

GETTING THERE

The entire area is well served by the metro with two main stations, Můstek and Muzeum in Wenceslas Square, and others at Karlovo náměstí and Národní třída. Tram routes from most parts of the city pass through Karlovo náměstí.

KEY

	Street-by-Street map *See pp144–5*
	Street-by-Street map *See pp150–51*
Ⓜ	Metro station
	Tram stop
P	Parking
	River boat boarding point

0 metres   250
0 yards   250

Street-by-Street: Wenceslas Square

HOTELS AND RESTAURANTS occupy many of the buildings around Wenceslas Square, though it remains an important commercial centre – the square began life as a medieval horse market. As you walk along, look up at the buildings, most of which date from the turn of this century, when the square was redeveloped. There are fine examples of the decorative styles used by Czech architects of the period. Many blocks have dark covered arcades leading to shops, clubs, theatres and cinemas.

Koruna Palace (1914) is an ornate block of shops and offices. Its corner turret is topped with a crown (*koruna*).

To Powder Gate

Statue of St Lawrence at U Pinkasů

U Pinkasů became one of Prague's most popular beer halls when it started serving Pilsner Urquell (*see pp196–7*) in 1843.

Můstek

Church of Our Lady of the Snows

The towering Gothic building is only part of a vast church planned during the 14th century ❷

Můstek

Můst

VODIČKOVA

Jungmann Square is named after Josef Jungmann (1773–1847), an influential scholar of language and lexicographer, and there is a statue of him in the middle. The Adria Palace (1925) used to be the Laterna Magika Theatre (*see p214*), which was where Václav Havel's Civic Forum worked in the early days of the 1989 Velvet Revolution.

Franciscan Garden

An old monastery garden has been laid out as a small park with this fountain, rosebeds, trellises and a children's playground ❸

Lucerna Palace

ŠTĚPÁN

Wiehl House, named after its architect Antonín Wiehl, was completed in 1896. The five-storey building is in striking Neo-Renaissance style, with a loggia and colourful *sgraffito*. Mikuláš Aleš designed some of the Art Nouveau figures.

STAR SIGHTS
★ Wenceslas Square
★ Hotel Europa
★ National Museum

★ **Wenceslas Square**
The dominant features of the square are the equestrian statue of St Wenceslas (1912) and the National Museum behind it **1**

LOCATOR MAP
See Street Finder, maps 3, 4 & 6

The Monument to the Victims of Communism consists of just a few simple wreaths, photographs of victims, crosses and candles. Since the Velvet Revolution in 1989 an unofficial shrine has been maintained here in front of the St Wenceslas Monument.

OBĚTEM KOMUNISMU

The Assicurazioni Generali Building was where Franz Kafka (see p68) worked as an insurance clerk for 10 months in 1906–7.

★ **Hotel Europa**
Both the façade and the interior of the hotel (1906) preserve most of their original Art Nouveau features **4**

St Wenceslas Monument

State Opera
Meticulously refurbished in the 1980s, the interior retains the luxurious red plush, crystal chandeliers and gilded stucco of the original late-19th-century theatre **6**

Fénix Palace

Muzeum

Former Federal Assembly

0 metres   100
0 yards   100

★ **National Museum**
The grand building with its monumental staircase was completed in 1890 as a symbol of national prestige **5**

KEY

– – – Suggested route

Wenceslas Monument in Wenceslas Square

Wenceslas Square ❶
VÁCLAVSKÉ NÁMĚSTÍ

Map 3 C5. Můstek, Muzeum. 3, 9, 14, 24.

T HE SQUARE HAS witnessed many key events in recent Czech history. It was here that the student Jan Palach burnt himself to death in 1969, and in November 1989 a protest rally in the square against police brutality led to the Velvet Revolution and the overthrow of Communism.

Wenceslas "Square" is something of a misnomer, for it is some 750 m (825 yd) long and only 60 m (65 yd) wide. Originally a horse market, today it is lined with hotels, restaurants, clubs and shops, reflecting the seamier side of Western consumerism. The huge equestrian statue of St Wenceslas that looks the length of the square from in front of the National Museum was erected in 1912. Cast in bronze, it is the work of Josef Myslbek, the leading Czech sculptor of the late 19th century. At the foot of the pedestal there are other statues of Czech patron saints. An improvised memorial near the statue commemorates the victims of the former regime.

Church of Our Lady of the Snows ❷
KOSTEL PANNY MARIE SNĚŽNÉ

Jungmannovo náměstí 18. **Map** 3 C5. 22 24 62 43. Můstek. **Open** 6am–7:30pm daily. 5:45pm Mon–Fri, 7pm Sat, 10am, noon (English), 8pm (7pm in winter) Sun.

C HARLES IV FOUNDED this church to mark his coronation in 1347. The name refers to a 4th-century miracle in Rome, when the Virgin Mary appeared to the pope in a dream telling him to build a church to her on the spot where snow fell in August. Charles's church was to have been over 100 m (330 ft) long, but was never completed. The towering building we see today was just the presbytery of the projected church. Over 33 m (110 ft) high, it was finished in 1397, and was originally part of a Carmelite monastery. On the northern side there is a gateway with a 14th-century pediment that decorated the entrance to the monastery graveyard.

In the early 15th century a steeple was added, but further building was halted by the Hussite Wars (*see pp26–7*). The Hussite firebrand Jan Želivský preached at the church and was buried here after his execution in 1422. The church suffered considerable damage in the wars and in 1434 the steeple was destroyed. For a long time the church was left to decay. In 1603 Franciscans restored the building. The intricate net vaulting of the ceiling dates from this period, the original roof having collapsed. Most of the interior decoration, apart from the 1450s pewter font, is Baroque. The monumental three-tiered altar is crowded with statues of saints, and is crowned with a crucifix.

Franciscan Garden ❸
FRANTIŠKÁNSKÁ ZAHRADA

Jungmannovo náměstí 18. **Map** 3 C5. Můstek. **Open** 6am–7pm daily.

O RIGINALLY the physic garden of a Franciscan monastery, the area was opened to the public in 1950 as a tranquil oasis close to Wenceslas Square. By the entrance is a Gothic portal leading down to a cellar restaurant – U františkánů (At the Franciscans). In the 1980s several of the beds were replanted with herbs, cultivated by the Franciscans in the 17th century.

Hotel Europa ❹
HOTEL EVROPA

Václavské náměstí 29. **Map** 4 D5. 24 22 81 17. Můstek. 3, 9, 14, 24. See **Where to Stay** pp182–9, **Restaurants, Pubs and Cafés** pp198–205.

T HOUGH A trifle shabby in places, the Europa Hotel is a wonderfully preserved reminder of the golden age

Art Nouveau decoration on façade of the Hotel Europa

Façade of the State Opera, formerly the New German Theatre

of hotels. It was built in highly decorated Art Nouveau style between 1903 and 1906. Not only has its splendid façade crowned with gilded nymphs survived, but many of the interiors on the ground floor have remained virtually intact, including all the original bars, large mirrors, panelling and light fittings.

National Museum ❺
NÁRODNÍ MUZEUM

Václavské náměstí 68. **Map** 6 E1. 📞 24 49 71 11. Ⓜ Muzeum. **Open** Oct–Apr 9am–5pm daily May–Sep 10am–6pm (but closed first Tue of month). 🎫 🚫

T HE VAST Neo-Renaissance building that dominates one end of Wenceslas Square houses the museum. Designed by Josef Schulz as a triumphal affirmation of the Czech national revival, the museum was completed in 1890. The entrance is reached by a ramp decorated with allegorical statues. Seated by the door are History and Natural History.

Inside, the rich marbled decoration is impressive, but overwhelms the collections devoted mainly to mineralogy, archaeology, anthropology, natural history and numismatics. The museum also has a Pantheon containing busts and statues of Czech scholars, writers and artists. It is decorated with many historical paintings by František Ženíšek, Václav Brožík and Vojtěch Hynais.

State Opera ❻
STÁTNÍ OPERA

Wilsonova 4. **Map** 4 E5. 📞 26 53 53 (box office). Ⓜ Muzeum. **Open** for performances only. See **Entertainment** pp210–15.

T HE FIRST THEATRE built here, the New Town Theatre, was pulled down in 1885 to make way for the present building. This was originally known as the New German Theatre, built to rival the Czechs' National Theatre (see pp156–7). A

Neo-Classical frieze decorates the pediment above the columned loggia at the front of the theatre. The figures include Dionysus and Thalia, the muse of comedy. The interior is stuccoed and original paintings in the auditorium and on the curtain have been preserved. In 1945 the theatre became the city's main opera house.

Mucha Museum ❼
MUCHOVO MUZEUM

Panskà 7. **Map** 4 D4. 📞 62 84 162. Ⓜ Můstek, Náměstí Republiky. 🚌 5, 14, 26. **Open** 10am–6pm daily. 📷 🚫 ♿ Ⓦ www.mucha.cz

T HE 18TH-CENTURY Kaunicky Palace is the long-overdue home to the first museum in the world dedicated to this Czech master of Art Nouveau. A selection of over 80 exhibits include paintings and drawings, sculptures, photographs and personal memorabilia. The central courtyard becomes a terrace for the café in the summer, and there is a museum shop offering exclusive gifts with Mucha motifs.

Main staircase of the National Museum

Art Nouveau in Prague

THE DECORATIVE STYLE known as Art Nouveau originated in Paris in the 1890s. It quickly became international as most of the major European cities quickly responded to its graceful, flowing forms. In Prague it was at its height in the first decade of the 20th century but died out during World War I, when it seemed frivolous and even decadent. There is a wealth of Art Nouveau in Prague, both in the fine and decorative arts and in architecture. In the New Town and the Jewish Quarter *(see pp80–93)*, entire streets were demolished at the turn of the century and built in the new style.

Façade detail, 10 Masaryk Embankment

Praha House
This house was built in 1903 for the Prague Insurance Company. Its name is in gilt Art Nouveau letters at the top.

ARCHITECTURE

ART NOUVEAU made its first appearance in Prague at the Jubilee exhibition of 1891. Architecturally, the new style was a deliberate attempt to break with the 19th-century tradition of monumental buildings. In Art Nouveau the important aspect was ornament, either painted or sculpted, often in the form of a female figure, applied to a fairly plain surface. This technique was ideally suited to wrought iron and glass, popular at the turn of the century. These materials were light but strong. The effect of this, together with Art Nouveau decoration, created buildings of lasting beauty.

Hotel Central
Built by Alois Dryák and Bedřich Bendelmayer in 1900, the façade of this hotel has plasterwork shaped like tree branches.

Hlahol Choir Building, 1905
The architect Josef Fanta embellished this building with mosaics and sculptures by Karl Mottl and Josef Pekárek (see also p142).

Hotel Evropa
Finished in 1904, this grand Art Nouveau building is notable for its fine detailing inside and out.

Ornate pilasters

Decorative statues

Brass and wrought-iron balustrade

Hlavní nádraží
Prague's main railway station was completed in 1901. With its huge interior glazed dome and elegant sculptural decoration, it shows many Art Nouveau features.

DECORATIVE AND FINE ARTS

MANY PAINTERS, sculptors and graphic artists were influenced by Art Nouveau. One of the most successful exponents of the style was the artist Alfons Mucha (1860–1939). He is celebrated chiefly for his posters. Yet he designed stained glass (see p102), furniture, jewellery, even postage stamps. It is perhaps here, in the decorative and applied arts, that Art Nouveau had its fullest expression in Prague. Artists adorned every type of object – doorknobs, curtain ornaments, vases and cutlery – with tentacle- and plant-like forms in imitation of the natural world from which they drew their inspiration.

Záboj and Slavoj

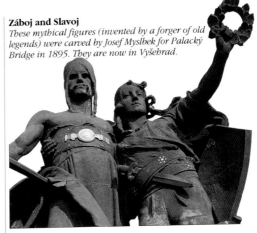

These mythical figures (invented by a forger of old legends) were carved by Josef Myslbek for Palacký Bridge in 1895. They are now in Vyšehrad.

Postage Stamp, 1918
A bold stamp design by Alfons Mucha marked the founding of the Czechoslovak Republic.

Glass Vase
This iridescent green vase made of Bohemian glass has relief decoration of intertwined threads. It is in the Museum of Decorative Arts.

Poster for Sokol Movement
Mucha's colour lithograph for the sixth national meeting of the Sokol gymnastic movement (1912) is in Tyrš's Museum (Physical Culture and Sports).

Curtain Ornament and Candlestick
The silver and silk ornament adorns the Mayor's room of the Municipal House. The candlestick by Emanuel Novák with fine leaf design is in the Museum of Decorative Arts.

WHERE TO SEE ART NOUVEAU IN PRAGUE

Detail of doorway, Široká 9, Jewish Quarter

ARCHITECTURE
Apartment Building, Na příkopě 7
Hanavský Pavilion *p161*
Hlahol Choir Building,
    Masarykovo nábřeží 10
Hlavní nádraží, Wilsonova
Hotel Central, Hybernská 10
    see also *p185*
Hotel Evropa *p146*
Industrial Palace *p162* and
    Four Guided Walks pp176–7
Ministerstvo Hospodářství *p67*
Municipal House *p64*
Palacký Bridge (Palackého most)
Praha House, Národní třída 7
Wiehl House *p144*

PAINTING
St Agnes's Convent *pp92–3*

SCULPTURE
Jan Hus Monument *p70*
Vyšehrad Garden *p160* and
    Four Guided Walks pp178–9
Vyšehrad Cemetery *p160* and
    Four Guided Walks pp178–9
Zbraslav Monastery *p163*

DECORATIVE ARTS
Museum of Decorative Arts *p84*
Prague Museum *p161*

Street-by-Street: Charles Square

Detail of house in Charles Square

THE SOUTHERN PART of the New Town resounds to the rattle of trams, as many routes converge in this part of Prague. Fortunately, the park in Charles Square (Karlovo náměstí) offers a peaceful and welcome retreat. Many of the buildings around the Square belong to the University and the statues in the centre represent writers and scientists, reflecting the academic environment. There are several Baroque buildings and towards the river stands the historic 14th-century Slavonic Monastery.

The Czech Technical University was founded here in 1867 in a grand Neo-Renaissance building.

Church of St Wenceslas

RESSLOVA

VÁCLAVSKÁ

Kar nám

To the river

NA MORÁNI

KARLOVO NÁ

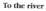

★ Church of St Cyril and St Methodius
A plaque and a bullet-scarred wall are reminders of the siege of the church in 1942, when German troops mounted an assault on the Czech and Slovak agents who were hiding there ⑪

★ Charles Square
The centre of the square is a pleasant 19th-century park with lawns, formal flowerbeds, fountains and statues ⑩

Church of St Cosmas and St Damian

VYŠEHRADSKÁ

POD SLOVANY

Slavonic Monastery
In 1965 a pair of modern concrete spires by František Černý were added to the church of the 14th-century monastery ⑭

TROJICKÁ

Church of St John on the Rock
This view of the organ and ceiling shows the dynamic Baroque design of Kilian Ignaz Dientzenhofer ⑬

STAR SIGHTS

★ Charles Square

★ Church of St Cyril and St Methodius

Church of St Ignatius

The sun rays and gilded cherubs on the side altars are typical of the gaudy decoration in this Baroque church built for the Jesuits **8**

Eliška Krásnohorská was a 19th-century poet who wrote the libretti for Smetana's operas. A statue of her was put up here in 1931.

LOCATOR MAP
See Street Finder, map 5

JECNÁ

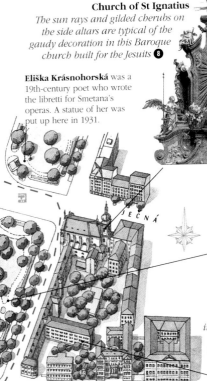

A statue of Jan Purkyně (1787–1869), an eminent physiologist and pioneer of cell theory, was erected in 1961. It is the most recent of the many memorials in the square.

Jesuit College

Founded in the mid-17th century, this imposing building has been a hospital since the suppression of the Jesuits in 1773 (see pp30–31) **9**

U NEMOCNICE

18th-century Institute of Gentlewomen (now a hospital)

Faust House

In the 18th century this house was owned by Count Ferdinand Mladota of Solopysky. The chemical experiments he performed reinforced the associations that gave the building its name **12**

BENÁTSKÁ

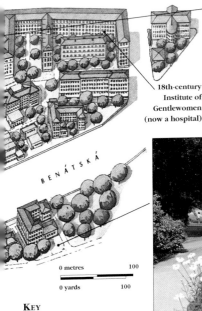

Botanical Gardens

Though part of the Charles University, the gardens are open to the public and are known for their profusion of rare plants. This is an agreeable place to relax **15**

| 0 metres | 100 |
| 0 yards | 100 |

KEY

– – – Suggested route

Sculptures on the façade of the Jesuit College by Tomasso Soldati

Church of St Ignatius ❽
KOSTEL SV. IGNÁCE

Ječná 2. **Map** 5 C2. 📞 *29 44 31.*
🚇 *Karlovo náměstí.* 🚋 *3, 4, 6, 14, 18, 22, 24.* **Open** *6am–6:30pm daily.* ✝ *frequent.* 📷

With its wealth of gilding and flamboyant stucco decoration, St Ignatius is typical of the Baroque churches built by the Jesuits to impress people with the power and glamour of their faith. The architects were the same two men responsible for the adjoining Jesuit College, Carlo Lurago, who started work on the church in 1665, and Paul Ignaz Bayer, who added the tower in 1687.

The painting on the high altar of *The Glory of St Ignatius* (St Ignatius Loyola, the founder of the Jesuit order) is by Jan Jiří Heinsch.

The Jesuits continued to embellish the interior right up until the suppression of their order in 1773, adding stuccowork and statues of Jesuit and Czech saints.

Jesuit College ❾
JEZUITSKÁ KOLEJ

Karlovo náměstí 36. **Map** 5 B2. 🚇 *Karlovo náměstí.* 🚋 *3, 4, 6, 14, 16, 18, 22, 24.* **Closed** *to the public.*

Half the eastern side of Charles Square is occupied by the former college of the Jesuit order in the New Town. As in other parts of Prague, the Jesuits were able to demolish huge swathes of the city to put up another bastion of their formidable education system. The college was built between 1656 and 1702 by Carlo Lurago and Paul Ignaz Bayer. The two sculptured portals are the work of Johann Georg Wirch who extended the building in 1770. After the suppression of the Jesuit order in 1773 the college was converted into a military hospital. It is now a teaching hospital and part of Charles University.

Charles Square ❿
KARLOVO NÁMĚSTÍ

Map 5 B2. 🚇 *Karlovo náměstí.* 🚋 *3, 4, 6, 14, 16, 18, 22, 24.*

Since the mid-19th century the square has been a park. Though surrounded by busy roads, it is a pleasant place to sit and read or watch people exercising their dachshunds.

The square began life as a vast cattle market, when Charles IV founded the New Town in 1348. Other goods sold in the square included firewood, coal and pickled herrings from barrels.

In the centre of the market Charles had a wooden tower built, where the coronation jewels were put on display once a year. In 1382 the tower was replaced by a chapel, from which, in 1437, concessions made to the Hussites by the pope at the Council of Basle were read out to the populace.

Church of St Cyril and St Methodius ⓫
KOSTEL SV. CYRILA A METODĚJE

Resslova 9. **Map** 5 B2. 📞 *29 55 95.*
🚇 *Karlovo náměstí.* 🚋 *3, 4, 6, 14, 16, 18, 22, 23, 24.* **Open** *10am–4pm Tue–Sun.* 🚫

This baroque church, with a pilastered façade and a small central tower, was built in the 1730s. It was dedicated to St Charles Borromeo and served as the church of a community of retired priests, but both the priests' home and the church were closed in 1783. In the 1930s the church was restored and given to the Czechoslovak Orthodox Church, and re-dedicated to St Cyril and St Methodius, the 9th-century "Apostles to the Slavs" (see pp20–21). In May 1942 parachutists who had assassinated Reinhard Heydrich, the Nazi governor of Czechoslovakia, hid in the crypt along with members of the Czech Resistance. Surrounded by German troops, they took their own lives rather than surrender.

Bullet holes made by the German machine guns during the siege can still be seen below the memorial plaque on the outer wall of the crypt, which now houses a museum of these times.

Main altar in the Church of St Cyril and St Methodius

Faust House ⓬
FAUSTŮV DŮM

Karlovo náměstí 40, 41. **Map** 5 B3.
Karlovo náměstí. 3, 14, 16.
Closed to the public.

PRAGUE THRIVES on legends of alchemy and pacts with the devil, and this Baroque mansion has attracted many. There has been a house here since the 14th century when it belonged to Prince Václav of Opava, an alchemist and natural historian. In the 16th century it was owned by the alchemist Edward Kelley. The chemical experiments of Count Ferdinand Mladota of Solopysky, who owned the house in the mid-18th century, gave rise to its association with the legend of Faust.

Baroque façade of Faust House

Church of St John on the Rock ⓭
KOSTEL SV. JANA NA SKALCE

Vyšehradská 49. **Map** 5 B3.
24 91 72 13, 24 91 53 71. 3, 4, 14, 18, 24. **Open** for services only.
7:30am, 11am Sun.

ONE OF PRAGUE'S smaller Baroque churches, St John on the Rock is one of Kilian Ignaz Dientzenhofer's most daring designs. Its twin square towers are set at a sharp angle to the church's narrow façade and the interior is based on an octagonal floorplan. The church was completed in

1738, but the double staircase leading up to the west front was not added until the 1770s. On the high altar there is a wooden version of Jan Brokof's statue of St John Nepomuk *(see p137)* which stands on the Charles Bridge.

Slavonic Monastery ⓮
KLÁŠTER NA SLOVANECH

Vyšehradská 49. **Map** 5 B3. 21 97 92 27. 3, 4, 14, 18, 24. **Closed** for reconstruction until 2002. **Cloisters open** by appointment. noon Mon, Wed, Fri.

BOTH THE MONASTERY and its church were almost destroyed in an American air raid in 1945. During their reconstruction, the church was given a pair of modern reinforced concrete spires.

The monastery was founded in 1347 for the Croatian Benedictines, whose services were held in the Old Slavonic language, hence its name "Na Slovanech". In the course of Prague's tumultuous religious history it has since changed hands many times. In 1446 a Hussite order was formed here, then in 1635 the monastery was acquired by Spanish Benedictines. In the 18th century the complex was given a thorough Baroque treatment, but in 1880 it was taken over by some German Benedictines, who rebuilt almost everything in Neo-Gothic style. The monastery has managed to preserve some historically important 14th-century wall paintings in the cloister, though many paintings were damaged in the air raid of World War II.

Remains of 14th-century wall paintings in the Slavonic Monastery

Botanical Gardens ⓯
BOTANICKÁ ZAHRADA

Na slupi 16. **Map** 5 B3. 29 51 67. 18, 24. 148. **Glasshouses open** 10am–4pm daily. **Gardens open** Jan–Feb: 8am–5pm daily; Mar–Oct: 8am–6pm daily; Nov–Dec: 8am–4pm daily.

CHARLES IV founded Prague's first botanical garden in the 14th century. This is a much later institution. The university garden was founded in the Smíchov district in 1775, but in 1897 it was moved to its present site. The huge greenhouses date from 1938.

Special botanical exhibitions and shows of exotic birds and tropical fish are often held here. One star attraction of the gardens is the giant water lily, *Victoria cruziana*, whose huge leaves can support a small child. During the summer it produces dozens of flowers which only survive for a day.

Entrance to the university's Botanical Gardens

Octagonal steeple of St Catherine's

Church of St Catherine ⓰

KOSTEL SV. KATEŘINY

Kateřinská. **Map** 5 C3. 🚋 *4, 6, 16, 22, 23.* **Closed** to the public.

ST CATHERINE'S stands in the garden of a former convent, founded in 1354 by Charles IV to commemorate his victory at the Battle of San Felice in Italy in 1332. In 1420, during the Hussite revolution *(see pp26–7)*, the convent was demolished, but in the following century it was rebuilt by Kilián Ignáz Dientzenhofer as an Augustinian monastery. The monks remained here until 1787, when the monastery was shut down. Since 1822 it has been used as a hospital. In 1737 a new Baroque church was built, but the slender steeple of the old Gothic church was retained. Its conspicuous octagonal shape has gained it the nickname of "the Prague minaret".

Chalice Restaurant ⓱

RESTAURACE U KALICHA

Na bojišti 14. **Map** 6 D3. 🕻 *29 07 01/ 29 19 45.* 🚇 *IP Pavlova.* 🚋 *4, 6, 16, 22.* **Open** *11am–3pm, 5–11pm daily.* 📷 🦽 *See* **Restaurants** *pp198–205.*

THIS PILSNER URQUELL beer hall owes its fame to the novel *The Good Soldier Švejk* by Jaroslav Hašek. It was Švejk's favourite drinking place and the establishment trades on the popularity of the best-loved character in 20th-century Czech literature. The staff dress in period costume from World War I, the era of this novel.

Dvořák Museum ⓲

MUZEUM ANTONÍNA DVOŘÁKA

Ke Karlovu 20. **Map** 6 D2. 🕻 *29 82 14.* 🚇 *IP Pavlova.* 🚌 *148.* **Open** *10am–5pm Tue–Sun.* 📷 📛 🦽 *also open for concerts.*

ONE OF THE most enchanting secular buildings of the Prague Baroque, this red and ochre villa now houses the Antonín Dvořák Museum. On display are Dvořák scores and editions of his works, plus photographs and memorabilia of the great 19th-century Czech composer, including his piano, his viola and his desk.

The building is by the great Baroque architect Kilián Ignaz Dientzenhofer *(see p129).* Just two storeys high with an elegant tiered mansard roof, the house was completed in 1720, for the Michnas of Vacínov and was originally known as the Michna Summer Palace. It later became known as Villa Amerika, after a nearby inn called Amerika. Between the two pavilions flanking the house is a fine iron gateway, a replica of the Baroque original. In the 19th century villa and garden fell into decay. The garden statues and vases, from the workshop of Matthias Braun, date from about 1735. They are original but heavily restored, as is the interior of the palace. The ceiling and walls of the large room on the first floor, often used for recitals, are decorated with 18th-century frescoes by Jan Ferdinand Schor.

Church of St Stephen ⓳

KOSTEL SV. ŠTĚPÁNA

Štěpánská. **Map** 5 C2. 🕻 *29 23 80.* 🚋 *4, 6, 16, 22.* **Open** *only for services.* ✝ *5pm Thu, 11am Sun.* 📛

FOUNDED BY CHARLES IV in 1351 as the parish church of the upper New Town, St Stephen's was finished in 1401 with the completion of the multi-spired steeple. In the late 17th century the Branberg Chapel was built on to the north side of the church. It contains the tomb of the prolific Baroque sculptor Matthias Braun.

Most of the subsequent Baroque additions were removed when the church was scrupulously re-Gothicized in the 1870s by Josef Mocker. There are several fine Baroque paintings,

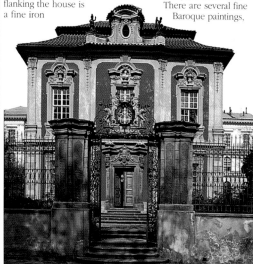

The Michna Summer Palace, home of the Dvořák Museum

Renaissance painted ceiling in the New Town Hall

however, including *The Baptism of Christ* by Karel Škréta at the end of the left hand aisle and a picture of St John Nepomuk *(see p137)* by Jan Jiří Heinsch to the left of the 15th-century pulpit. The church's greatest treasure is undoubtedly a beautiful Gothic panel painting of the Madonna, known as *Our Lady of St Stephen's*, which dates from 1472.

Gothic pulpit in St Stephen's

New Town Hall ⍐
NOVOMĚSTSKÁ RADNICE

Karlovo náměstí 23. **Map** 5 B1. ⍐⍐ Karlovo náměstí. ⍐⍐ 3, 4, 6, 14, 16, 18, 22, 24. ⍐ 24 91 28 10. **Tower open** May–Sep: 10am– 6pm Tue–Sun.

IN 1960 A STATUE of Hussite preacher Jan Želivský was unveiled at the New Town Hall. It commemorates the first and bloodiest of many defenestrations. On 30 July 1419 Želivský led a crowd of demonstrators to the Town Hall to demand the release of some prisoners. When they were refused, they stormed the building and threw the Catholic councillors out of the windows. Those who survived the fall were finished off with pikes.

The Town Hall already existed in the 14th century, the Gothic tower was added in the mid-15th century and contains an 18th century chapel. In the 16th century it acquired an arcaded courtyard. After the joining-up of the four towns of Prague in 1784 the Town Hall ceased to be the seat of the municipal administration and became a courthouse and a prison. It is now used for cultural and social events, and its splendid Gothic hall can be hired for wedding receptions.

U Fleků ㉑

Křemencova 11. **Map** 5 B1. ⍐ 24 91 51 18. ⍐⍐ Národní třída, Karlovo náměstí. ⍐⍐ 6, 9, 17, 18, 22. **Museum open** 10am–5pm Mon–Fri. See **Restaurants** pp198–205.

RECORDS INDICATE that beer was brewed here as early as 1459. This archetypal Prague beer hall has been fortunate in its owners, who have kept up the tradition of brewing as an art rather than just a means of making money. In 1762 the brewery was purchased by Jakub Flekovský, who named it U Fleků (At the Fleks). The present brewery, the smallest in Prague, makes a special strong, dark beer, sold only on the premises. The restaurant now also features a small museum of Czech brewing history.

Church of St Ursula ㉒
KOSTEL SV. VORŠILY

Ostrovní 18. **Map** 3 A5. ⍐ 29 37 30. ⍐⍐ Národní třída. ⍐⍐ 6, 9, 18, 22. **Open** only for services. ⍐ 5pm daily, 10am Sun. ⍐

THE DELIGHTFUL Baroque church of St Ursula was built as part of an Ursuline convent founded in 1672. The original sculptures still decorate the façade and in front of the church stands a group of statues featuring St John Nepomuk (1747) by Ignaz Platzer the Elder. The light airy interior has a frescoed, stuccoed ceiling and on the various altars there are lively Baroque paintings. The main altar has one of St Ursula.

The adjoining convent has recently been returned to the Ursuline order and has now become a Catholic school. One part of the ground floor is still used for secular purposes – the Klášterní Vinárna (Convent Restaurant).

National Theatre ㉓
NÁRODNÍ DIVADLO

See pp156–7.

U Fleků, Prague's best-known beer hall

National Theatre ㉓

NÁRODNÍ DIVADLO

THIS GOLD-CRESTED THEATRE has always been an important symbol of the Czech cultural revival. Work started in 1868, funded largely by voluntary contributions. The original Neo-Renaissance design was by the Czech architect Josef Zítek. After its destruction by fire *(see opposite)*, Josef Schulz was given the job of rebuilding the theatre and all the best Czech artists of the period contributed towards its lavish and spectacular decoration. During the late 1970s and early 80s the theatre was restored and the New Stage was built by architect Karel Prager.

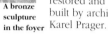

A bronze sculpture in the foyer

The theatre from Marksmen's Island

A bronze three-horse chariot, designed by Bohuslav Schnirch, carries the Goddess of Victory.

The New Stage auditorium

★ **Auditorium**
The elaborately-painted ceiling is adorned with allegorical figures representing the arts by František Ženíšek.

STAR FEATURES

★ **Auditorium**

★ **Lobby Ceiling**

★ **Stage Curtain**

The five arcades of the loggia are decorated with lunette paintings by Josef Tulka, entitled *Five Songs*.

★ **Lobby Ceiling**
This ceiling fresco is the final part of a triptych painted by František Ženíšek in 1878 depicting the Golden Age of Czech Art.

★ **Stage Curtain**
This sumptuous gold and red stage curtain, showing the origin of the theatre, is the work of Vojtěch Hynais.

Façade Decoration
This standing figure on the attic of the western façade is one of many figures representing the Arts sculpted by Antonín Wagner in 1883.

The startling sky-blue roof covered with stars, is said to symbolize the summit all artists should aim for.

The President's Box
The former royal box, lined in red velvet, is decorated with famous historical figures from Czech history by Václav Brožík.

NATIONAL THEATRE FIRE

On 12 August, 1881, just days before the official opening, the National Theatre was completely gutted by fire. It was thought to have been started by metalworkers on the roof. But just six weeks later, enough money had been collected to rebuild the theatre. It was finally opened two years late in 1883 with a performance of Czech composer Bedřich Smetana's opera *Libuše (see p79)*.

FURTHER AFIELD

Visitors to Prague, finding the old centre packed with sights, tend to ignore the suburbs. It is true that once you start exploring away from the centre, the language can become more of a problem. However, it is well worth the effort, firstly to escape the crowds of tourists milling around the Castle and the Old Town Square, secondly to realize that Prague is a living city as well as a picturesque time capsule. Most of the museums and other sights

Vaulting in Church of St Barbara, Kutná Hora

in the first part of this section are easily reached by Metro, tram or even on foot. If you are prepared to venture a little further, do not miss the grand palace at Troja or the former monastery at Zbraslav, which houses the modern Czech sculpture collection of the National Gallery. The Day Trips *(pp168–70)* include visits to castles close to Prague and the historic spa towns of Marienbad and Karlsbad, which attracted the first tourists to Bohemia during the 19th century.

SIGHTS AT A GLANCE

Museums and Galleries
Mozart Museum ❶
Prague Museum ❻
National Technical Museum ❽
Trades Fair Palace pp164–5 ❾
Zbraslav Monastery ⓯

Monasteries
Břevnov Monastery ⓭

Historic Districts
Vyšehrad ❷
Žižkov ❹
Náměstí Míru ❺

Cemeteries
Olšany Cemeteries ❸

Historic Sites
White Mountain and
Star Hunting Lodge ⓮

Historic Buildings
Troja Palace pp166–7 ⓫

Parks and Gardens
Letná Park ❼
Exhibition Ground and
Stromovka Park ❿
Zoo ⓬

KEY

▨	Central Prague
▢	Greater Prague
✈	Airport
▬	Major road
═	Minor road

15 km = 10 miles

 Part of the garden staircase at the 17th-century Troja Palace

Bertramka, the villa that houses the Mozart Museum

Mozart Museum ❶
BERTRAMKA

Mozartova 169. 54 38 93/54 00 12. *Anděl*. 4, 7, 9. **Open** 9:30am–6pm daily.

THOUGH SLIGHTLY off the beaten track, the museum is well signposted because of Prague's reverence for Mozart. Bertramka is a 17th-century farmhouse, enlarged in the second half of the 18th century to convert it into a comfortable suburban villa. Mozart and his wife Constanze stayed here as the guests of the composer František Dušek and his wife Josefina in 1787, when Mozart was working on *Don Giovanni*. He composed the overture to the opera in the

garden pavilion just a few hours before its premiere at the Nostitz (now the Estates) Theatre *(see p65)*. The house contains a small exhibition of Mozart and his various visits to Prague. The villa is best visited in the late afternoon when it is at its most tranquil. During the summer recitals take place on the terrace.

Vyšehrad ❷

Map 5 B5. *Vyšehrad*. 7, 18, 24.

A ROCKY OUTCROP above the Vltava, Vyšehrad means "castle on the heights" *(see pp178–9)*. It was fortified in the 10th century and, at times, used as the seat of the Přemyslid princes. The area has great historical and mythological significance for the Czech people, and in the 1870s it was chosen as the site for a national cemetery.

Olšany Cemeteries ❸
OLŠANSKÉ HŘBITOVY

Vinohradská 153, Jana Želivského. *Želivského*. 67 31 06 52. 11, 16, 19, 26. **Open** Mar–Sep: 9am–6pm; Oct–Feb: 9am–4pm.

AT THE NORTHWEST corner of the main cemetery stands the small Church of St Roch (1682), protector against the plague – the first cemetery was founded here in 1679 specifically for the burial of plague victims. In the course of the 19th century, the old cemetery was enlarged and

new ones developed, including a Russian cemetery, distinguished by its old-fashioned Orthodox church (1924–5), and a Jewish one, where Franz Kafka *(see p68)* is buried. Tombs include those of painter Josef Mánes (1820–71) who worked during the Czech Revival movement *(see pp32–3)*, and Josef Jung-mann (1773–1847), compiler of a five-volume Czech-German dictionary.

Žižkov ❹

Jiřího z Poděbrad, Želivského, Flóra. **National Monument**, U památníku. 133, 168, 207. **Closed** to the public.

Equestrian statue of Jan Žižka

THIS QUARTER of Prague was the scene of a historic victory for the Hussites *(see pp26–7)* over Crusaders sent by the Emperor Sigismund to destroy them. On 14 July 1420 on Vítkov hill, a tiny force of Hussites defeated an army of several thousand well-armed men. The determined, hymn-singing Hussites were led by the one-eyed Jan Žižka.
In 1877 the area around Vítkov was renamed Žižkov in honour of Žižka's victory, and in 1950 a bronze equestrian statue of Žižka by Bohumil Kafka was erected on the hill. About 9m (30 ft) high, this is the largest equestrian statue in the world. It stands in front of the equally massive National Monument (1927–32), built as a symbol of the struggle for independence of the Czecho-slovak people. The Monument later served as a mausoleum for Klement Gottwald and other Communist leaders. Their remains have since been removed, but the future of the building is uncertain.

Well-tended grave in the eastern part of the Olšany Cemeteries

Relief by Josef Myslbek on portal of St Ludmilla in Náměstí Míru

An even more conspicuous landmark is a giant television transmitter, 260 m (850 ft) high. The locals have always been somewhat suspicious of the rays emanating from this great tube of reinforced concrete, built in 1984–8.

Náměstí Míru ❺

Map 6 F2. Ⓜ *Náměstí Míru.* 🚃 *4, 16, 22.* 🚌 *135, 148, 272.* **Church of St Ludmilla open** only for services.

Tʜɪs ᴀᴛᴛʀᴀᴄᴛɪᴠᴇ sǫᴜᴀʀᴇ, with a well-kept central garden, is the focal point of the Vinohrady quarter. At the top of its sloping lawns stands the attractive, brick Neo-Gothic Church of St Ludmilla (1888– 93), designed by Josef Mocker, architect of the west end of St Vitus's Cathedral *(see pp100–3).* Its twin octagonal spires are 60 m (200 ft) high. On the tympanum of the main portal is a relief of Christ with St Wenceslas and St Ludmilla by the great 19th-century sculptor Josef Myslbek. Leading artists also contributed designs for the stained-glass windows and the church's colourful blue and gold interior.

The outside of the square is lined with attractive buildings, the most conspicuous being the Vinohrady Theatre, a spirited Art Nouveau building completed in 1907. The façade is crowned by two huge winged figures sculpted by Milan Havlíček, symbolizing Drama and Opera.

Prague Museum ❻
MUZEUM HLAVNÍHO MĚSTA PRAHY

Na Poříčí 52. **Map** 4 F3.
Ⓒ *24 81 67 72/24 81 67 73.*
Ⓜ *Florenc.* 🚃 *3, 8, 24.*
Open 9am–6pm Tue–Sun
(9am–8pm 1st Thu of every month).
🖾 🚫

Tʜᴇ ᴄᴏʟʟᴇᴄᴛɪᴏɴ records the history of Prague from primeval times. A new museum was built to house the exhibits in the 1890s. Its Neo-Renaissance façade is rich with stucco and sculptures, and the interior walls are painted with historic views of the city. On display are examples of Prague china and furniture, relics of the medieval guilds and paintings of Prague through the ages. The most remarkable exhibit is the paper and wood model of Prague by Antonín Langweil. Completed in 1834, it covers 20 sq m (25 sq yards). The scale of the extraordinarily accurate model is 1:500.

Letná Park ❼
LETENSKÉ SADY

Map 3 A1. Ⓒ *32 57 92.*
Ⓜ *Malostranská, Hradčanská.*
🚃 *1, 8, 12, 18, 22, 25, 26.*

Aᴄʀᴏss ᴛʜᴇ ʀɪᴠᴇʀ from the Jewish Quarter, a large plateau overlooks the city. It was here that armies gathered before attacking Prague Castle. Since the mid-19th century it has been a wooded park.

On the terrace at the top of the granite steps that lead up from the embankment stands a curious monument – a giant metronome built in 1991. It was installed after the Velvet Revolution on the pedestal formerly occupied by the gigantic stone statue of Stalin leading the people, which was blown up in 1962. Nobody likes the metronome any more than they did Stalin and it may soon be replaced. A far more durable monument is the Hanavský Pavilion, a Neo-Baroque cast iron structure, built for the 1891 Exhibition. It was later dismantled and erected on its present site in the park, where it houses a popular restaurant and café.

View of the Vltava and bridges from Letná Park

National Technical Museum ❽
NÁRODNÍ TECHNICKÉ MUZEUM

Kostelní 42. 📞 20 39 91 11.
🚋 1, 8, 25, 26. **Open** 9am–5pm
Tue–Sun. 📷 🚫 🎥 ♿

THOUGH IT TRIES to keep abreast of all scientific developments, the museum's strength is its collection of machines from the Industrial Revolution to the present day, the largest of its kind in Europe. The section that attracts the most visitors is the History of Transportation in the vast central hall. This is filled with locomotives, railway carriages, bicycles, veteran motorcars and motorcycles, with aeroplanes and a hot-air balloon suspended overhead.

The photography and cinematography section is well worth a visit, as is the collection of astronomical instruments. The section measuring time is also popular, especially on the hour when everything starts to chime at once. In the basement there is a huge reconstruction of a coal mine, with an assortment of tools tracing the development of mining from the 15th to the 19th century.

Trades Fair Palace ❾
VELETRŽNÍ PALÁC

See pp164–5.

Exhibition Ground and Stromovka Park ❿
VÝSTAVIŠTĚ A STROMOVKA

🚋 1, 8, 25, 26. **Exhibition Ground open** 10am–11pm daily. 📷
Stromovka Park open 24hrs daily.
Lapidárium 📞 37 31 98. **Open** noon–6pm Tue–Fri, 10am–6pm Sat, Sun. ♿

LAID OUT for the Jubilee of 1891, the Exhibition Ground has been used for trade fairs, sports and artistic events ever since. With its lively funfair, it is the obvious destination for a day out from central Prague with the children. All kinds of exhibitions, sporting events,

The Industrial Palace, centrepiece of the 1891 Exhibition Ground

spectacles and concerts are staged throughout the summer. The large park to the west was the former royal hunting enclosure and deer park, first established in the late 16th century. The name Stromovka means "place of trees", a reminder that a large area of the park was once a flourishing tree nursery. Opened to the public in 1804, the park is still a pleasant wooded area and an ideal place for a walk. The Lapidarium holds an exhibition of 11th–19th century sculpture, including some originals from the Charles Bridge (see pp136–9).

Troja Palace ⓫
TROJSKÝ ZÁMEK

See pp164–5.

Zoo ⓬
ZOOLOGICKÁ ZAHRADA

U trojského zámku 3. 📞 6880 480.
🚇 Holešovice, then 🚌 112.
Open May–Oct 9am–7pm daily; Nov–Apr: 9am–4pm daily. 📷 📷 ♿ 🍴

ATTRACTIVELY SITUATED on a rocky slope overlooking the right bank of the Vltava, the zoo was founded in 1924.

It now covers an area of 64 hectares (160 acres) and there is a chair lift to take visitors to the upper part. To travel on the lift, you can use an ordinary metro/tram ticket.

The zoo's 2,500 animals represent 500 species, 50 of them extremely rare in the wild. It is best known for its breeding programme of Przewalski's horses, the only species of wild horse in the world. It has also enjoyed considerable success in breeding big cats, wolves, antelopes, giraffes, flamingoes, gorillas and orang-utans. Two new pavilions have recently opened – one for lions, tigers and other beasts of prey and one for elephants.

Red panda, relative of the famous giant panda, in Prague Zoo

Břevnov Monastery

BŘEVNOVSKÝ KLÁŠTER

Markétská. ☎ 35 15 20/35 34 61.
🚌 8, 22. ☑ only, 10am & 2pm Sat
& Sun other times by arrangement.
🖼 🚫

FROM THE surrounding sub-urban housing, you would never guess that Břevnov is one of the oldest inhabited parts of Prague. A flourishing community grew up here around the Benedictine abbey founded in 993 by Prince Boleslav II *(see p20)* and Bishop Adalbert (Vojtěch) – the first monastery in Bohemia. An ancient well called Vojtěška marks the spot where prince and bishop are supposed to have met and decided to found the monastery.

The gateway, courtyard and most of the present monastery buildings are by the great Baroque architects Christoph and Kilian Ignaz Dientzen-hofer *(see p129)*. The monastery Church of St Margaret is the work of Christoph. Completed in 1715, it is based on a floorplan of overlapping ovals, as ingenious as any of Bernini's churches in Rome. In 1964 the crypt of the original 10th-century church was discovered below the choir and is open to the public. Of the other buildings, the most interesting is the abbey's meeting hall, or Theresian Hall, with a painted ceiling dating from 1727.

White Mountain and Star Hunting Lodge

BÍLÁ HORA A HVĚZDA

🚌 8, 22 (White Mountain), 18 (Star Hunting Lodge). *White Mountain enclosure open* 24hrs daily. *Star Hunting Lodge open* 10am–5pm Tue–Sun. 🖼 🚫

THE BATTLE of the White Mountain *(see p30–31)*, fought on 8 November 1620, had a very different impact for the two main communities of Prague. For the Protestants it was a disaster that led to

Star Hunting Lodge

300 years of Habsburg domination; for the Catholic supporters of the Habsburgs it was a triumph, so they built a memorial chapel on the hill. In the early 18th century this was converted into the grander Church of Our Lady Victorious and decorated by leading Baroque artists, including Václav Vavřinec Reiner.

In the 16th century the woodland around the battle site had been a royal game park. The hunting lodge, completed in 1556, survives today. This fascinating build-ing is shaped as a six-pointed star – *hvězda* means star. It was converted into a museum in 1950 and dedicated to the writer of historical novels, Alois Jirásek (1851–1930), and the painter, Mikoláš Aleš

(1852–1913). Part of the museum also has exhibits relating to the Battle of the White Mountain.

Zbraslav Monastery

ZBRASLAVSKÝ KLÁŠTER

Zámek Zbraslav ☎ 57 92 19 29.
🚌 129, 240, 241, 243, 255, 360.
Open 10am–6pm Tue –Sun.
🖼 🚫 ♿

IN 1279 WENCESLAS II founded a monastery to serve as the burial place for the royal family, though only he and Wenceslas IV were ever buried here. Destroyed during the Hussite Wars *(see pp26–7)*, the monastery was rebuilt in 1709 to be abolished in 1785 and made into a factory. Earlier this century it was restored and in 1941 was given to the National Gallery. It now houses a unique collection of Asian art with exhibits including art and artefacts from China, Japan, India, South East Asia and Tibet. A collection of Japanese sculpture is featured which visually impaired visitors are encouraged to touch. The exhibition also includes a section dedicated to Islamic art. Informative guided tours are available.

Zbraslav Monastery, home to the National Gallery's Asian Art Collection

Trades Fair Palace ⑨

VELETRŽNÍ PALAC

THE NATIONAL GALLERY IN PRAGUE opened its Centre for Modern and Contemporary Art in 1995, housed in a reconstruction of a former Trades Fair building of 1929. Its vast, skylit spaces make an ideal backdrop for the collection, which ranges from French 19th-century art through superb examples of Impressionist and Post-Impressionist painting, to works by Munch, Klimt, Picasso and Miró, and a splendid collection of Czech modern art.

Grand Meal *(1951–55)*
Mikuláš Medek's works range from post-war Surrealism to 1960s Abstraction.

Screening
Room

Fourth
Floor

★ Torso *(1936)*
Zdeněk Pešánek was a pioneer of kinetic art, here combining an organic form with neon lighting.

Pomona *(1910)*
Aristide Maillol was a pupil of Rodin. This work is part of an exceptional collection of bronzes.

Third
Floor

Second
Floor

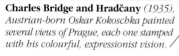

Charles Bridge and Hradčany *(1935),*
Austrian-born Oskar Kokoschka painted several views of Prague, each one stamped with his colourful, expressionist vision.

★ Myself: Portrait-Landscape
The only existing self-portrait by Henri "Le Douanier" Rousseau (1890) has the same surreal quality as all his works. Note the Eiffel Tower in the background.

STAR SIGHTS

★ **Self-Portait by Picasso**

★ **Myself: Portrait-Landscape by Rousseau**

★ **Torso by Pesanek**

★ **Self-Portrait by Pablo Picasso**
This was painted in 1907, a period during which the artist's work was being strongly influenced by primitive sculpture and art.

Cognition and Amazement (1969)
This haunting Figurative work by Květoslava Válová was painted in a year when artistic freedom was being crushed.

Three Axes (1966)
Radoslav Kratina was part of a movement called "New Sensitivity", one of a succession that dominated post-war Czech art.

Stairs to all floors

Stairs to all floors

Stairs to all floors

First Floor

Mezzanine Floor

Ground Floor

Main entrance

The fascia's concrete and glass bands are typical of 1920s Functionalism.

KEY

- Czech art 1965 - 1995
- Czech art 1900 - 1965
- French art 19th, 20th centuries
- European art of the 20th century
- Performance art 1960-1990
- Special exhibition space
- Non-exhibition space

Troja Palace ⓫

TROJSKÝ ZÁMEK

ONE OF THE MOST STRIKING summer palaces in Prague, Troja was built in the late 17th century by Jean-Baptiste Mathey for Count Sternberg, a member of a leading Bohemian aristocratic family. Situated at the foot of the Vltava Heights, the exterior of the palace was modelled on a Classical Italian villa, while its garden was laid out in formal French style. The magnificent interior took over 20 years to complete and is full of extravagant frescoes expressing the Sternberg family's loyalty to the Habsburg dynasty. Troja has recently been restored and houses a good collection of 19th-century art.

Defeat of the Turks
This turbaned figure, tumbling from the Grand Hall ceiling, symbolizes Leopold I's triumph over the Turks.

Belvedere turret

Statue of Olympian God

Terracotta urn on the garden balustrade

Statues of sons of Mother Earth

Personification of Justice
Abraham Godyn's image of Justice gazes from the lower east wall of the Grand Hall.

★ **Garden Staircase**
The two sons of Mother Earth which adorn the sweeping oval staircase (1685–1703) are part of a group of sculptures by Johann Georg Heermann and his nephew Paul, depicting the struggle of the Olympian Gods with the Titans.

VISITORS' CHECKLIST

U trojského zámku 1, Prague 7.
68 90 761. 112 from
Holešovice metro. summer
only (see p55). **Open** Apr–Oct:
10am–6pm Tue–Sun.

★ Grand Hall Fresco

The frescoes in the Grand Hall (1691–7), by Abraham Godyn, depict the story of the first Habsburg Emperor, Rudolph I, and the many victories of Leopold I over the archenemy of Christianity, the Sublime Porte (Ottoman Empire).

Stucco decoration

★ LANDSCAPED GARDENS

Palace entrance
To the maze
Main entrance
Café
Grand fountain

Orangery

STAR FEATURES

★ Grand Hall Fresco

★ Landscaped Gardens

★ Garden Staircase

Chinese Rooms
Several rooms feature 18th-century murals of Chinese scenes. This room makes a perfect backdrop for a ceramics display.

Sloping vineyards were levelled, hillsides excavated and terraces built to fulfil the elaborate and grandiose plans of French architect, Jean-Baptiste Mathey, for the first Baroque French-style formal gardens in Bohemia. The palace and its geometric network of paths, terracing, fountains, statuary and beautiful terracotta vases, is best viewed from the south of the garden between the two orangeries. The gardens have been carefully restored according to Mathey's original plans.

Day Trips from Prague

T HE SIGHTS THAT ATTRACT most visitors away
from the city are Bohemia's picturesque
medieval castles. Karlstein, for example, stands
in splendid isolation above wooded valleys
that have changed little since the Emperor
Charles IV hunted there in the 14th century.
We have chosen four castles, very varied in
character. There are regular organized tours
(see p219) to the major sights around Prague,
to the historic mining town of Kutná Hora
and, if you have more time to spare, to
the famous spa towns of Karlsbad and
Marienbad in western Bohemia.

St George and Dragon, Konopiště

25 km = 16 miles

Veltrusy Château ❶
VELTRUSKÝ ZÁMEK

20 km (12 miles) north of Prague. 📞
0205 78 11 44/46. 🚋 from Smíchov
to Kralupy nad Vltavou, then local bus.
Open May–Sep: 8am–5pm Tue–Sun;
Oct–Apr: 9am–4pm Sat & Sun (phone
to make an appointment for week
days). 📷 🚫 ♿ (park only).

V ELTRUSY is a small town
beside the Vltava, famous

for the 18th-century château
built by the aristocratic
Chotek family. The building is
in the shape of a cross, with a
central dome and a grand
staircase decorated with statues
representing the months of the
year and the four seasons.

The estate was laid out as
an English-style landscaped
deer park, covering an area
of 300 hectares (750 acres).
Near the entrance there is still

an enclosure with a herd of
deer. The Vltava flows along
one side and dotted around
the grounds are several
summer houses. The Doric and
Maria Theresa pavilions, the
orangery and the grotto date
from the late 18th century.
The park is planted with
some 100 kinds of tree.

Karlstein Castle ❷
KARLŠTEJN

25 km (16 miles) southwest of Prague.
📞 0311 68 16 17/95.
🚋 from Smíchov to Karlštejn
(1.5 km/1 mile) from castle).
🚌 from Anděl to Karlštejn (1 km
(0.6 miles) from castle). **Closed** until
Feb 2001. 📷 📞 compulsory. 🚫
Chapel of the Holy Rood
📞 74 00 81 54. **Open** by reservation
only.

T HE CASTLE WAS founded by
Charles IV as a country
retreat, a treasury for the
imperial crown jewels and a
symbolic expression of his
divine right to rule the Holy
Roman Empire. It stands on a

Karlstein Castle, built by Emperor Charles IV in the 14th century

crag above the River Berounka. When you reach the castle what you see is largely a 19th-century reconstruction by Josef Mocker. The original building work (1348–67) was supervised by French master mason, Matthew of Arras, and after him by Peter Parler. You can still see the audience hall and the bedchamber of Charles IV in the Royal Palace. On the third floor, the Emperor's quarters are below those of the Empress.

The central tower houses the Church of Our Lady, decorated with faded 14th-century wall paintings. A narrow passage leads to the tiny Chapel of St Catherine, Charles's private place of meditation. The walls are adorned with semiprecious stones set into the plaster.

The same extravagance was used in the Chapel of the Holy Rood in the Great Tower, with its gilded vaulting studded with glass stars. Charles IV housed the crown jewels and relics of the crucifixion here. Unfortunately it is no longer open to the public. It contained 127 panels painted by Master Theodoric (1357–65). These were damaged both by acts of vandalism and by the visitors' breath. Some restored panels can be seen at St George's Convent (see pp106–9).

Konopiště Castle ❸

40 km (25 miles) southeast of Prague. 📞 0301 213 66. 🚂 from Hlavní nádraží to Benešov, then local bus. **Open** Apr, Oct: 9am–noon, 1–3pm Tue–Fri, 9am–noon, 1–4pm Sat–Sun; May–Aug: 9am–noon, 1–5pm Tue–Sun; Sep: 9am–noon, 1–4pm Tue–Sun. 📷 🚫

Though it dates back to the 13th century, this moated castle is essentially a late 19th-century creation. In between, Konopiště had been rebuilt by Baroque architect František Kaňka and in front of the bridge across the moat is a splendid gate (1725) by Kaňka and sculptor Matthias Braun.

In 1887 Konopiště was bought by Archduke Franz Ferdinand, who later became heir to the Austrian throne. It was his assassination in 1914

View of the castle at Křivoklát, dominated by the Great Tower

in Sarajevo that triggered off World War I. His wife was assassinated with him. To escape the Habsburg court's harsh disapproval of his wife, Ferdinand spent much of his time at Konopiště. He amassed arms, armour and Meissen porcelain, all on display in the fine furnished interiors. However, the abiding memory of the castle is of the hundreds of stags' heads lining the walls.

Hunting trophies at Konopiště

Křivoklát Castle ❹

45 km (28 miles) west of Prague. 📞 0313 55 81 20. 🚂 from Smíchov to Křivoklát (1 km /0.6 miles) from castle). 🚌 from Anděl. **Open** Mar, Nov, Dec: 9am–noon, 1–3pm Tue–Sun; May, Sep: 9am–noon, 1–4pm Tue–Sun; Jun–Aug: 9am–noon, 1–5pm Tue–Sun. 📷 🚫

This castle, like Karlstein, owes its appearance to

the restoration work of Josef Mocker. It was originally a hunting lodge belonging to the early Přemyslid princes and the seat of the royal master of hounds. In the 13th century King Wenceslas I built a stone castle here, which remained in the hands of Bohemia's kings and the Habsburg emperors until the 17th century.

Charles IV spent some of his childhood here and returned from France in 1334 with his first wife Blanche de Valois. Their daughter Margaret was born in the castle. To amuse his queen and young princess, Charles ordered the local villagers to trap nightingales and set them free in a wooded area just below the castle. Today you can still walk along the "Nightingale Path".

The royal palace is on the eastern side of the triangular castle. This corner is dominated by the Great Tower, 42 m (130 ft) high. You can still see some 13th-century stonework, but most of the palace dates from the reign of Vladislav Jagiello. On the first floor there is a vaulted Gothic hall, reminiscent of the Vladislav Hall in the Royal Palace at Prague Castle (see pp104–5). It has an oriel window and a beautiful loggia that was used by sentries. Also of interest is the chapel, which has a fine Gothic altar carving. Below the chapel lies the Augusta Prison, so-called because Bishop Jan Augusta of the Bohemian Brethren was imprisoned here for 16 years in the mid-16th century. The dungeon now houses a grim assortment of instruments of torture.

Kutná Hora **❺**

70 km (45 miles) east of Prague. **ℂ**
0327 51 23 78. (tourist information).
⬚ *from Hlavní nádraží, Masarykovo
nádraží or Holešovice.* **▦** *from Florenc.*
Church of St Barbara open *Jan–Mar,
Nov–Dec: 9–11:30am, 2–3:30pm Tue–
Sun; Apr & Oct: 9–11:30am, 1–4pm
Tue–Sun; May–Sep: 9am–5:30pm.* **▨**
Italian Court open *Nov–Feb: 10am–
4pm daily; Mar, Oct: 10am–5pm daily;
Apr– Sep: 9am–6pm daily.* **▨ Hrádek
open** *Apr, Oct: 9am–5pm Tue–Sun;
May, Sep: 9am–6pm Tue–Sun; Jun–
Aug 10am–6pm Tue–Sun.* **▨ Stone
House open** *Apr (phone for times).*

T HE TOWN ORIGINATED as a
small mining community
in the second half of the 13th
century. When rich deposits of
silver were found, the king
took over the licensing of the
mines and Kutná Hora became
the second most important
town in Bohemia.
   In the 14th century five to
six tonnes of pure silver were
extracted here each year,
making the king the richest
ruler in Central Europe. The
Prague *groschen*, a silver coin
that circulated all over Europe,
was minted here in the Italian
Court (Vlašský dvůr), so-called
because Florentine experts
were employed to set up the
mint. Strongly fortified, it was
also the ruler's seat in the
town. In the late 14th century

a superb palace was
constructed with
reception halls and the
Chapel of St Wenceslas
and St Ladislav, below
which lay the royal
treasury.
   When the silver started
to run out in the 16th
century, the town began
to lose its importance;
the mint finally closed in
1727. The Italian Court
later became the town
hall. On the ground floor
you can still see a row
of forges. Since 1947 a
mining museum has
been housed in another
building, the Hrádek,
which was originally a
fort. A visit includes a
tour of a medieval mine.
There is museum in the
Stone House (Kamenný dům),
a restored Gothic building of
the late 15th century.
   To the southwest of the
town stands the Church of St
Barbara, begun in 1380 by the
workshop of Peter Parler, also
the architect of St Vitus's
Cathedral *(see pp100–3)*. The
presbytery (1499) has a fine
net vault and windows with
intricate tracery. The slightly
later nave vault is by royal
architect Benedikt Ried. Catch
the murals in the nave, many
of which show mining scenes.
The cathedral, with its three

The Italian Court, Kutná Hora's first mint

massive and tent-shaped spires
rising above a forest of flying
buttresses, is a wonderful
example of Bohemian Gothic.

Karlsbad **❻**
KARLOVY VARY

140 km (85 miles) west of Prague.
⬚ *from Masarykovo nádraží.*
▦ *from Florenc.*

L EGEND HAS IT that Charles IV
(see pp24–5) discovered
one of the sources of mineral
water that would make the
town's fortune when one of his
staghounds fell into a hot
spring. In 1522 a medical
description of the springs was
published and by the end of
the 16th century over 200 spa
buildings had been built there.
Today there are 12 hot mineral
springs – *vary* means hot
springs. The best-known is the
Vřídlo (Sprudel), which rises to
a height of 12 m (40 ft). At
72˚C, it is also the hottest. The
water is good for digestive
disorders, but you do not have
to drink it; you can take the
minerals in the form of salts.
   The town is also known for
its Karlovy Vary china and
Moser glass, and for summer
concerts and other cultural
events. The race course is
popular with the more sporting
invalids taking the waters.
   Outstanding among the local
historic monuments is the
Baroque parish church of Mary

The three steeples of Kutná Hora's great Church of St Barbara

Magdalene by Kilian Ignaz Dientzenhofer (1732–6). More modern churches built for foreign visitors include a Russian church (1896) and an Anglican one (1877). The 19th-century Mill Colonnade (Mlýnská kolonáda) is by Josef Zítek, architect of the National Theatre *(see p156–7)* in Prague. There have been many royal visitors over the centuries – from Peter the Great of Russia in 1711 to England's Edward VII in 1907.

Marienbad ❼

MARIÁNSKÉ LÁZNĚ

170 km (105 miles) west of Prague.
🚉 from Hlavní nádraží.
🚌 from Florenc.

Bronze statue of a chamois at Jeleni skok (Stag's Leap), with a view across the valley to the Imperial Sanatorium, Karlsbad

T HE ELEGANCE of Marienbad's hotels, parks and gardens has faded considerably since it was the playground of kings and princes at the turn of the century. The area's health-giving waters – *lázně* means bath (or spa) – have been known since the 16th century, but the spa was not founded until the beginning of the last century. The waters are used to treat all kinds of disorders; mud baths are also popular.

Most of the spa buildings date from the latter half of the 19th century. The great cast-iron colonnade with frescoes by Josef Vyletěl is still an impressive sight. In front of it is a "singing fountain", its jets of water now controlled by computer. Churches were provided for visitors of all denominations, including an Evangelical church (1857), an Anglican church (1879) and the Russian Orthodox church of St Vladimír (1902). Visitors can learn the history of the spa in the house called At the Golden Grape (U zlatého hroznu), where the German poet Johann Wolfgang von Goethe stayed in 1823. Musical visitors during the 19th century included the composers Weber, Wagner and Bruckner, while writers such as Ibsen, Gogol, Mark Twain and Rudyard Kipling also found its treatments beneficial. King Edward VII came here frequently. In 1905 he agreed to open the golf course (Bohemia's first), even though he hated the game.

There are many pleasant walks in the countryside around Marienbad, especially in the protected Slavkov Forest.

The cast-iron colonnade at Marienbad, completed in 1889

THREE GUIDED WALKS

RAGUE OFFERS some good opportunities for walking. In the centre of the city, many streets are pedestrianized and the most important sights are confined to quite a small area *(see pp14–15)*. Here are three guided walks of varied character. The first passes through a main artery of the city, from the Powder Gate on the outskirts of the Old Town to St Vitus's Cathedral in Prague Castle, crossing the wonderful Charles Bridge at its mid-point. This is the Royal Coronation Route, followed for

House sign in Celetná Street
(See Royal Route Walk pp174–5)

centuries by Bohemian kings. Away from the busy centre, the second of the walks takes in the peace and tranquility of one of Prague's loveliest parks. Petřín Park is especially rewarding, also, for its spectacular views of the city. The final walk is in Vyšehrad. This is a peaceful, ancient fortress which is steeped in history and atmosphere, and the route includes a visit to the resting place of some of Prague's most famous citizens. The views from Vyšehrad of the Vltava and Prague Castle are unparalleled.

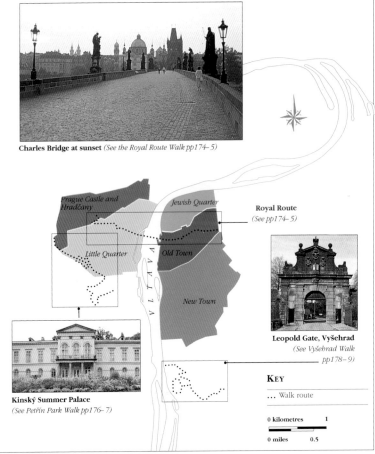

Charles Bridge at sunset *(See the Royal Route Walk pp174–5)*

Prague Castle and Hradčany

Jewish Quarter

Royal Route
(See pp174–5)

Little Quarter

Old Town

VLTAVA

New Town

Leopold Gate, Vyšehrad
(See Vyšehrad Walk pp178–9)

Kinský Summer Palace
(See Petřín Park Walk pp176–7)

KEY

··· Walk route

0 kilometres 1

0 miles 0.5

◁ **View of the New Town from Petřín Park with the Church of St Lawrence in the foreground**

A 90-Minute Walk along the Royal Route

THE ROYAL ROUTE ORIGINALLY linked two important royal seats; the Royal Court – situated on the site of the Municipal House and where the walk starts – and Prague Castle, where the walk finishes. The name of this walk derives from the coronation processions of the Bohemian kings and queens who passed along it. Today, these narrow streets offer a wealth of historical and architecturally interesting sights, shops and cafés, making the walk one of Prague's most enjoyable. For more details on the Old Town, the Little Quarter and Hradčany turn to pages 60–79; 122–41 and 94–121 respectively.

History of the Royal Route

The first major coronation procession to travel along this route was for George of Poděbrady (see p26) in 1458. The next large procession took place in 1743, when Maria Theresa was crowned with great pomp – three Turkish pavilions were erected just outside the Powder Gate. September 1791 saw the coronation of Leopold II. This procession was led by cavalry, followed by mounted drummers, trumpeters and soldiers and Bohemian lords. Some 80 carriages came next, carrying princes and bishops. The most splendid were each drawn by six pairs of horses, flanked by servants with red coats and white leather trousers, and carried the ladies-in-waiting.

Figural *sgraffito* covers the façade of the Renaissance House at the Minute

The last great coronation procession along the Royal Route – for Ferdinand V – was in 1836 with over 3,391 horses and four camels.

From the Powder Gate to Old Town Square

At Náměstí Republiky turn towards the Municipal House (see p64) and walk under the Gothic Powder Gate ① (see p64). Here, at the city gates, the monarch and a large retinue of church dignitaries, aristocrats, and foreign ambassadors were warmly welcomed by leading city representatives. The gate leads into one of Prague's oldest streets, Celetná (see p65). It was here the Jewish community and the crafts guilds, carrying their insignia, greeted their king.

The street is lined with Baroque and Rococo houses with unusual house signs. Behind the façades are Gothic buildings. At house No. 36 was the Mint ②. It moved

here after the mint at Kutná Hora (see p168) was occupied by Catholic troops in the Hussite Wars (see pp26–7). It minted coins from 1420 to 1784. The House of the Black Madonna ③ contains a museum of Czech Cubist art (see p65). Revellers would watch processions from the taverns, At the Spider ④ and At the Vulture ⑤.

At the end of Celetná Street is the Old Town Square ⑥ (see pp66–9). Here, the processions halted beside Týn Church ⑦ (see p70) for pledges of loyalty from the university. Keep to the left of the square, past No. 20, At the Unicorn ⑧. This is where Smetana began a music school in 1848. Proceed to the Old Town Hall ⑨ (see pp72–4).

House at the Black Madonna ③

The distinct Baroque façade of the House at the Golden Well in Karlova Street ⑪

Here, the municipal guard and a band waited for the royal procession and city dignitaries cheered from the temporary balcony around the hall.

Along Karlova Street and across Charles Bridge

Walk past the sgraffitoed façade of the House at the Minute and into Malé náměstí ⑩, where merchants waited with members of the various religious orders. Turn right down gallery-filled Karlova

months later he died. Walk under the Old Town Bridge Tower ⑫ and over Charles Bridge ⑬ and then under the Little Quarter Towers ⑭ *(see pp136–9).*

The Little Quarter

The walk now follows Mostecká Street. On entering the Little Quarter the mayor handed the city keys to the king and the artillery fired a salute. At the end of this street is Little Quarter Square ⑮ *(see p124)* and the Baroque church, St Nicholas's ⑯ *(see pp128–9).*

Sculpture of Moor by Ferdinand Brokof on Morzin Palace

sharp right and walk up the Castle ramp which leads you to Hradčanské Square. The route ends at the Castle's Matthias Gate *(see p48)* ⑲. The procession ended with the coronation held at St Vitus's Cathedral.

The Old Town from Charles Bridge ⑬

Powder Gate

Street. Beyond Husova Street is an attractive Baroque house, At the Golden Well ⑪. Further on is the 16th-century Clementinum *(see p79),* where the clergy stood. You then pass into Knights of the Cross Square *(see p79).* When Leopold II's procession passed through here the clouds lifted, which was considered to be a good omen. But only a few

The procession passed the church to the sound of its bells ringing.

Leave this picturesque square by Nerudova Street ⑰ *(see p130).* Poet and writer Jan Neruda, who immortalized hundreds of Little Quarter characters in books like *Mala Strana Tales,* grew up and worked at No. 47 ⑱. At the end of this street you turn

KEY

••• Walk route

🔆 Good viewing point

Ⓜ Metro station

🚊 Tram stop

━ Castle wall

0 metres	300
0 yards	300

TIPS FOR WALKERS

Starting point: Náměstí Republiky.

Length: 2.4 km (1.5 miles).

Getting there: Line B goes to Náměstí Republiky metro station. At Hradčany you can get tram 22 back into town.

Stopping-off points: Rest beneath the sunshades of the outdoor cafés on Old Town Square in the summer. Karlova Street has one of the most popular cafés in Prague, At the Golden Snake (U Zlatého hada). There are also cafés in the lower part of Malostranské Square.

Coronation procession passing through the Knights of the Cross Square

A Two-Hour Walk through Petřín Park

PART OF THE CHARM of this walk around this large and peaceful hillside park are the many spectacular views over the different areas of Prague. The Little Quarter, Hradčany and the Old Town all take on a totally different aspect when viewed from above. The tree-covered gardens are dotted with châteaux, pavilions and statues and crisscrossed by winding paths leading you to secret and unexpected corners. For more on the sights of Petřín Hill see pages 140–41.

One of the gateways in the Hunger Wall ⑤

A 17th-century statue of Hercules that stands in the lower lake ②

Kinský Square to Hunger Wall

The walk starts at náměstí Kinských in Smíchov. Enter Kinský Garden through a large enclosed gateway. This English-style garden was founded in 1827 and named after the wealthy Kinský family, supporters of Czech culture in the 19th century.

Take the wide asphalt path on your left to the Kinský Summer Palace ①. This 1830s pseudo-classical building was designed by Jindřich Koch and its façade features Ionic columns terminating in a triangular tympanum. Inside the building is a large hall of columns with a triple-branched staircase beautifully-decorated with statues. The Ethno-graphical Museum is housed here; however, it is closed at present for reconstruction.

Next to the museum is a 1913 statue of the actress Hana Kvapilová.

About 50 m (150 ft) above the palace is the lower lake ② with a Baroque sandstone statue of Hercules. Walk left around the lake and continue up the hill to the Church of St Michael ③, on your left. This 18th-century wooden folk church was moved here from a village in the Ukraine.

Follow the path up the hill for about 20 m (60 ft), then go to the top of the steps to a wide asphalt path known as the Observation Path for its beautiful views of the city. Turn right and further on your left is the upper lake ④ with a 1950s bronze statue of a seal at its centre. Keep following the Observation Path; ahead of you stands a Neo-Gothic gate. This allows you to pass through the city's old Baroque fortifications.

Hunger Wall to Observation Tower

Continue along the path to the Hunger Wall ⑤ *(see pp140–41)*. This was a major part of the Little Quarter's fortifica-tions; the wall still runs from Újezd

Church of St Michael ③

Kinský Summer Palace

Street across Petřín Hill and up to Strahov Monastery. Passing through the gate in the wall brings you to Petřín Park. Take the wide path to the left below the wall and walk up the hill beside the wall until you cross the bridge which spans the funicular railway *(see p141)*. Below on your right you can see the

Sunbathers on Petřín Hill

Nebozízek restaurant *(see p202)* famed for its views. On either side of the path are small sandstone rockeries. Most are entrances to reservoirs, built in the 18th and 19th centuries, to bring water to Strahov Monastery; others are left over from the unsuccessful attempts at mining the area. Walk up to the summit of the hill. On your right is the Mirror Maze ⑥ *(see p140)*. Facing the maze is the 12th-century St Lawrence's Church ⑦ *(see pp140–41)*, renovated in 1740 in the Baroque style.

KEY

* * * Walk route

☼ Good viewing point

Tram stop

Funicular railway

Hunger Wall

0 metres	300
0 yards	300

Observation Tower to Strahov Monastery

A little further on stands the Observation Tower ⑧ *(see p140)*. This steel replica of the Eiffel Tower in Paris is 60 m (200 ft) high. Opposite the tower is the main gate of the Hunger Wall. Pass through, turn left and follow the path to the Rose Garden ⑨.

The garden was planted by the city of Prague in 1932, and features a number of attractive sculptures. When you look down to the far end of the garden you can see The Observatory *(see p140)*. This was rebuilt from a municipal building in 1928 by the Czech Astronomical Society and was then modernized in the 1970s. It now houses a huge telescope and is open in the evenings to the public.

Returning to the Observation Tower, follow the wall on the left, passing some chapels of the Stations of the Cross dating from 1834. Then pass through a gap in the Hunger Wall, turn right, and walk past a charming Baroque house. About 50 m (150 ft) beyond this, you pass through another gap in the Hunger Wall on your right. Turn left into a large orchard above Strahov Monastery ⑩ *(see pp120–21)* for spectacular views of Prague. Continue onto a wide path which leads slightly downwards along the wall, through the orchard and past tennis courts to the

Sgraffitoed façade of the Calvary Chapel next to the Church of St Lawrence ⑦

Strahov Monastery courtyard. You can catch tram 22 from here, or linger in the peaceful monastery grounds. If you feel energetic you can walk back down the hill.

TIPS FOR WALKERS

Starting point: náměstí Kinských in Smíchov.
Length: 2.7 km (1.7 miles). The walk includes steep hills.
Getting there: The nearest metro station to the starting point is Anděl. Trams 6, 9 and 12 take you to Kinský Square.
Stopping-off points: There is a restaurant, Nebozízek, half way up Petřín Hill and during the summer a few snack bars are open at the summit of the Hill near the Observation Tower.

Hradčany and the Little Quarter from the summit of Petřín Hill

A 60-Minute Walk in Vyšehrad

ACCORDING TO ANCIENT LEGEND, Vyšehrad was the first seat of Czech royalty. It was from this spot that Princess Libuše is said to have prophesied the future glory of the city of Prague *(see pp20–21)*. However, archaeological research indicates that the first castle on Vyšehrad was not built until the 10th century. The fortress suffered a turbulent history and was rebuilt many times. Today, it is above all a peaceful place with parks and unrivalled views of the Vltava valley and Prague. The fascinating cemetery is the last resting place of many famous Czech writers, actors, artists and musicians.

Decorative sculpture on the Baroque Leopold Gate ⑤

The ruin of Libuše's Baths on the cliff face of Vyšehrad Rock ⑩

V Pevnosti

From Vyšehrad metro ① make your way up the steps facing the metro exit to the complex of the Palace of Culture ② straight ahead. Walk west along its large granite terrace, go down the incline and straight ahead into the quiet street Na Bučance. Turn right at the end, cross the road and you find yourself on V Pevnosti, facing the brick walls of the original Vyšehrad Citadel. Ahead of you is the west entrance to the fortress, the mid-17th-century Tábor Gate ③. Past this gate on the right are the ruins of

the 14th-century fortifications built by Charles IV. Further on are the ruins of the original Gothic gate, Špička ④. Pass that and you get to the sculpture-adorned Leopold Gate ⑤, one of the most impressive parts of these 17th-century fortifications. It adjoins the brick walls ⑥ that were widened during the French occupation of 1742.

K rotundě to Soběslavova Street

Turn right out of the gate and just after St Martin's Rotunda, turn left into K rotundě. A few metres on your left, almost concealed behind high walls, is the New Deanery, now the Vyšehrad Museum ⑦. This is used to house archaeological remains found around Vyšehrad. Situated at the corner of K rotundě and Soběslavova streets is the Canon's House ⑧.

Turn left down Soběslavova to see the excavations of the foundations of the Basilica of St Lawrence ⑨. This was built by Vratislav II in the late 11th century, but was destroyed by the Hussites *(see pp26–7)* in 1420. At the basilica turn right on to the fortified walls for a stunning view of Prague.

KEY

••• Walk route

☆ Good viewing point

🚇 Metro station

🚊 Tram stop

— Castle wall

| 0 metres | 200 |
| 0 yards | 200 |

18th-century engraving by I G Ringle, showing Vyšehrad and the Vltava

Vyšehrad Rock

The wooded outcrop of rock on which Vyšehrad was built drops in the west to form a steep rock wall to the river – a vital defensive position. On the summit of the rock are the Gothic ruins of the so-called Libuše's Baths ⑩. This was a defence bastion of the medieval castle. Further on your left is a grassy patch where the remains of a 14th-century Gothic palace ⑪ have been found.

Vyšehrad Park

The western part of Vyšehrad has been transformed into a park. Standing on the lawn south of the Church of St Peter and St Paul are four groups of statues ⑫ by the 19th-century sculptor Josef Myslbek. The works

The elaborate memorial to the composer Antonín Dvořák in Vyšehrad Cemetery ⑭

represent figures from early Czech history – including the legendary Přemysl and Libuše (see pp20–21). The statues were originally on Palacký Bridge, but were damaged during the US bombardment of February 1945. After being restored, they were taken to Vyšehrad Park. The park was the site of a Romanesque palace, which was connected by a bridge to the neighbouring church. Another palace was built here in the reign of Charles IV (see pp24–5).

The Church of St Peter and St Paul

This twin-spired church ⑬ totally dominates Vyšehrad. It was founded in the latter half of the 11th century by Prince Vratislav II and was enlarged in 1129. In the mid-13th century it burned down and was replaced by an Early Gothic church. Since then it has been redecorated and restored many times in a variety of styles. In 1885, it was finally rebuilt in Neo-Gothic style, the twin steeples being added in 1902. Note the early-12th-century stone coffin, thought to be of St Longinus, and a mid-14th-century Gothic panel painting Our Lady of the Rains on the altar in the third chapel on the right.

Vyšehrad Cemetery and the Pantheon

The cemetery ⑭ was founded in 1869 as the burial place for some of the country's most famous figures, such as Bedřich Smetana (see p79). Access is through a gate to the right of the church. On the east side of the cemetery is the Slavín (Pantheon) – a great tomb built in 1890 for the most honoured personalities of the Czech nation, including the sculptor Josef Myslbek.

Leave the cemetery by the same gate and walk back down K rotundě. On your left is the Devil's Column ⑮, said to be left by the devil after losing a wager with a priest. At the end of this street is St Martin's Rotunda (see p44) ⑯. This is a small Romanesque church built at the end of the 11th century and restored in 1878. Turn left, walk downhill through the Cihelná (Brick) Gate ⑰, which was built in 1741, and down Vratislavova Street to the Výtoň tram stop on the Vltava Embankment.

The Neo-Gothic Church of St Peter and St Paul ⑬

Statue of Přemysl and Princess Libuše by Josef Myslbek in Vyšehrad Park ⑫

TIPS FOR WALKERS

Starting point: Vyšehrad metro station, line C.
Length: 1.5 km (1 mile).
Getting there: The walk starts from Vyšehrad metro station and ends at No. 17 tram which takes you back to the city centre.
Stopping-off points: The park in front of the church of St Peter and St Paul is a lovely place to relax. There is a café opposite the Basilica of St Lawrence.

TRAVELLERS' NEEDS

WHERE TO STAY

SINCE THE "VELVET REVOLUTION" of 1989, Prague has become one of the most visited cities in Europe. Despite investment in new hotels, helped by huge injections of foreign capital, the city is struggling to meet the demand for accommodation. Many old hotels have been rebuilt; others have just re-vamped the reception area, and the impression quickly fades as you climb the stairs. Most of the renovated hotels are as smart as any in Europe – and often just as expensive. Unfortunately there is

Doorman at the exclusive Palace hotel *(see p189)*

little for the budget traveller. The few cheap hotels tend to be old-fashioned places in the centre of the city or smaller, pension-type hotels in the suburbs. We have inspected over 100 hotels in every price bracket and on pages 187–9 recommend 30 that offer good value. The chart on page 186 will help you select a hotel. A cheap alternative is to stay in a flat or a room in a private home, which is usually booked by an agency *(see p184)*. Hostels and campsites offer other budget options *(see p185)*.

The elegant Ungelt hotel *(see p187)*

WHERE TO LOOK

AS PRAGUE is such a small city, it is best to stay near the centre close to all the main sights, restaurants and shops. Most hotels are found around Wenceslas Square. Here you are at the hub of everything, and the prices of some (but not all) of the hotels reflect this. Another popular area is the nearby Náměstí Republiky, but the best area is around Old Town Square, a few minutes' walk from Charles Bridge. Hotels here include large, international establishments, old-fashioned Czech places, and some small, much more exclusive hotels.

To the south, in the New Town, there are a few cheaper hotels only a few metro stops from Old Town Square. But the area is less picturesque and some of the streets suffer from heavy volumes of traffic.

For a view of the river Vltava, stay in the Jewish Quarter, although most hotels here are new and expensive. There are also a few botels (floating hotels) moored along the embankments away from the city centre. They are a bit cheaper, but the small cabins are very cramped and uncomfortable, and most of the boats would benefit from some renovation.

Over Charles Bridge, in the Little Quarter, you will find a handful of interesting hotels in delightful surroundings, but there are far fewer by Prague Castle in Hradčany. Further north of this area, there are some large and particularly unappealing hotels. The city's suburbs too, have a number of rather nondescript places a few of these being new. These have some good facilities, but

are often as expensive as their equivalents in the centre with the added inconvenience of travelling time and cost – the metro stops at midnight and taxis can become expensive.

HOW TO BOOK

TRYING TO BOOK hotels in Prague in advance can be frustrating. Most middle-range hotels have a contracted room allocation with a tour operator. If no other rooms are available, the hotel will ask you to call a week or two before you travel, by which time they will know if the rooms have been filled by tour groups. This may be nerve-racking for those who prefer to book in advance. It is important to receive written confirmation of your booking by letter or

Pool-side bar at the luxury Praha Renaissance *(see p187)*

fax. This can save trouble on arrival. Phone and fax communication with the Czech Republic has improved over the last few years, but the response from hotels can still be slow. If you would like to let someone else make the arrangements, a number of UK tour operators specialize in Prague *(see p184)*.

FACILITIES

FOLLOWING the refurbishment programme, most rooms now have en suite WC and shower or bath, telephone and TV, which may also offer video and satellite channels. Many hotels offer a reasonably-priced laundry service, and the larger hotels usually have 24-hour room service and mini bars. Guests are expected to vacate rooms by midday, but most hotels are happy to keep luggage safe if you are leaving later. Foreign-owned hotels sometimes import managers, but the Czech staff generally speak good English so you should encounter few communication problems.

DISCOUNT RATES

THE PRICE STRUCTURE for hotels in Prague is fairly flexible, but unfortunately not to the tourist's advantage. Rooms are usually twice as expensive for foreigners as for nationals, whether booked independently or through a tour operator. The only way to get a cheap rate is to turn up at the hotel and negotiate. The popular seasons are Christmas and New Year, and between Easter and October, when rooms are often hard to find.

HIDDEN EXTRAS

MOST HOTELS include tax (currently at 23%) and service charges in their tariff, but do check these details when you book. Telephone charges can be a shock when you receive your bill so be aware of the mark-up rate. A number of telephone boxes in the city take international phone cards and credit cards; they will cost you much less

The Paříž is a national monument *(see p187)*

(see p224). Some expensive hotels charge an extra fee for breakfast, others include a continental breakfast, but hot dishes cost extra. Buffet-style continental breakfasts are popular, and usually offer fresh fruit, cereals, yogurt, muesli, cold meat and cheese, and juice, jugs of coffee and tea.

Tipping is now common and is expected in all hotels. As in most countries, single travellers receive no favours.

The ultra-modern Atrium hotel dominates the area *(see p189)*

There are few single rooms, particularly in newer hotels, and a supplement is charged for single occupancy of a double room; expect to pay about 80% of the standard rate.

DISABLED TRAVELLERS

WHEELCHAIR accessibility to hotels on pages 187–9 represents each hotel's own assessment. For information on accommodation for the disabled, write to the Czech Association of Persons with Disabilities *(see p226)*, or contact the Embassy of the Czech Republic in your country.

TRAVELLING WITH CHILDREN

CHILDREN are accommodated by most hotels, either in family rooms or with extra beds, but Prague is not geared to their needs. Hotel breakfasts offer plenty of choice, and although all the fresh milk is pasteurized, hotels also provide long life milk. Few places offer high-chairs or baby-sitters. It is worth asking if there are discounts, or if children can stay free in parents' rooms.

DIRECTORY

UK AGENCIES

British Airways Holidays
London Road,
Crawley, West Sussex
RH10 2XA.
℄ 01293-723180.
FAX 01293-722650.

Čedok Tours
53–54 Haymarket,
London
SW1Y 4RP.
℄ 020-7839 4414.
FAX 020-7839 0204.

Cresta Holidays
Tabley Court,
32 Victoria Street,
Altrincham,
Cheshire WA14 1E2.
℄ 0161-927 7000.
FAX 0870-169 0797.

Crystal Holidays
Kings Place,
Wood Street,
Kingston-upon-Thames,
Surrey KT1 1JY.
℄ 020-8241 5040.

Czech Tourist Centre
16 Frognal Parade,
Finchley Road,
London NW3 5HG.
℄ 020-7794 3263.
FAX 020-7794 3265.

JMB "Opera Holidays"
Rushwick,
Worcester WR2 5SN.
℄ 01905-425628.
FAX 01905-420219.

Osprey Holidays
Broughton Market,
Edinburgh
EH3 6NU.
℄ 0131-557 1555.
FAX 0990-502 020.

Page & Moy Ltd.
136 & 140 London Road,
Leicester
LE2 1EN.
℄ 0116-250 7000.
FAX 0116-254 9949.

Peltours
Sovereign House,
11–19 Ballards Lane,
Finchley,
London N3 1UX.
℄ 020-8346 9144.
FAX 020-8343 0579.

Prospect Music and Art Tours
36 Manchester Street,
London W1M 5PE.
℄ 020-8995 2151.
FAX 020-7486 5868.

Thomson Tour Operations Holiday Shop
Albert House,
Tindall Bridge,
Edward Street,
Birmingham B1 2RA.
℄ 0121-252 3669.
FAX 0121-236 7030.

Travelscene
Travelscene House
11–15 St Ann's Road,
Harrow,
Middlesex HA1 1LQ.
℄ 020-8427 4445.
FAX 020-8861 4154.

US AGENCIES

Čedok Czechoslovak Travel
10 E. 40th St.
NY NY. 10016.
℄ 212-689-9720.

Czechoslovak Health Tours
321 E. 75th St.
NY NY. 10021.
℄ 212-861-7393.

Duna Travel Inc.
213 E. 82nd St.
NY NY. 10028.
℄ 212-737-0150.

FLATS AND ROOMS IN PRIVATE HOMES

IN UK

The Czechbook
Jopes Mill,
Trebrownbridge,
Nr. Liskard,
Cornwall PL14 3PX.
℄ & FAX 01503 240629.

Regent Holidays
15 John Street,
Bristol BS1 2HR.
℄ 0117-921 1711.
FAX 0117-925 4866.

Rose Jackson Travel
PO Box 13664,
London SW14 8WD.
℄ 020-8878 0088.
FAX 020-8878 0464.

IN PRAGUE

Akasi
Václavské náměstí 17.
Map 3 C3.
℄ 24 23 61 18.
FAX 24 23 72 35.

American Express Travel Service
Václavské náměstí 56.
Map 3 C5.
℄ 22 21 01 06.
FAX 22 21 11 31.

Autotourist Travel Agency
Londýnská 62. Map 6 F4.
℄ 22 51 20 53.
FAX 24 22 27 52.

AVE Ltd
Hlavní nádraží (main station). Map 4 E5.
℄ 24 22 32 26.
FAX 24 23 07 83.

Balnea Travel Agency
Národní 28. Map 3 B5.
℄ 21 10 53 14.
FAX 24 94 67 47.

Čedok
Na příkopě 18. Map 4 D4.
℄ 24 19 71 11.

Estec
Vaníčkova 5, Prague 6.
℄ 57 21 04 10.
FAX 57 21 52 63.

Pragoscan Travel Agency
Husova 9. Map 3 B4.
℄ 422 41 92.
FAX 24 91 16 12.

Pragotur
Za Poříčskou Branou 7.
Map 4 D3.
℄ 24 81 61 20.
FAX 24 81 61 72.

Prague Information Service (PIS)
Na příkopě 20.
Map 3 C4.
℄ 26 40 22/
54 44 44/187.
W www.prague-info.cz
Staroměstské
náměstí 1. Map 3 B3.
℄ 54 44 44.
Hlavní nádraží (main station). Map 4 E5.

SCS Ltd
Botičská 4, Prague 2.
℄ 29 76 98.
FAX 29 99 52/29 33 64.

Tom's Travel
Ostrovní 1.
Map 3 B5.
℄ 24 99 09 90.
FAX 24 99 09 99.

Top Tour
Rybná 3. Map 3 C2.
℄ 232 10 77.
FAX 24 81 14 00.
Registration charge.

Travel Agency of České Dráhy
Hybernská 5. Map 3 C4.
℄ 24 22 58 49.
FAX 24 22 36 00.

HOSTELS

CKM Youth Agency
Jindřišská 28.
Map 5 C1.
℄ & FAX 26 86 23.

Universitas Tours
Opletalova 38.
Map 4 D5.
℄ 26 04 26.

CAMPING

Aritma Džbán
Kemp Džbán 3,
Vokovice.
℄ 36 90 06.
FAX 36 13 65.
Open all year.

Kotva Braník
U ledáren 55,
Braník.
℄ 44 46 17 12.
FAX 46 61 10.
Open Apr–Oct.

Troja
Trojská 157, Troja.
℄ 83 85 04 87.
FAX 854 29 45.
Open mid-Apr–Nov.

DISABLED TRAVELLERS

Czech Association of Persons with Disabilities
Karlínské náměstí 12,
Prague 8.
℄ 24 81 59 15.
FAX 24 81 69 76.

Embassy of the Czech Republic
26 Kensington Palace
Gardens,
London W8 4QY.
℄ 0171-243 1115.
FAX 0171 727 9654.

**Pension Páv, in a quiet street of a
historic neighbourhood** *(see p188)*

PRIVATE ROOMS AND SELF-CATERING APARTMENTS

OVER THE PAST few years, the number of private rooms to rent in Prague has grown enormously. Although cheap and popular, they may be some distance from the centre. Private rooms in homes start at about Kč600 per person per night, usually with breakfast. There are also self-contained apartments – a fairly central one-bedroom apartment costs about Kč2,200 per night. Most agencies that offer private rooms also rent out apartments *(see Directory opposite)*.

To book a room or apartment, tell the agency exactly what you want, for how many, when and in which area. The agency will suggest places. Find out the exact location and the nearest metro before accepting; if you are in Prague, see it yourself. Make sure you receive written or faxed confirmation of a booking to take with you. On arrival in Prague, pay the agency in cash; they give you a voucher to take to the room or apartment (sometimes you can pay the owner directly). If the agency requires advance payment by banker's draft or Eurocheque, go direct to the accommodation with your receipt. Agencies may ask for a deposit on bookings from abroad, or charge a registration fee payable in Prague.

HOSTELS

THERE AREN'T many hostels in Prague, but the CKM Youth Agency in the New Town provides up-to-date information on availability. The official IYHF hostel is the Juniorhotel, also in the New Town. It offers basic but clean, cheap accommodation, with reductions for members.

CAMPING

MOST CAMPSITES in or near Prague are closed from November to the start of April. They are very cheap with basic facilities, but are well served by transport. The largest site is at Troja *(see pp164–5)*, 3 km (1.5 miles) north of the centre. Aritma Džbán, 4 km (2.5 miles) west, is open all year for tents, and Kotva Braník is 6 km (4 miles) south of the city on the banks of the Vltava. For details contact the PIS *(see Directory opposite)*.

The smartly refurbished City Hotel Moran *(see p188)*

Choosing a Hotel

Tʜᴇ ʜᴏᴛᴇʟs ʟɪsᴛᴇᴅ on the following pages have all been inspected and assessed. This chart shows some of the factors which may affect your hotel choice. For more information on each hotel see pages 187–9. The hotels are listed by area and appear alphabetically within their price categories.

Hotel	Price	Number of Rooms	Large Rooms	Business Facilities	Children's Facilities	Recommended Restaurant	Close to Shops and Restaurants	Quiet Location	24-Hour Room Service
OLD TOWN *(see p187)*									
Axa	Ⓚ	131	●	■					
Atlantic	Ⓚ	60	●				●		
Central	Ⓚ	68	●				●	■	
Harmony	Ⓚ	60	●	■			●		
Meteor	ⓀⓀ	88	●			■	●		
Praha Renaissance	ⓀⓀⓀ	309	●	■	●		●		
Ungelt	ⓀⓀⓀ	9	●				●	■	●
Paříž	ⓀⓀⓀⓀ	98	●	■		■	●		
JEWISH QUARTER *(see p187)*									
Intercontinental	ⓀⓀⓀⓀ	364	●	■			●		●
President	ⓀⓀⓀⓀ	100		■			●		
LITTLE QUARTER *(see p187–8)*									
Kampa	Ⓚ	83	●				●	■	
U Páva	ⓀⓀ	11	●	■			●	■	
U Tří pštrosů	ⓀⓀⓀ	18	●			■	●		
NEW TOWN *(see p188–9)*									
Luník	Ⓚ	35	●				●	■	
Evropa	Ⓚ	85	●	■			●		
Pension Páv	Ⓚ	8	●	■				■	●
Esplanade	ⓀⓀⓀ	74	●				●	■	●
Adria	ⓀⓀⓀ	66	●				●		●
City Hotel Moráň	ⓀⓀⓀ	57	●					■	
Interhotel Ambassador and Zlatá Husa	ⓀⓀⓀ	174	●	■			●		
Jalta Praha	ⓀⓀⓀⓀ	89	●	■	●		●		
Palace	ⓀⓀⓀⓀ	124	●	■			●	■	●
FURTHER AFIELD *(see p189)*									
Belvedere	Ⓚ	142	●	■			●		
Carol	Ⓚ	40	●	■	●				●
Esprit	Ⓚ	63	●					■	
Praha	ⓀⓀⓀ	124	●	■				■	●
Atrium Hilton	ⓀⓀⓀⓀ	800	●	■					●
Corinthia Towers	ⓀⓀⓀⓀ	551	●	■	●	■	●		●
Diplomat Praha	ⓀⓀⓀⓀ	382	●	■	●				

Price categories for a double room per night in high season, with breakfast, tax and service:
Ⓚ Kč up to 4,000
ⓀⓀ Kč4–5,000
ⓀⓀⓀ Kč5–6,000
ⓀⓀⓀⓀ Kč6–7,000
ⓀⓀⓀⓀⓀ over Kč7,000

CLOSE TO SHOPS AND RESTAURANTS Within a 5-minute walk of good shops, bars, cafés and restaurants.

BUSINESS FACILITIES *(see p185).*

CHILDREN'S FACILITIES *(see p185).*

OLD TOWN

Axa

Na poříčí 40, 110 00 Praha 1.
Map 4 E3. 24 81 25 80.
FAX 232 21 72. **Rooms:** 131.
AE, DC, MC, V.

This old-style hotel opposite the Harmony is slightly dispiriting, yet reasonably priced and central. The rather uninviting exterior opens into a clean, efficient entrance hall. All the rooms have been renovated. A large open-plan public restaurant and bar overlooks the road. It is light and airy, but lacks character. The big bonus is the basement swimming pool..

Atlantic

Na poříčí 9, 110 00 Praha 1.
Map 4 D3. 24 81 10 84.
FAX 24 81 23 78. **Rooms:** 60.
AE, DC, MC, V, JCB.

A few minutes walk from Náměstí Republiky along a busy road, this hotel is well placed for exploring the city. Reconstructed in 1988–9, it is neat and modern, if lacking in character, and the bedrooms are functional and comfortable enough, with most facilities. The restaurant overlooks the main road and at the back there is a bistro cum bar serving lighter snacks and drinks.

Central

Rybná 8, 110 00 Praha 1. **Map** 3 C2.
24 81 20 41. FAX 232 84 04.
Rooms: 68.
breakfast only. AE, MC, JMB, V.

The chief advantage of the Central is its location. Situated in a quiet backstreet with a minimal outlook, it is an old-style hotel, with reasonable prices. The lobby and reception have had a cursory face-lift, but this fades as you climb the stairs. The bedrooms, though old-fashioned and a bit rickety, are neat and clean with a mix of old and new furniture. The small bathrooms are immaculate.

Harmony

Na poříčí 31, 110 00 Praha 1.
Map 4 E3. 232 00 16,
FAX 231 00 09. **Rooms:** 60.
AE, DC, MC, V.

Not far from the Atlantic, the Harmony is in pristine condition after complete reconstruction. A compact place, it is run by young, friendly staff. Two small restaurants, one with tables on the pavement, give a choice of Czech or international cuisine.

Meteor

Hybernská 6, 110 00 Praha 1. **Map** 4
D3. 24 19 21 11. FAX 24 21 30 05.
Rooms: 88. AE, DC, MC, V.

Though part of the international Best Western group, the Meteor still has a cosy, old-fashioned feel. Some parts are slightly scruffy, but most of it has been well modernized and made comfortable. Many of the bedrooms are on the small side, as are the marble showers. In the cellar there is an attractive restaurant.

Praha Renaissance

V celnici, PO Box 726, 110 00 Praha
1. **Map** 4 E3. 21 82 21 00.
FAX 21 82 22 00. **Rooms:** 309.
AE, DC, V, JCB.

The gleaming glass front of this smart new hotel takes over one corner of Náměstí Republiky. Young men in bright uniforms buzz around the guests, giving friendly and efficient service. The luxurious bedrooms include soft furnishings, plump bedcovers and fluffy bathrobes. There is a choice of restaurants, a beer hall and a very smart pool and health club.

Ungelt

Štupartská 7, 110 00 Praha 1. **Map**
C3. 24 82 86 86. FAX 24 82 81
81. **Rooms:** 9. AE, MC, V.

Tucked away in a quiet street just behind the Old Town Square, this discreet, elegant hotel has an air of exclusivity. The accommodation is in suites, simply but stylishly fitted out with spacious, airy rooms and useful kitchenettes. Some of the rooms feature magnificent wooden ceilings. The restaurant is neat and simple with plain wooden chairs on a marble floor softened with rugs, and there is a shady terrace.

Paříž

U Obecního domu 1, 110 00 Praha 1.
Map 4 D3. 24 22 21 51. FAX 24
22 54 75. **Rooms:** 98.
AE, DC, MC, V.

This turn-of-the-century hotel just off Náměstí Republiky was built by the celebrated architect Jan Vejrych. A Neo-Gothic building with Art Nouveau elements, it was declared a historic monument in 1984 and displays examples of beautiful craftsmanship. The restaurant is particularly attractive, with superb doors and fine decoration on the ceiling. The

rooms have been well modernized in international style – that is, fairly characterless but extremely comfortable – and everything is in pristine condition.

JEWISH QUARTER

Intercontinental

Náměstí Curieových 43–45, 110 00
Praha 1. 24 88 11 11.
FAX 24 81 12 16. **Rooms:** 364.
AE, MC, DC, V, JCB.

An imposing 1970s building set right on the bank of the Vltava, this hotel is catching up with the competition by adding health and fitness facilities and a swimming pool. There is nothing particularly Czech about the place, but it is a good example of a five-star international hotel. Many of the rooms have lovely views over the river, but although comfortable enough, they are hardly inspired, the best features being the chic grey marble bathrooms.

President

Náměstí Curieových 100, 116 88
Praha 1. **Map** 3 B2. 231 48 12.
FAX 231 82 47. **Rooms:** 100.
AE, DC, MC, V, JCB.

The central location more than compensates for the President's aesthetic shortcomings. Built over 20 years ago for trade unionists, it has been thoroughly refurbished internally and is comfortable, if slightly package-tour-like. The bustling centre of the hotel is its large, airy reception area with lots of sofas, rugs and some bright original paintings. There is a choice of two restaurants, one Czech and one "international", and a roof terrace where, drink in hand, you can enjoy the view across the Vltava to Prague castle.

LITTLE QUARTER

Kampa

Všehrdova 16, 118 00 Praha 1.
Map 2 E5. 57 32 04 04.
FAX 57 32 02 62. **Rooms:** 83.
AE, DC, MC, V.

Built originally as an armoury at the beginning of the 17th century, the Kampa opened recently as a hotel after a complete renovation. Five minutes from Charles Bridge, it is tucked away in a peaceful side street, surrounded by trees and gardens. In the large reception hall, a bar and restaurant are combined under a huge Baroque vaulted

For key to symbols see p185

ceiling. The effect is far from cosy, and the whole hotel has a slightly institutional feel but it is excellent value. The decor and furnishings are simple and the bedrooms are immaculately clean and neat with whitewashed walls, plain curtains and dark wooden furniture.

U Páva

U lužického semináře 32, 110 00 Praha 1. **Map** 2 F3. **[** 57 32 07 43. **FAX** 53 33 79. **Rooms:** 11. 🛏 🔛 TV ⚑ 🛗 P 🍷 ▮▮ 🍽 AE, MC, V. Ⓚ Ⓚ

U Páva translated means "At The Peacock". The hotel is only a few minutes walk from Charles Bridge through a pretty, quiet part of the Little Quarter. It provides a smart and stylish stay. The historical features of the house have been enhanced by traditional dark wooden furniture, crystal chandeliers and attractive rugs. Lots of personal touches give it an original and individual feel and the bedrooms, similarly furnished, are both spacious and comfortable.

U Tří pštrosů

Dražického náměstí 12, 118 00 Praha 1. **Map** 2 F3. **[** 57 32 05 65. **FAX** 57 32 06 11. **Rooms:** 18. 🛏 ▮ 🔛 TV ⚑ P 🍷 ▮▮ 🍽 AE, V, MC. Ⓚ Ⓚ Ⓚ

Just beside Charles Bridge, the hotel "At The Three Ostriches" began life as the home of Jan Fux, a dealer in ostrich feathers (see p134). It is one of the best known hotel/ restaurants in Prague. Family run, the place has a special, intimate atmosphere and refuses to get involved with tour operators. The restaurant has an excellent reputation, so book ahead. The bedrooms have recently been refurbished and are extremely spacious and also comfortable, being decorated in keeping with the style of the place.

NEW TOWN

Luník

Londýnská 50, 120 00 Praha 2. **Map** 6 E2. **[** 24 25 39 74. **FAX** 24 25 39 86. **Rooms:** 35. 🛏 ▮ 🔛 🛗 🛗 🍷 MC, V, JCB, AE. Ⓚ

Located in a quiet street lined with trees, the Luník is 15 minutes' walk or two metro stops from Wenceslas Square, but well worth it for the price. The hotel is in immaculate condition. There is simple but smart decor throughout with whitewashed walls and good quality wooden furnishings. Bedrooms are pristine, albeit rather small and functional, with few frills but every necessity.

Evropa

Václavské náměstí 25, 110 00 Praha 1. **Map** 4 D5. **[** 24 22 81 17. **FAX** 24 22 45 44. **Rooms:** 85. 🛏 30. ▮ 🔛 🛗 🍷 🍷 ▮▮ 🍽 AE, DC, MC, V. Ⓚ

The Evropa's exterior outshines its neighbours in Wenceslas Square. It is the city's most beautiful hotel, with superb Art Nouveau decor. The wonderful old dining room boasts stunning glasswork and the hotel's café/bar is the most famous in Prague (see p146). It remains reasonably priced. Yet the bedrooms are rather disappointing. Each one varies enormously in size, style and facilities; the best are those on the first and second floors, with French windows and high ceilings. But even these bedrooms are not really grand – the furniture is a mish-mash of pieces dating from the 1970s and earlier, and the bathrooms, where they exist, are pretty basic.

Pension Páv

Křemencova 13, 110 00 Praha 1. **Map** 5 B1. **[** 24 91 32 86. **FAX** 24 91 05 74. **Rooms:** 8. 🛏 24 TV ▤ 🍽 Ⓚ

Located in a fairly quiet street in a historic part of Prague, this hotel is a compact place with just a few rooms and apartments. These are simple but quite stylishly decorated, and all are of a good size. The pension has its own cosy bar and a reasonable restaurant; both are ideal for those evenings when you feel too exhausted to venture out.

Esplanade

Washingtonova 19, 110 00 Praha 1. **Map** 4 E5. **[** 24 21 17 15. **FAX** 24 22 93 06. **Rooms:** 74. 🛏 ▮ 24 TV ⚑ P 🍷 ▮▮ 🍽 AE, DC, MC, V, JCB. Ⓚ Ⓚ Ⓚ

This refined, almost stately hotel is run with old-fashioned service and courtesy. The location in a wide tree-lined street just off Wenceslas Square is marred by the view of a freeway, but you are not aware of this once inside. Built early this century, the hotel has high ceilings with some glorious Art Nouveau features. There are two restaurants: the rather bizarre one down in the basement has the advantage of staying open till 2am – extremely useful after operas or concerts and very unusual for Prague. The decoration of the rooms varies, but each is large and comfortable.

Adria

Václavské náměstí 26, 110 00 Praha 1. **Map** 4 D5. **[** 21 08 11 11. **FAX** 21 08 13 00. **Rooms:** 66. 🛏 ▮ 🔛 24 TV ⚑ 🛗 🍷 P 🍷 ▮▮ 🍽 AE, DC, MC, V, JCB. Ⓚ Ⓚ Ⓚ Ⓚ

After being completely rebuilt, the Adria is bright and chic with a dazzling yellow awning above its entrance on Wenceslas Square. Electric doors slide back to admit you to the marble-tiled reception. Clever use of glass and mirrors make this seem bigger than it is and with plenty of gleaming brass the overwhelming impression is light and up-beat. The bedrooms are also bright and cheery with yellow walls and smartly co-ordinated furnishings.

City Hotel Moráň

Na Moráni 15, 120 00 Praha 2. **Map** 5 A3. **[** 24 91 52 08. **FAX** 24 92 06 25. **TX** 12 21 34. **Rooms:** 57. 🛏 ▮ 🔛 TV ⚑ 🛗 P 🍷 ▮▮ 🍽 AE, DC, MC, V. Ⓚ Ⓚ Ⓚ Ⓚ

The City Hotel Moráň is another reconstruction made to meet the higher standards of today's visitors to Prague. It has been beautifully decorated in an understated style with whitewashed walls with soft green carpets in some areas, smart sofas and chairs on pale marble floors in others. There is also a smart café/ restaurant and bar overlooking the street. Although the bedrooms vary in size, the standard of comfort is high throughout: equipped with all the conveniences you would expect to find in a modernized hotel.

Interhotel Ambassador/ Zlatá Husa

Václavské náměstí 5–7, 110 00 Praha 1. **Map** 3 C5. **[** 24 19 31 11/ 24 21 21 85. **FAX** 24 23 06 20. **Rooms:** 174. 🛏 ▮ 🔛 24 TV ⚑ 🛗 🍷 P 🛗 🍷 ▮▮ ▮ 🍽 AE, DC, MC, V. Ⓚ Ⓚ Ⓚ Ⓚ

In the centre of Wenceslas Square, neighbouring hotels are now under the same owner-ship. The result is rather a muddle, but it gives you a choice of bars and restaurants, some of which stay open until midnight or later, without having to leave the building. The lounge and reception areas look scruffy and rather old-fashioned, but the other public rooms are reasonably comfortable. Although all the bedrooms are the same price, the standard varies enormously, so insist on a recently refurbished room.

Palace

Panská 12, 110 00 Praha 1. **Map** 4 D4. **[** 24 09 31 11. **FAX** 24 22 12 40. **TX** 12 33 37. **Rooms:** 124. 🛏 ▮ 24 TV ⚑ ⚑ ▤ 🛗 ⚑ 🛗 P 🍷 ▮▮ ▮ 🍽 AE, DC, MC, V, JCB. Ⓚ Ⓚ Ⓚ Ⓚ Ⓚ

A short walk from Wenceslas Square, located in a quiet side street, this hotel reopened in 1989 after a complete refurbishment. The unusual mixture of styles – modern, Art Nouveau and traditional – with lashings of brass, glass, mirrors and fake flowers, may not be to everyone's taste, and in places the decor does go a touch over the top, but the hotel succeeds in its aim to provide any luxury its guests may require.

Jalta Praha

Václavské náměstí 45, 110 00 Praha 1.
Map 4 D5. 22 82 21 11. **FAX** 24 21 38 66. **Rooms:** 89.
TV ⊹ 🖩 🗗 🛌 🖧 🗘 P 🕑 🍴
🛎 🖳 AE, DC, MC, V, JCB.
Ⓚ Ⓚ Ⓚ Ⓚ Ⓚ

One of Prague's old-fashioned hotels, the Jalta Praha has a central position on Wenceslas Square. The reception is chillingly unadorned with just a small desk at one end. Other parts of the hotel, however, have undergone some reconstruction: the exterior has been renovated and the main restaurant redesigned. The bedrooms have also been refurbished. They are comfortable, good-sized rooms that are attractively decorated, with modern bathrooms attached.

FURTHER AFIELD

Belvedere

Milady Horákové 19, 170 00 Praha 7.
20 10 61 11. **FAX** 33 37 23 68.
Rooms: 142. 🖩 🗗 🖧 🗘 TV ⊹
⊹ 🗗 🛌 🗘 P 🕑 🍴 🛎 🖳
🖳 AE, DC, MC, V, JCB. Ⓚ

Just one metro stop north from Florenc, this area buzzes with activity – shops, restaurants, cafés. It has a life very much of its own, and shows you a more intimate side of Prague. The hotel is on a main corner and the bar/café opens onto the street. It is a friendly, relaxed place, which is why it is popular with groups. Although there is nothing special about the hotel and it can be slightly gloomy, it is clean, neat, reasonably central and moderately priced. The rooms are simple but comfortable, with good modern shower rooms.

Carol

Kurta Konráda 547 / 12, 190 Praha 9.
66 31 13 16. **FAX** 684 42 76.
Rooms: 40. 🖩 🗗 🖧 🗘 TV ⊹
🗗 🛌 🗘 P 🍴 🍴 🛎 🖳
AE, DC, MC, V, JCB. Ⓚ

This hotel is Dutch owned, which perhaps explains why the simple, but chic restaurant and bar often remain open until 11pm and 3am respectively. It isn't exactly a pit of reckless hedonism and sybaritic shenanigans, but the atmosphere is relatively relaxed for Prague. Bedrooms continue the somewhat minimalist decor, but are immaculate and comfortable. Like its neighbour the Esprit, its only real disadvantage is its distance from the city centre, but, of course, that weakness can easily become a strength.

Esprit

Lihovarská 1098, 190 00 Praha 9.
683 04 55. **FAX** 684 59 17.
Rooms: 63. 🖩 🗗 🖧 ⊹ 🗘 P
🍴 🗗 🖳 AE, V,. Ⓚ

The owners of this neat, modern hotel have converted the house next door, adding 10 bedrooms to its capacity. The breakfast-room/bar/restaurant is cheerfully decorated and kept pristine. The well-kept bedrooms are simple but smart with pine furniture, whitewashed walls and pale cotton duvet covers - hot in winter, cool in summer. The hotel's only possible drawback is its distance from the centre of Prague: a 10-minute walk from the last stop on the metro B line, and 5 minutes from a direct bus route in an area of uninspiring, dusty, residential suburbs. But, of course, it is also quite peaceful. If you can, avoid booking this hotel through a travel agent, as it will have the effect of almost doubling the price.

Praha

Sušická 20, 166 35 Praha 6.
24 34 11 11. **FAX** 24 31 12 18.
Rooms: 124. 🖩 🗗 🖧 🗘 TV ⊹
🗗 🖳 🛌 🗘 P 🕑 🍴 🍴
🍴 🖳 AE, DC, MC, V, JCB.
Ⓚ Ⓚ Ⓚ Ⓚ

If you can't bear the noise of traffic or city smells 24 hours a day, then this large modern hotel surrounded by lovely gardens may be the place for you. Its disadvantages, apart from the price, are its distance from the centre. Way beyond the last metro stop on the B line, it is a good 15 minute walk to the nearest bus stop. But once you are there it has all the facilites you would expect of a big, modern hotel. It is less huge than it looks because all the bedrooms have a view towards the city and are a generous size. All that it offers in space, with acres of empty marble floors and small clusters of modern seating, it lacks in atmosphere. It is effeciently run and comfortable, if slightly clinical.

"Atrium Hilton"

Pobřežní 1, 186 00 Praha 8.
Map 4 F2. 24 84 11 11.
FAX 24 84 23 78. **Rooms:** 800. 🖩
🗗 🖧 🖳 TV ⊹ 🗗 🍴 🛎 🗗 🛌
🗘 P 🕑 🍴 🍴 🗗 AE, DC, V,
JCB. Ⓚ Ⓚ Ⓚ Ⓚ Ⓚ

The first atrium-type hotel to be built in the Czech Republic, this gleaming building stands out like a beacon of modernity against the background of the surrounding drab apartment buildings. French-owned and designed, it is the biggest hotel in the country, and despite the huge size, it does have a certain style. Sit in the airy, marble hall surrounded by plants and allow yourself to be lulled by the sound of running water and watch the transparent lift capsules zoom quaking residents up and down the atrium. The bedrooms are tastefully decorated with all the comforts you would expect to find in a large international hotel. In fact, you could be in any such hotel anywhere in the world.

Corinthia Towers

Kongresová 1, 140 69 Praha 4.
61 19 12 18. **FAX** 61 21 16 73.
TX 12 21 00. **Rooms:** 551. 🖩 🗗
🗗 TV ⊹ 🖧 🖳 🍴 🗗 🛎 🗗 🛌
🗘 P 🕑 🍴 🍴 🗗 AE, DC, MC, V,
JCB. Ⓚ Ⓚ Ⓚ Ⓚ Ⓚ

Situated beside the Vyšehrad metro stop, the Corinthia Towers is only a few minutes' from the city centre. Built in 1988 as a modern high-rise filled with glass, brass and marble, it features an impressive sports and health centre and a beautiful indoor swimming pool with stunning views over the city. Sit in the lounge on roomy leather sofas and watch the water cascade from the marble fountain, or choose to eat in either the French or Czech restaurants or the snack bar. The good-sized bedrooms are all well decorated and comfortable.

Diplomat Praha

Evropská 15, 160 00 Praha 6. 24 39 41 11. **FAX** 24 39 42 15. **Rooms:** 382. 🖩 🗗 🖧 TV ⊹ 🖳 🍴
🗗 🛌 🗘 P 🕑 🍴 🍴 🖳
AE, DC, MC, V, JCB. Ⓚ Ⓚ Ⓚ Ⓚ Ⓚ

This hotel is located right at the end of metro line A, but is only 12 minutes from the city centre. It opened in 1990 and still looks and feels very new, with lots of shiny marble and brass, and huge open spaces. Very efficiently run by Austrians, the hotel offers excellent facilities including a nightclub, numerous restaurants, shops, and even a whirlpool in the health club. It is popular with tour operators, and is very comfortable.

For key to symbols see p185

RESTAURANTS, CAFÉS AND PUBS

RESTAURANTS in Prague, just like the economy, seem to be getting better. For 40 years state-licensed eating and drinking establishments had little incentive to experiment or improve. But attitudes are rapidly changing. Fuelled by the booming tourist industry, new restaurants are opening constantly, many of them foreign-owned, offering the discerning eater an ever-increasing choice. The restaurants described in this

The Good Soldier Švejk at U Kalicha *(see p154)*

section reflect the change, though many only serve a limited range of standard Western dishes as well as staple Czech meals. *Choosing a Restaurant* on pages 198–9 summarizes the key features of the restaurants and cafés, listed by area. Full listings can be found on pages 200–4 and information on pubs, beer halls and bars appears on page 205. Compared to Western prices, eating out in Prague is still cheap.

TIPS ON EATING OUT

BECAUSE OF the huge influx of tourists, eating out has changed in character. The traditional lunch hour is still taken very early – between 11am and 1pm, and for most Czechs the normal time for the evening meal is around 7pm. However, many of the restaurants stay open late and it is possible to get a meal at any time from 10am until 2am. Until recently, these late hours were almost unheard of.

During spring and summer, the large numbers of visitors tend to put a strain on many of Prague's more popular restaurants. To be certain of a table, especially in the very well-known restaurants, book two or three days in advance. Although most restaurants are

in the city centre, quite a few are off the normal tourist track, away from Wenceslas and Old Town Squares, and worth the extra journey. Prices also tend to be lower the further you go from the centre.

PLACES TO EAT

THE IMPORTANCE of a stylish yet comfortable setting, and food which is inspired rather than just prepared, is slowly beginning to trickle down to Prague's better and more innovative restaurants. The places which follow this maxim are generally the best.

One of the simplest places to eat is the sausage stand, a utilitarian establishment, very common in Central Europe. It offers Czech sausages, which can either be eaten standing at

Vinárna v Zátiší *(see p201)*

the counter or taken away cold. For a late-night meal your best bet is often a snack bar *(bufet)*. But beware, even if a snack bar boasts a 24-hour sign, it may sometimes close before midnight.

For greater comfort, head for a café *(kavárna)*. Cafés range from loud, busy main street locations to quieter bookstore establishments. All have fully stocked bars and serve a variety of food from simple pastries and sandwiches to full-blown meals. Opening hours differ widely, but many open early in the morning and are good for a quick, if not quite a Western-style, breakfast.

A restaurant may be called a *restaurace* or a *vinárna* (one that sells wine). The best are those geared to non-Czech clientele. While usually cheap by Western standards, they are pricier than Czech places, but in return offer better service and higher quality food.

Plain Czech food is normally available at the local beer hall or pub *(pivnice)*, though the emphasis there is normally on drinking rather than eating.

Diners enjoying their meal at U Kalicha *(see p203)*

Tourists eating at the outdoor cafés in the Old Town Square

READING THE MENU

NEVER JUDGE a restaurant by the standard of its menu translations – mistakes are common in every class of restaurant. Many menus still list the weight of meat served (a relic of wartime rationing). Bear in mind that most main courses come with potatoes, rice or dumplings. Salads and other side dishes must be ordered separately. *(See pp194–5 for What to Eat in Prague.)*

Restaurant sign

THINGS TO BEWARE OF

IN EXPENSIVE RESTAURANTS the waiter may bring nuts to your table. Yes, they are for you to eat, but at a price equal to, or higher than, an appetizer. You will not insult

Fine dining amid stained-glass Art Deco splendour

anybody by telling the waiter to take them away. The same applies to appetizers brought round by the waiter.

It's advisable not to order a meal on a waiter's suggestion. The chances are it will be the most expensive dish in the house, and if you have not seen the menu the price may be even higher still.

Check your bill carefully, because extra charges are often added – this is quite a common practice in Prague. However, legitimate extra costs do exist. Cover charges range from Kč10–25 and such basic items as milk, ketchup, bread and butter might be charged for. Finally, a 23% tax, normally included in the menu, is occasionally added to the total bill.

ETIQUETTE

YOU DON'T HAVE to wait to be seated in snack bars and smaller eateries. It is also quite normal for others to join your table if there is any room. No restaurant has an official dress code, but people tend to dress up when dining in up-market restaurants.

PAYMENT AND TIPPING

THE AVERAGE PRICE for a full meal in the centre of Prague is about Kč600. The waiter may write your order on a piece of paper and then leave it on your table for the person who comes around

when you are ready to pay. Levels of service vary – it can be very slow – but generally a 10% tip is appropriate. Add the tip to the bill, do not leave the money on the table.

More and more restaurants now accept major credit cards, but always ask before the meal to make sure. Traveller's cheques and Eurocheques are rarely accepted.

VEGETARIANS

VEGETARIANS are not well catered for in Prague. In the past, fresh vegetables were rare in winter. But they are becoming more common throughout the year, although variable in quality. Even when a dish is described as meatless, it's always worth double checking. Vegans and those with special dietary needs will have a difficult time eating.

DISABLED

RESTAURANTS do not cater specifically for the disabled. The staff will almost always try and help, but Prague's ubiquitous stairs and basements will defeat all but the most determined.

USING THE LISTINGS
Key to symbols in the listings on pp200–4.

¶◎¶ fixed-price menu
V vegetarian dishes
T formal dress
♬ live music
▦ outdoor tables
♗ good wine list
★ highly recommended
▨ credit cards accepted:
AE American Express
DC Diners Club
MC Mastercard/Access
V Visa
JCB Japanese Credit
Bureau

Price categories for a three-course meal including a half-bottle of house wine, tax and service:
ⓚ   under Kč250
ⓚⓚ   Kč250–450
ⓚⓚⓚ   Kč450–650
ⓚⓚⓚⓚ over Kč650

Prague's Best: Restaurants and Cafés

THE VARIETY AND NUMBER of places to eat and drink in Prague has increased considerably in recent years. But despite a massive influx of discerning diners, some of the restaurants may disappoint visitors with their uninspired cuisine. The following restaurants, chosen from the listings on pages 200–4, will guide you to sample tasty, interesting meals while relaxing in venues which not only provide a pleasant atmosphere, but also offer reasonably priced, good quality food.

U Tří pštrosů
High-quality and traditional Czech dishes are found at this exclusive restaurant. (See p202.)

Peklo
The 12th-century beer cellars and delicious Italian fare make this well worth a visit. (See p201.)

Prague Castle and Hradčany

Little Quarter

Nebozízek
The spectacular view over Prague from this café terrace ensures the popularity of this establishment. (See p202.)

Café Savoy
A small, but delicious, selection of snacks can be enjoyed at this classy café. (See p201.)

U Malířů
This converted 16th-century house has an excellent reputation for its exquisite French dishes, in an atmosphere of discreet luxury. The murals and painted ceilings add to the romantic mood. (See p202.)

Chez Marcel
This is a little corner of Paris in the heart of Prague's Jewish Quarter. (See p200.)

U Červeného kola
Steaks and mouth-watering desserts are a speciality in this quiet restaurant, tucked away in a side street near St Agnes's Convent. (See p201.)

Opera Grill
French nouvelle cuisine is served in an intimate and exclusive atmosphere. (See p200.)

La Perle de Prague
La Perle de Prague serves haute cuisine in an elevated setting at the top of the stylish "Ginger and Fred" building. (See p203.)

Hotel Evropa Café
A pause for coffee is a good way to enjoy this beautiful Art Nouveau hotel. (See p202.)

What to Eat in Prague

Czech cookery is very similar to Austrian – lots of meat (usually pork or beef) served with dumplings, potatoes or rice, in a sauce. Meat, poultry, fish, cabbage and potatoes are all prepared simply and without strong spices; meat tends to be fried, roasted, or oven-baked in stock. On special occasions, game is usually the main course: venison, boar steaks or quails. Standard dishes tend to be served in copious quantities, and main courses are virtually meals in themselves. The most common dish is pork served with dumplings and sauerkraut (vepřové, knedlíky a zelí). Dumplings are traditionally served with most hot dishes and gravy. Vegetable portions can be small, although there has been a slight increase in the consumption of fresh vegetables in recent years. Salads are variable in quality. Hot soups are the traditional start to a meal, and range from broth with liver dumplings to cabbage soup with sausage.

"Stuffed eggs" are a popular appetizer

Žitný chléb (rye bread)

Rohlík (finger roll)

Pletená
houska (knot roll)

Chléb and Pečivo (breads)
An assortment of breads is served with most meals.

Uzený losos (smoked salmon)

Paštika (pâté)   gherkin

Sardinka (sardines)

Tvaroh s ředkvičkami (cream cheese with radishes)

Chlebíčky
These open sandwiches arranged on sliced baguette (French bread) can be found in any Lahůdky (delicatessen) and Bufet (snack bar) in Prague. They are popularly served to guests in Czech homes. Ham, fish, salami, roast beef, egg and cheeses are used, often with mayonnaise or garnished with a gherkin (nakládaná okurka). Unfortunately western-style fast food is encroaching on this snack's popularity.

Klobásy (grilled sausages)

Párky (frankfurters)   mustard

Klobásy and Párky
Klobásy are grilled sausages; párky are boiled frank-furters (hot dogs). Both are sold with mustard (hořčice) from street stalls and in special sausage shops.

Plněná šunka
An appetizer of stuffed ham, filled with a mix of whipped cream and coarsely grated horseradish, which gives it a kick.

Polévka
Simple vegetable soups – pea, potato, cauliflower, cabbage or tomato – are popular starters.

Hovězí polévka s játrovými knedlíčky
Liver dumplings in beef broth is a warming soup for all seasons.

Pečená kachna
Roast duck with bacon dumplings (špekové knedlíky) and red sauerkraut is a popular main course.

Uzené
Smoked pork is mostly served with slices of potato dumplings (bramborové knedlíky) and white sauerkraut.

Vepřový řízek
Breaded and fried pork steak (schnitzel) is usually accompanied by hot potatoes or a cold potato salad. It often has a salad garnish and a slice of lemon.

Houskové knedlíky (sliced bread dumplings)

Brusinky (cranberries)

Hovězí (beef)

Svíčková na smetaně
Pot-roasted fillet of beef (svíčková) is served in a rich, creamy, slightly sweet vegetable sauce (na smetaně) and is garnished with either cranberries or a dollop of whipped cream.

Salát
In winter, salads are often pickled; in summer, they are simply-dressed mixtures of tomato, lettuce, cucumbers and peppers.

Jablkový strudel
Thin apple slices are wrapped in a light pastry case. Other strudel fillings include cherries or cream cheese.

Ovocné knedlíky
Fruit dumplings, in this case švestkové (plum), are served with melted butter, icing sugar and ground poppy seeds.

Vdolek
This round yeast pastry is served with redcurrant or plum jam and whipped cream.

Palačinky
Crêpe pancakes can be filled with ice cream and/or stewed fruit or jam, and coated in sugar, chocolate or almonds.

What to Drink in Prague

'Golden Tiger' beer mat

CZECH BEERS ARE FAMOUS around the world, but nowhere are they drunk with such appreciation as in Prague. The Czechs take their beer (*pivo*) seriously and are very proud of it. Pilsner and its various relations originate in Bohemia. It is generally agreed that the best Pilsners are produced close to the original source – and all the top producers are not far from Prague. Beers can be bought in cans, in bottles, and best of all, on draught. Canned beer is made mostly for export, and no connoisseur would ever drink it. The Czech Republic also produces considerable quantities of wine, both red and white, mainly in Southern Moravia. Little of it is bottled for export. Mineral water can be found in most restaurants; Mattoni and Dobrá voda (meaning good water) are the two most widely available brands.

Gambrinus, legendary King of Beer, and trademark of a popular brand of Pilsner

PILSNER AND BUDWEISER

Traditional copper brew-kettles in Plzeň

THE BEST-KNOWN CZECH BEER is Pilsner. Clear and golden, with a strong flavour of hops, Pilsner is made by the lager method: top-fermented and slowly matured at low temperatures. The word "Pilsner" (which is now a generic term for similar lagers brewed all over the world) is derived from Plzeň (in German, Pilsen), a town 80 km (50 miles) southwest of Prague, where this type of beer was first made in 1842. The brewery that developed the beer still makes Plzňské pivo as well as the slightly stronger Plzňský prazdroj (original source), which is better known by its German name Pilsner Urquell. A slightly sweeter beer, Budweiser Budvar (which is no relation to the American beer of the same name), is brewed 150 km (100 miles) south of Prague in the town of České Budějovice (in German, Budweis).

Budweiser logo

Pilsner Urquell logo

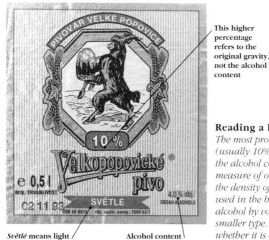

This higher percentage refers to the original gravity, not the alcohol content

Světlé means light   Alcohol content

Reading a Beer Label
The most prominent figure on the label (usually 10% or 12%) does not refer to the alcohol content. It is a Czech measure of original gravity, indicating the density of malt and other sugars used in the brew. The percentage of alcohol by volume is usually given in smaller type. The label also states whether it is a dark or a light beer.

BEER AND BEER HALLS

| Staropramen | Plzeňské | Velkopopovický kozel | Budweiser Budvar | Plzňský prazdroj (Pilsner Urquell) |

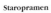

THE REAL PLACE TO ENJOY Czech beer is a pub or beer hall (*pivnice*). Each pub is supplied by a single brewery (*pivovar*), so only one brand of beer is available, but several different types are on offer. The major brands include Plzeňské and Gambrinus from Plzeň, Staropramen from Prague, and Velkopopovické from Velké Popovice, south of Prague. The usual drink is draught light beer (*světlé*), but a number of beer halls, including U Fleků (*see p155*) and U Kalicha (*see p154*) also serve special strong dark lagers (ask for *tmavé*). Another type you may encounter is *kozel*, a strong light beer like a German *bock*.

A half litre of beer (just under a pint) is called a *velké* (large), and a third of a litre (larger than a half pint) is called a *malé* (small). The waiters bring beers and snacks to your table and mark everything you eat and drink on a tab. In some pubs (*see p205*) there is a tacit assumption that all the customers want to go on drinking until closing time, so don't be surprised if more beers arrive without your ordering them. If you don't want them, just say no. The bill is totted up when you leave.

Beer gardens, such as U Fleků, serve "dark" lagers on draught

WINES

CZECH WINE PRODUCERS have not yet emulated the success of other East European wine-makers. The main wine-growing region is in Moravia, where most of the best wine is produced for local consumption. Some wine is also made in Bohemia, around Mělník, just north of Prague. The whites, made mostly from Riesling and Müller-Thurgau grapes, tend to be oversweet, though Rulandské is an acceptable dry white. The reds are slightly better, the main choices being Frankovka and

Rulandské, white and red

Vavřinecké. In the autumn, a semi-fermented young white wine called *burčák* is sold and drunk across the capital; despite its sweet, juice-like taste, it is surprisingly intoxicating.

CZECH SPIRITS AND LIQUEURS

IN EVERY RESTAURANT and pub you'll find Becherovka, a bitter-sweet, yellow herbal drink served both as an aperitif and a liqueur. It can also be diluted with tonic. Other local drinks include Borovička, a juniper-flavoured spirit, and plum brandy or Slivovice. The latter is clear and strong and rather an acquired taste. Imported spirits and cocktails are expensive.

Becherovka

Choosing a Restaurant or Café

THE RESTAURANTS listed have been selected for their good value or exceptional food. This chart highlights some of the main factors which may influence your choice of places to eat, such as fixed-price menus, tables outside, late opening and Czech specialities. The entries appear alphabetically within the price category, and any special features are indicated. For more details about each restaurant, see pages 200–4, and refer to page 205 for further information about bars and beer halls.

	Price	Fixed-Price Menu	Attractive Setting	Tables Outside	Czech Specialities	Seafood Specialities	Late Opening	Live Music at Night
OLD TOWN (see pp200–1)								
Café Four	®							
Klub Architektů	®		■				■	
Pizzeria	®							
Na Poříčí	®®				●			
Pivnice Skořepka	®®				●	■		
Red, Hot and Blues	®®		■				●	●
Restaurant Marie Teresie	®®		■			■		
Restaurace Století	®®®		■				■	
U Zlaté uličky	®®®	●					■	
Bellevue	®®®®	●	■					
Le Saint-Jacques	®®®®	●				●	■	
Opera Grill	®®®®	●					■	
Vinárna v Zátiší	®®®®	●						
JEWISH QUARTER (see p201)								
Valentin	®	●						
Chez Marcel ★	®®®	●				●	■	
King Solomon	®®®							
U Maxima ★	®®®	●		●	■		■	●
Barok	®®®®						■	
U Červeného kola	®®®®	●	■					
PRAGUE CASTLE AND HRADČANY (see p201)								
Palffy Palace ★	®®®®		■	●				
U Labutí	®®®®		■		■			
U Zlaté Hrusky	®®®®	●	■	●	■		■	
LITTLE QUARTER (see pp201–2)								
Café Savoy	®	●	■				●	
Pizza Canzone	®							
U Černeho Orla	®®		■		■		■	
U Schnellů	®®		■					
Nebozízek	®®®	●	■	●	■	●		
Valdštejnská hospoda	®®®	●	■	●	■			
Kampa Park ★	®®®®	●	●	●			●	●
U Malířů	®®®®	●					■	
U Modré kachničky ★	®®®®	●	■					
U Tří pštrosů	®®®®	●			●	■		

Price categories

These have been calculated to represent the cost of an average three-course meal for one, including half a bottle of house wine, and all unavoidable extra charges such as cover, service and tax:

Ⓚ under Kč250
ⓀⓀ Kč250–450
ⓀⓀⓀ Kč450–650
ⓀⓀⓀⓀ over Kč650.

★ Means highly recommended.

FIXED-PRICE MENU
A restaurant which offers a set menu: usually three or four courses without wine or coffee, for a fixed price.

ATTRACTIVE SETTING
A restaurant with an unusual or historic interior, or with a beautiful view.

TABLES OUTSIDE
A restaurant where you can dine out-of-doors during the warmer months.

CZECH SPECIALITIES
A good selection of traditional dishes.

LATE OPENING
Last orders taken at or after 11:30pm.

	Price	FIXED-PRICE MENU	ATTRACTIVE SETTING	TABLES OUTSIDE	CZECH SPECIALITIES	SEAFOOD SPECIALITIES	LATE OPENING	LIVE MUSIC AT NIGHT
NEW TOWN (see pp202–3)								
Hotel Evropa Café	Ⓚ		■					
Kavárna Velryba	Ⓚ						■	
Kmotra	Ⓚ						■	
Radost FX Café	Ⓚ						■	
Vltava	Ⓚ		■	●		●		
Café Restaurant Louvre	ⓀⓀ		■		■			
U Kalicha	ⓀⓀ				■			●
Esplanade	ⓀⓀⓀ		■		■			
French Restaurant in Obecní Dům	ⓀⓀⓀ	●	■		■			
Pod Křídlem	ⓀⓀⓀ				■		■	●
U Čížků	ⓀⓀⓀ		■		■			
Perle de Prague ★	ⓀⓀⓀⓀ	●	■					
FURTHER AFIELD (see pp203–4)								
The Globe Bookstore Café	Ⓚ		■				■	
Na Ořechovce	Ⓚ		■	●	■		■	
Na Slamníku	Ⓚ		■		■		■	
U Koleje	Ⓚ							
U Tří hrochů	Ⓚ			●				
U Mikuláše Dačického	ⓀⓀ		■				■	
U Sloupu	ⓀⓀ	●			■			
Letensky Zamecek	ⓀⓀⓀ		■	●	■			
Rio's Beachclub	ⓀⓀⓀ		■				■	
U Blaženky	ⓀⓀⓀ		■	●	■			
U Cedru ★	ⓀⓀⓀ		■					
Zlatý Drak	ⓀⓀⓀ							
Rhapsody	ⓀⓀⓀⓀ						■	●

OLD TOWN

Café Four

Soukenická 2 **Map** 4 D2.
(231 25 24. **Open** 9am–11pm
daily. **☺** AE, DC, MC, V. **Ⓚ**

Many different teas and coffees
are available at this café, and
the setting, just off the beaten
track, makes it a pleasant, chic
place to escape from the bustle
of central Prague. The food is
standard, but reasonably priced.

Klub Architektů
THE ARCHITECTS' CLUB

Beltemske nam 5a. **Map** 3 B4. **(** 24
40 12 14. **Open** 11:30am–midnight
daily. **Ⓥ ☺** AE, MC, V. **Ⓚ**

This hidden gem is tucked away
in a warren of tunnels and
arches, reached through a
courtyard near the Bethlehem
Chapel. Eager diners who have
tracked it down tend to keep it
something of a secret, but still it
fills up with those in the know,
and you may have to explore its
lamplit corners to find a space.
Having done so, settle down to
enjoy plentiful servings of hearty
cuisine, with a good choice for
vegetarians as well as carnivores.

Pizzeria

Benediktská 16. **Map** 4 D3.
(231 57 27. **Open** 11am–11.30pm
daily. **☺** AE, MC, V, EURO. **Ⓚ**

The first real pizzeria in Prague
after the revolution, Mikulka's
established its reputation early
and has worked hard to retain it.
Pizzas and huge bowls of pasta
keep the restaurant full. At first it
was only popular with the
foreign community, so it is a
tribute to the quality of the
food and low prices that you
now meet as many Czechs here
as foreigners. Finding space
can be difficult, but the wait is
never long.

Na Poříčí

Na poříčí 20. **Map** 4 E3. **(** 24 81 13
63. **Open** 11am–11pm Mon–Sat,
noon–1ppm Sun. **☺** MC, V. **ⓀⓀ**

Choose your setting in this large
restaurant. It is part pub, part
wine bar, and part elegant
restaurant, with papered walls
adorned with framed prints.
The menu offers traditional
Czech meals, poultry and fish,
plus an attempt at more original
cuisine (lobster and brandy
soup). Being one of the few
good,inexpensive restaurants in
the neighbourhood, it tends to be
very busy at lunchtime.

Pivnice Skořepka

Skořepka 1. **Map** 3 B4.
(24 21 47 15. **Open**
11am–midnight daily. **☺** MC, V,
JCB. **ⒼⓀ**

This high-ceilinged, wood-panelled
restaurant serves numerous Czech
dishes, but most people go to eat
the large pork knees – joints like
those at a Tudor banquet. Served
with mustard and horseradish,
they make a memorable meal.
Those who wish to eat less meat
can choose a good chicken cutlet
stuffed with ham and blue cheese.
Wash it all down with either a
light or dark beer.

Red, Hot and Blues

Jakubská 12. **Map** 3 C3.
(231 46 39. **Open** 9am–11pm
daily. **Ⓥ Ⓙ ⓈⓉ ☺** AE, MC, V.
ⓀⓀ

Located in what were the king's
stables 500 years ago, this place
draws a crowd largely from the
expatriate community who come
for the good, home-town New
Orleans and Creole cooking: chilli,
chowder, burgers with all the trim-
mings, and étouffé. Seafood,
salads and chicken are also
prepared with imagination and
there is a weekend brunch
American-style. Live jazz or blues
each night and happy hour
specials are additional attractions.
To hear live music (cover added),
you will have to stay past 7:30pm.

Restaurant Marie Teresie

Na příkopě 23. **Map** 3 C4.
(& **FAX** 24 22 98 69. **Open**
11am–11pm daily. **☺** AE, DC, MC, V.
ⒼⓀ

Located right in the heart of Prague
on a busy pedestrianized street,
Restaurant Marie Teresie is a stylish
and comfortable throwback to the
14th century. The menu offers a
range of authentic Czech cuisine,
light and dark Staropramen beer
and a good selection of local wines.

Restaurance Století
CENTURY RESTAURANT

Karoliny Světlé 21. **Map** 3 A4. **(** 22
22 00 08. **Open** noon–midnight daily.
☺ MC, V. **ⓀⓀⓀ**

Arched ceilings, sepia prints and
shelves lined with dried flowers
and old china suggest a step back
in time, but the food at this quiet,
intimate restaurant is up to the
minute, with unusual dishes such
as avocado stuffed with whipped
roquefort and marzipan. The service is slow but you won't mind.

U Zlaté uličky
BY GOLDEN LANE

Masná 9. **Map** 3 C3. **(** 232 08 84.
Open 11am–midnight daily. **ⓀⓀⓀ**

Figurines line the window of this
restaurant. Yugoslavian cuisine,
specializing in veal, is the main
fare, but there are pork and steak
dishes too. The palačinka (fluffy
whipped crêpe filled with cream
and covered with chocolate sauce)
is probably the best in town. A bar
completes the cosy restaurant.

Bellevue

18 Smetanovo nábřeží 2. **Map** 3 A5.
(22 22 14 49. **Open** 11:30am–
3pm, 5:30–11pm daily. **Ⓣ ☺** AE,
MC, V. **ⓀⓀⓀⓀ**

This Art Deco masterpiece has
more going for it than inlaid wood
walls and marble floors. By the
river, it has a view of Prague
Castle. The menu is the same as
Vinárna v Zátiší (see p201), with
the same owners. A few Czech
dishes are on offer, but the fare is
mostly international, and includes
Beef Wellington and Norwegian
salmon. Each dish is delightfully
prepared, if rather uninspiring, so
don't expect any surprises beyond
the high standard of service. On
Sundays there is a buffet brunch.

Le Saint-Jacques

Jakubská 4. **Map** 3 C3.
(232 26 85. **Open** noon–3pm
Mon–Fri, 6pm–midnight Mon–Sat.
☺ AE, DC, MC, V. **ⓀⓀⓀⓀ**

This restaurant represents a taste
of France, in terms of cuisine if
not in decor (the establishment is
a hybrid of austerity and
attempted modernity which does
not quite come off and is all the
more fascinating for it). It is
managed by a French proprietor
who is as attentive as his cuisine is
charming. Try any fish dish from
the constantly-evolving menu.

Opera Grill

Karolíny Světlé 35. **Map** 3 A4. **(** 22
22 05 18. **Open** 6pm–1am daily. **ⓉⓀ**
Ⓣ Ⓙ ☺ AE, DC, MC, V. **ⓀⓀⓀⓀ**

With only seven tables, surrounded by armchairs, a pianist
playing softly, and a serene,
candle-lit elegance, it is easy to
imagine that you are in a private
dining room. The menu features
international dishes: rack of
lamb, pasta, salmon, chicken
and steak. The prices do not
reflect the exclusive ambience,
nor do all the clientele dress
formally. This is a dining
experience to be tried before it
becomes too exclusive.

Vinárna v Zátiší
IN SECLUSION

Liliová 1, Betlémské náměstí.
Map 3 B4. **[** 22 22 06 27.
Open noon–3pm, 5.30–11pm daily.
T 🍽 *AE, MC, V.* ⓀⓀⓀ⒦

Located near both Charles Bridge
and the Old Town Square,
Vinárna v Zátiší was Prague's first
Western-owned and run
restaurant. The British owner
concentrated on quality of both
food and service, and it rapidly
became the hub of the foreign
business community. Today, the
place is crowded as word has
spread about the tasty Beef
Wellington and Norwegian
salmon. White walls and colourful
prints create a relaxing ambience.
Buffet lunch is served on Sundays.
brunch is served.

JEWISH QUARTER

Valentin

Valentinská 9. **Map** 3 B3. **[** 26 02
94. **Open** 10am–10pm daily. **V**
🍽 Ⓚ

This modern restaurant calls itself a
"day bar". While there is a complete
selection of alcohol, most people do
not come for inebriation but for the
food or just coffee and a chat. The
ultra-modern interior features black
and white triangles, from the tiled
floor, to the wood on the walls, to
the lights. As well as chicken breasts
with mushrooms and cream, and
pepper steak, there are several
vegetarian options.

Chez Marcel

Haštalská 12. **Map** 3 C2.
[231 56 76. **Open** 8am–1am
Mon–Fri, 9am–1am Sat, Sun. 🍽 🍽
★ ⓀⓀ⒦

A touch of France in the centre of
Prague, this is where business
people and students alike come
for regional plats du jour, steak au
poivre, fresh mussels and the best
French fries in the city. The mood
is bustling and gallic, the service
can be variable. Desserts are
especially memorable.

King Solomon

Široká 8. **Map** 3 B3. **[** 24 81 87 52.
Open 11am–11 pm Sun–Thu,
11am–90 minutes before sunset Fri.
🍽 *AE, MC, V.* ⓀⓀ⒦

Prague's only strictly kosher restaurant is formal, comfortable and
quiet, with a decor of booths and
canopies. The light lunch and more
substantial dinner menu are com-
plemented by Israeli and Moroccan
wines. No dairy foods are served.

U Maxima

Bilkova 4. **Map** 3 B2. **[** 231 77 61.
Open 11–midnight daily. 🍽 **V** **T**
🎵 🍽 ★ 🍽 *AE, DC, MC, V.*
ⓀⓀ⒦

This elegant restaurant is situated
just off one of the most popular
tourist streets, yet retains an air of
tranquility and charm, enhanced by
live piano music which adds an
ivory elegance. Specialities include
the hearty "Czech plate" – pork,
duck, smoked meat, cabbage and
dumplings. Be sure to book.

Barock

Pařížská 24. **Map** 3 B2. **[** 232 92 21.
Open 8:30am–4pm, 6–11pm Mon–Fri,
10am–1am Sat, Sun. 🍽 *AE, DC, MC,
V, JCB.* ⓀⓀⓀ⒦

There's not a jarring element in this
stylish venue's approach, and it has
fast become one of the places to
see and be seen on the Prague
fashion circuit. But it's not merely a
trendy venue; the atmosphere, food
and service really are up to
international standards. An excellent
range of Thai and Japanese cuisine
is served by smart, efficient staff.

U Červeného kola
AT THE RED WHEEL

Anežská 2. **Map** 3 C2. **[** 24 81 11
18. **Open** 11am–11pm daily. **T** 🍽
🍽 *AE, DC, MC, V, JCB.* ⓀⓀⓀ⒦

Though hard to find, this elegant
restaurant, behind the cloister of St
Agnes's (see pp92–3), is worth the
search. Red carpets and upholstered
seats provide the setting for finely
laid tables and antique clocks.
Steaks predominate – the speciality
is with garlic. A few chicken and
fish dishes complete the offerings.
There is also a garden room.

PRAGUE CASTLE AND
HRADČANY

Palffy Palace

Valdštejnská 14. **Map** 2 E2 **[** 57 31
22 43. **Open** noon– 11pm daily. **V**
🍽 ★ 🍽 *AE, MC, V.* ⓀⓀⓀ⒦

The faded elegance of an 18th-
century palace, shared with a con-
servatory of music, is the setting
for innovative continental cuisine
served with great, but unhurried,
style. Dishes such as beef tender-
loin with gorgonzola butter and
scallops with red onion and fennel
sauce follow the free appetizer of
roasted garlic with crusty bread.
Dine on the lovely terrace in
summer. Don't be put off by the
dingy entrance and stairs.

U Labutí
AT THE SWANS

Hradčanské náměstí 11. **Map** 1 C3.
[20 51 11 91. **Open** noon–11pm
daily. **V** 🍽 *AE, MC.*
ⓀⓀⓀ⒦

This establishment, which prides
itself on being more of a club
than a restaurant, offers a
comfortable setting with antique
tables and chairs. The cuisine is
traditional Czech, with
international dishes, including
steak and chicken.

U Zlaté Hrušky
AT THE GOLDEN PEAR

Nový Svět 3. **Map** 1 B2.
[20 51 53 56 **Open** 11:30am–
3:30pm, 6:30pm–midnight daily.
🍽 **T** 🍽 *AE, DC, MC, V.*
ⓀⓀ⒦

Situated in one of a group of 16th-
century houses near the castle, this
quite formal restaurant attracts an
upmarket clientele including
politicians and visiting dignitaries.
Specialities include venison with
pears and gnocchi. In summer,
request a table in the garden.

LITTLE QUARTER

Café Savoy

Vítězná 5. **Map** 2 E5. **[** 53 50 00.
Open 9am–midnight daily.
🍽 *AE, V.*

This popular café is stunningly
decorated with restored murals.
The attentive waiters and mellow
music make it comfortably classy,
if a little pricey. Although the food
selection is not that large, the hors
d'oeuvres alone make any trip
well worthwhile.

Pizza Canzone

Josefská 2. **Map** 2 E3.
Open 10am–midnight daily. Ⓚ

Pizza, pasta, Italian desserts and
coffees are served here in a bright,
clean environment. Although it is
nothing spectacular, it is a nice place
to drop into towards the end of a
day spent exploring the Castle or
Little Quarter. No phone, but no
need to reserve in advance.

U Cerneho Orla
AT THE BLACK EAGLE

Malostranské náměstí 14.
Map 2 E3. **[** 53 63 73. **Open**
10am–midnight daily. 🍽 *AE, DC,
MC, V.* Ⓚ⒦

A quiet and cozy atmosphere makes this a comfortable place to relax, even though it is located in the busy Malá Strana area. The food is traditional Czech, but well-prepared and generously served. Leave room for an excellent dessert – especially the fruit dumplings.

U Schnellů
AT THE SCHNELL'S

Tomášská 7. **Map** 2 E3.
⦗ *53 20 04 .*
Open *11am–11pm daily.* ⓚⓚ

Attentive staff and delicious food make this restaurant worth a visit. Entrées are reasonably priced, the Pilsner Urquell beer is well chilled, and the nearby St Thomas's Church provides an attractive backdrop.

Nebozízek
LITTLE AUGER

Petřínské sady 411. **Map** 2 D5.
⦗ *53 79 05.* **Open** *11am–11pm daily.* 🖼 🍷 V. ⓚⓚⓚ

The view of Prague from this restaurant is fantastic. During spring and summer months the outdoor patio is very popular. Inside, the place is cosy and elegant. The menu is wide-ranging, offering seafood, Chinese and Czech dishes, steaks and more. Be sure to book four days in advance.

Valdštejnská hospoda
WALDSTEIN INN

Valdštejnská nám 7. **Map** 2 E3. **⦗** *53 61 95.* **Open** *11:30am–11:30pm daily.* 🔽 ⓚⓚⓚ

A favourite with the staff of the British embassy, this was once a typical local pub, but it has been re-vamped and re-themed in order to highlight some of the original architectural features of the 15th-century building. The present-day finery combines with the older vaulted ceilings and exposed stonework to create an old-world atmosphere in which you can enjoy all the traditional Czech favourites as well as a fabulous assortment of international dishes.

Kampa Park

Na Kampě 8b. **Map** 2 F4.**⦗** *57 31 34 93.* **Open** *11:30am–1am daily.* 🍴⦿ 🔽 🖼 ★ 🍷 AE, DC, MC, V. ⓚⓚⓚⓚ

This pastel-pink house in a delightful setting right on the Vltava river features seafood flown in fresh from Scandinavia, with turbot and salmon especially recommended. Seasonal dishes and local goat's cheeses are also highly praised. The clientele was originally

power diners and visiting celebrities, but the great food, romantic atmosphere and friendly service now draw in the locals and tourists as well, especially for the good-value weekend brunch menu.

U Malířů
AT THE PAINTER'S

Maltézské náměstí 11. **Map** 2 E4.
⦗ *57 53 00 00.* **Open** *6pm–midnight daily.* 🔽 🍷 AE, MC, V, JCB. ⓚⓚⓚⓚ

U Malířů is the only authentic French gastronomic restaurant in the country. The French chef Daniel Mutel uses only the freshest ingredients, brought in twice a week from France, to concoct such original dishes as roasted young pigeon in puff pastry and rack of lamb. There are also traditional French delicacies. Bread is baked on the premises, and home-made sorbets are another speciality. The restaurant was founded in 1543 and the beautiful ceilings were first painted many centuries ago. All in all, the ambience is romantic and beautiful, thanks to Gothic windows and elegant table settings.

U Modré kachničky
AT THE BLUE DUCKLING

Nebovidská 6. **Map** 2 E4. **⦗** *57 32 03 08.* **Open** *noon–4pm, 6:30–11:30 daily.* ★ 🍷 AE, DC, V. 🔽 ⓚⓚⓚⓚ

On a quiet street in the Little Quarter, this restaurant reflects the intimate, romantic and charming nature of this part of town. It is worth a visit for the hand-painted walls boast Prague's best display of modern Art Nouveau. The restaurant has three rooms, each with its own fabulous mural, and each more stunning than the last. Beautiful wooden antiques combine with framed prints to add an eclectic feel. The fare is strictly game and meat; those who love duck, boar, veal, venison and salmon are guaranteed fresh, succulent flavours and generous portions.

U Tří pštrosů
AT THE THREE OSTRICHES

Dražického náměstí 12. **Map** 2 E3.
⦗ *57 32 05 65.* **Open** *noon–11pm daily.* 🔽 ⓚⓚⓚⓚ

Plants and flowers adorn the walls of the two small, elegant dining rooms on the ground floor of the hotel of the same name *(see p134 & p188)*. Situated at the base of Charles Bridge, it boasts a good selection of Czech and international fare, although its pricey offerings appear to be predominantly Czech and central European, with carp, goulash and beef dishes available.

Hotel Evropa Café
HOTEL EUROPA CAFE

Václavské náměstí 25. **Map** 4 D5.
⦗ *24 22 81 17.* **Open** *11am–11pm, daily.* 🍷 AE, DC, MC, JCB. ⓚ *(See p146.)*

With its large windows facing onto Wenceslas Square, this is a good place to enjoy a cup of coffee and a bite to eat while watching people stroll by. The café is part of the larger Hotel Evropa restaurant, a grand old structure that has seen better days. The price of a snack or drink reflect its tourist clientele.

Kavárna Velryba
CAFE WHALE

Opatovická 24. **Map** 5 B1. **⦗** *24 91 23 91.* **Open** *11am–2am daily.* ⓚ

This subterranean café-cum-restaurant is a trendy hangout for Prague's young. It has a lively, comfortable atmosphere as well as good cheap food. A new addition are the televisions on the walls. The food is basic, including chicken breast sandwiches, beefburgers, fried mushrooms, lentil dishes and decent salads. It tends to get very smoky and the front door is likely to be locked when it gets too crowded inside, but the place boasts the largest whisky selection in Prague. Though the café is open late, the kitchen closes at 11pm.

Kmotra
GODMOTHER

V jirchářích 12. **Map** 5 B1.
⦗ *24 91 58 09.* **Open** *11am–midnight daily.* ⓚ

This basement pizzeria became an overnight success by following a simple recipe: large, tasty pizzas at cheap prices. Czech students, travellers, couples and business people all rub elbows within the whitewashed, vaulted rooms.

Radost FX Café

Bělehradská 120. **Map** 6 E2.
⦗ *24 25 47 76.* **Open** *11am–5am Mon–Sat, 10:30am–2am Sun.* 🔽 ⓚ

This small, vegetarian café is popular with Czechs and foreigners. It is connected to the nightclub Radost FX (see p215) and people tend to stop and eat before and after clubbing. As a result, getting a table can be difficult, especially during the evenings. The menu includes salads, fresh soup, sandwiches (including marinated tofu and humous in pitta bread), vegetarian pizzas, nachos and delicious home-made pastries.

Vltava

Rašínovo nábřeží. **Map** 5 A2.
【 29 49 64. **Open** 11am–10pm
daily. 🏧 Ⓚ

Located on the bank of the Vltava
river, the outdoor patio of this
restaurant provides a wonderful
setting during the warmer months
to view Prague Castle and watch
the tour boat activity on the river.
When it is too cold to sit outside,
the small restaurant is cosy and
warm. It is ostensibly a fish
restaurant (the speciality being
whole trout baked with garlic) and
there is a wonderful fish soup, but
the menu covers a great deal of
ground and also includes Chinese
food, chicken, pork and steak.

Café Restaurant Louvre

Národní třída 20. **Map** 3 B5. 【 29 72
23, 29 76 65. **FAX** 24 29 74 72. **Open**
8am–11pm. 🗐 AE, DC, MC, V, JCB.
ⓀⓀ

Come here to relax in the airy
1930s-style dining hall. There is a
good selection of both local and
international newspapers, which
you can browse through while
you eat. Choose from a menu
which includes such specialities as
goulash, sweet pancakes and
authentic Radegast beer. The
relaxed and friendly atmosphere is
matched by the good-value prices.

U Kalicha
AT THE CHALICE

Na bojišti 14. **Map** 6 D2.
【 29 07 01/29 19 45. **Open** 11am–
11pm daily. Ⓥ 🎵 🗐 AE, DC, V, JCB.
ⓀⓀ (see p154)

From selections like beefsteak à la
Lieutenant Lukáš to cartooned walls,
practically everything in here will
make you feel part of the famous
Czech novel The Good Soldier
Švejk, the theme on which the
restaurant is based. Traditional
Czech cuisine is available at
inflated prices, and the in-house
souvenir shop, selling everything
from Švejk T-shirts and beer steins
to postcards discourages the
locals from coming in.

Esplanade Hotel French Restaurant

Washintonova 19. **Map** 4 E5. 【 24 21
36 96. **Open** noon–3pm, 6:30–11pm
daily. 🗐 AE, MC, DC, V, JCB. ⓀⓀⓀ

One of the best places to go for
fine hotel dining of the old school
– lots of silver-domed salvers and
table-side flambéing amid a setting
of Art Nouveau splendour and
fabulous floral arrangements.
An air of quiet – though not
understated – luxury pervades the
dining room. This is the type of
venue at which to wine and dine
an older business associate if you
really want to impress.

French Restaurant in Obecní Dum

Náměstí Republiky 5. **Map** 4 D3.
【 22 00 27 77. **Open** noon–3pm,
6–11pm daily. 🗐 AE, DC, MC, JCB.
ⓀⓀⓀ

The main attraction is the decor of
this opulent and airy restored fin-
de-siècle restaurant, but the cuisine
– international spiced with Czech
specialities – is no less rewarding
in itself. Sharing a building with a
major concert hall, it is ideal for a
pre- or post-entertainment meal.

Pod Křídlem
UNDER THE WING

Narodní Třída 10. **Map** 3 B5. 【 24 91
23 771/24 95 17 41. **Open** 10am–
midnight Mon–Fri, 11:30am–midnight Sat, Sun. 🎵 🗐 AE, DC, MC, V,
JCB. ⓀⓀⓀ

Shiny, bright and white, this seems
more like an international bistro
than an ethnic eatery. But the
decor and pianist create an entirely
enjoyable atmosphere. Try the
roast duck or pork dumplings and
sauerkraut. This bistro is a popular
venue after an evening at the
National Theatre (see pp156–7) –
only a few minutes' walk away.

U Čížků

Karlovo náměstí 34. **Map** 5 B2. 【 22
23 22 57. **Open** noon–3:30pm, 5pm–
10pm daily. 🗐 AE, MC, V. ⓀⓀⓀ

Designed in the style of a typical
Bohemian farmhouse, and serving
the most traditional Czech foods,
U Čížků provides an opportunity
to get a taste of Czech cuisine and
culture at the same time. Try the
red cabbage soup with sausage, or
if you're very hungry, go for the
assortment dish with two kinds of
pork, duck, sausage, two types of
dumplings and two varieties of
sauerkraut. Combined with its low
prices, all the above features make
the restaurant popular with large
tour groups, so book early.

La Perle de Prague

Rašín Building, Rašínovo nábřeží 18.
Map 5 A2. 【 21 98 41 60. **Open**
noon–2:30pm Tue–Sat, 7–10:30pm
Mon–Sat. 🍴Ⓠ🍷🎩🍺★ Ⓥ🗐 AE,
DC, MC, V. ⓀⓀⓀⓀ

Prague's most talked-about modern
building is home to Prague's most
talked-about new restaurant. Here
on the top two floors of architect
Frank Gehry's fabulous "Ginger
and Fred" building, the bar and
restaurant that is the Perle de
Prague offers Parisian-style haute
cuisine in a striking post-modern
setting, combined with fabulous
views of the city. Within the chic,
formal restaurant there is no music
to disturb the serious gourmet, but
the separate cocktail bar offers you
the chance to dance cheek to
cheek in a building whose fluid
lines were inspired by the graceful
movements of its namesakes on
the dance floor.

FURTHER AFIELD

The Globe Bookstore Café

Janovského 14. 【 66 71 26 10
Open 10am– midnight daily. Ⓚ

Cheap, good food, a great library
of English-language books and a
charming atmosphere keep the
expatriates coming back to this
café. The limited menu consists
mainly of sandwiches, bagels,
pasta and Greek salads, but the
comfortable armchairs and latest
editions of English-language
magazines make it very popular.

Na Ořechovce

Vychodni 7. 【 312 35 94.
Open noon–11pm daily.
🏧 🗐 AE, MC, V. Ⓚ

Hearty roast dishes are the key
items here, accompanied by
traditional dumplings and washed
down with Pilsner beer. The
peacefulness of the suburban
location is reflected in the leafy
garden in which you can dine in
summer, when you might want to
choose slightly lighter dishes from
the more international end of the
menu's range.

Na Slamníku
ON THE STRAW MATTRESS

Wolkerova 12. 【 33 32 25 94.
Open 3pm–midnight daily. Ⓚ

The preparation and presentation
of the food here is simple, in
keeping with the decor and
atmosphere of a typical 300-year-
old Czech pub. Apart from the
pool table in the back "salon", it
has remained untouched, and the
Czech treats like pan-fried pork
are the tasty staples. One of the
best deals in town.

U Koleje
AT THE COLLEGE

Slavíkova 24. 【 627 41 63. **Open**
11am–10pm Mon–Thu, 11am–5pm
Fri. Ⓚ

Floral tablecloths and low lamps
hanging over each table give this

former pub a cheerful but quiet, intimate feel. Named after a student dormitory, the restaurant features a menu that is not as international as its clientele. Yet for unpretentious cooking at reasonable prices U Koleje has few equals. The daily soup specials are always good, and for a treat try the spicy pork rolled in a potato pancake. The menu is geared towards meat-eaters, but a few fish dishes are also offered.

U Tří hrochů
AT THE THREE RHINOS

Bubenečská 8. 24 31 47 61. **Open** 11:30am–10pm Mon–Fri, 5–10pm Sat & Sun.

Though the atmosphere isn't great, this restaurant offers courteous service and pizzas with a good choice of toppings. It is mainly frequented by locals, and its close proximity to Prague's main launderette makes it an excellent place to visit between cycles. Lentil and bean salads are on offer, and bread lovers should not miss the delicious home-made cheese rolls, served piping hot straight from the oven.

U Mikuláše Dačického

Viktora Huga 2. 54 93 12. **Open** 4pm–1am Mon–Fri, 6pm–1am Sat.

As a token of appreciation, this restaurant was decorated by set-designers from the Barandov film studios during the 1930s. They chose a medieval motif, which provides a courtly ambience. Dark-stained panelled walls, large wooden tables, chairs upholstered in red leather, and murals depicting noblemen, knights and a host of courtesans feasting, make the restaurant a unique place to eat in. The food portions are large, and although the menu is similar to that found in other restaurants, the food is prepared with more care. The house speciality is a shish kebab which consists of mixed meats and vegetables, and while some rave about the fish dishes, they can vary in quality.

U Sloupu
AT THE PILLAR

Lucemburská 11. 22 71 31 51. **Open** 11am–11pm Mon–Fri, noon–11pm Sat, Sun.

Located on a quiet street outside the city centre, this dignified restaurant serves traditional Czech meals in a modern Art Deco-style environment. While favourites such as fried carp and svíčková (beef with a cream sauce) are all

available à la carte, there is also a fixed-price menu, and this is recommended as a starting point for those who are unfamiliar with traditional Czech fare.

Letensky Zamecek

Letenské sady 341. **Map** 3 A1. 33 37 56 04. **Open** noon–midnight daily.

The "little castle" is actually three restaurants in one. The elegant first floor caters primarily to a business and foreign clientele; the ground floor serves Czech dishes (including fruit dumplings to die for) to locals at a fraction of the price; and the beer garden offers a friendly atmosphere and cheerful service to a wide range of diners, many of whom are resting their weary feet and enjoying a refreshing drink after a walk in Letná Park. The setting is attractive, with views of the river and the Old Town, and the standard of cooking is generally high, with dishes ranging from goulash to seafood.

Rio's Beach Club

Ostrov Štvanice 38. **Map** 4 F1. 231 13 84. **Open** 11–1am daily.

Set on an island in the Vltava, this pretty restaurant really does offer diners the evocative sound of waves lapping on a beach – though Prague's riverside could not be mistaken for the Copacabana even in the best of weather. It also offers a very appealing choice of dishes, including – in keeping with its name – some with an appetizing Brazilian influence. Worth seeking out for something a bit different, in terms of both setting and cuisine.

U Blaženky

U Blaženky 1. 57 32 09 24. **Open** 11am–11pm daily.

Nestling in the delightful setting of a wooded hilltop overlooking the city, this is a real find, not just for the views from its terrace in summer, but for the food and service all year round. French and Czech dishes rub shoulders on the menu – you can choose between such delicacies as light and flavoursome salmon in herb butter and hearty garlic-roast mutton chops. The Czech speciality of duck breast in raspberry sauce is also worth sampling here, as is the house dessert of fried apples with vanilla ice-cream.

U Cedru
AT THE CEDAR

Národni Obrany 27. 312 29 74. **Open** 11am–1pm daily. ★ AE, DC, MC, V, JCB.

Although it is situated out of the centre of town, this restaurant is easily accessible by metro, and it is well worth the trip. Humous (chickpea dip), felafel (chickpea balls), baba ganuj (aubergine dip), stuffed vine leaves and other staple Lebanese favourites are served. Most people who eat here do not even order a main course: they find that a large selection of appetizers (all served with pitta bread) is usually more than enough. The high quality of the food and its consistent freshness have turned the place into a hot spot for the foreign community. The restaurant is small, with a decor that does not in any way reflect the ethnic nature of its menu, and, as it fills up quickly, reservations are strongly recommended.

Zlatý Drak
GOLDEN DRAGON

Anglická 6. **Map** 6 E2. 24 21 81 54. **Open** 11:30am–3pm, 6–10:30pm daily. DC, V, JCB.

Unlike other Chinese restaurants in Prague, Zlatý Drak underplays the Chinese theme, and its glossy atmosphere is enhanced by large wall mirrors. This is the best Chinese restaurant to be found in town, although the portions are so small that you might decide to order an additional main course. The dishes range from tofu to duck, and there is also a variety of vegetarian options on offer.

Rhapsody

Dukelskych hrdinu 46. 80 67 68. **Open** 6pm–2am Mon–Sat. AE, DC, MC, V, JCB.

As the name suggests, music is an integral part of the drinking and dining experience in this tastefully appointed wine bar and restaurant. Live piano music accompanies your drinking and dining experience. The range of international wines is extremely good. The food is straight-forward – hearty steaks and pasta predominate – but is well-cooked and simply presented. A comfortable, welcoming and laid-back place in which to spend a leisurely evening or at which to round off the night.

Pubs, Beer Halls and Bars

PUBS IN PRAGUE ARE EITHER drinking pubs, which usually serve food as well; traditional beer halls, large enterprises dedicated to the mass consumption of beer; or pubs where people go mainly to eat. *Hostinec* and *hospoda* indicate a pub with food, whereas a *pivnice* serves only beer, but over time the distinctions have faded. Bars usually serve beer as well as wine and spirits. Most of them open at 10 or 11am and close at 10pm. Don't wait to be seated – just look for a free chair. If you sit at an empty table, don't be surprised if others join you. A waiter will bring more beer as you finish, until you say otherwise. Remember that imported spirits can be expensive.

TRADITIONAL PUBS AND BEER HALLS

THERE ARE a variety of drinking establishments in Prague, to suit all tastes. Recommended for the brave, **U Zlatého tygra** is *the* loud Czech literati pub, wall-to-wall with (mostly male) regulars. **U Fleků** has brewed its unique dark beer, Flekovské, since 1499. For authenticity, and Budvar, try **U Medvídků**, which is not too far away from the National Theatre (*see pp156–7*) and Old Town Square, or **Krušovická pivnice**, an airy local pub serving some food. The **U Vejvodů** looks the worse for four centuries' wear, but the interior is new and it also boasts a non-smoking room. The **Hospoda u Goldexu** shares its kitchen with a restaurant, so the food is good. Although this is seldom visited by out-of-towners, it is very popular with ex-pats. In the Castle area, **U Kocoura** most resembles a traditional pub, serving Prazdroj beer and fried cheese, while **Vinárna U Čerta** is more upmarket. A spacious former chapel, **U Betlémské kaple** serves a selection of wholesome Czech food and cold beer from Velké Popovické. **Konírna** is an atmospheric pub down a cobbled lane, and is just the place to go for a quiet pint of beer.

THEME BARS

A RECENT NOVELTY is the theme bar with a foreign atmosphere. The would-be English **John Bull Pub** is pleasant and affordable. The food, big on dumplings and meat, tastes better washed down with a pint of John Bull bitter. With the Municipal House concert hall a block away (*see p214*), it is a good pre-concert venue. The secret of **Jo's Bar** is a US clientele and good Mexican food. The margaritas are excellent and Sunday brunch very popular. The **Nike Sports Bar** is for sports enthusiasts. TVs show the latest action, there is a shoe shop, and the salads, burgers and snacks are good.

CAFÉ SOCIETY

THE CITY IS also embedded in café society, ranging from old-fashioned smoky joints to cafés within bookstores, boutiques and billiard halls. Some are restaurants, others focus on drinking (see listings), but all serve alcohol. **Lávka** has the finest setting in the city. Situated at the foot of Charles Bridge, it offers a spectacular view of the Castle. It is more a place to see and be seen, like **Dolce Vita** and **Slavia** recently reopened by the river opposite the National Theatre. In contrast, **U Zeleného Čaje** is a Zen-like tea house with more than 100 varieties of tea. For a perfect meeting place, try the **Café Milena** opposite the clock tower in the old town square.

DIRECTORY

Slavia
Smetanovo nábř. 2.
Map 3 A5.
24 22 09 57.

Dolce Vita
Široká 15. **Map** 3 B3.
232 91 92.

Hospoda u Goldexu
Vinohradská 25.
Map 6 E1.
24 21 18 06.

Jo's Bar
Malostranské náměstí 7.
Map 2 E3.
53 09 42.

John Bull Pub
Senovážné náměstí 8.
Map 4 E4.
24 22 60 05.

Konírna
Hybernská 8.
Map 3 A4.
24 21 19 59.

Krušovická pivnice
Široká 20. **Map** 3 B3.
231 66 89.

Lávka
Novotného lávka 1.
Map 3 A4.
24 21 47 97.

Nike Sports Bar
Ve smečkách 30.
Map 6 D1.
24 19 63 66.

U Betlémské kaple
Betlemské náměstí 2.
Map 3 B4.
24 21 18 79.

U Fleků
Křemencova 11.
Map 5 B1.
24 91 51 18.

U Kocoura
Nerudova 24. **Map** 2 D3.
53 89 62.

U Medvídků
Na Perštýně 7. **Map** 3 B5.
24 22 09 30.

U Pinkasů
Jungmannovo náměstí 15/16. **Map** 3 C5.
24 22 29 65.

Café Milena
Staroměstské nam. 22.
Map 3 B3.
21 63 26 02.

U Zeleného Čaje
Nerudova 19. **Map** 2 D3.
57 53 00 27.

U Zlatého tygra
Husova 17. **Map** 3 B4.
22 22 11 11.

Vinárna U Čerta
Nerudova 4. **Map** 2 D3.
57 53 15 26-7.

SHOPS AND MARKETS

FOLLOWING THE TRANSITION to a market economy, and the breaking down of barriers between the West and East, the range of goods available in Prague's shops has increased enormously. A number of leading US and West European firms have established businesses in the city, and the quality of goods manufactured in the Czech Republic has improved considerably. Most of Prague's best shops are conveniently located in the city centre, especially in and around

Bohemian crystal

Wenceslas Square. Many of these areas have been pedestrianized, making for leisurely window-shopping, although they can get rather crowded. There are a number of department stores which sell an eclectic range of Czech and Western items. For a different shopping experience, the few traditional markets in the city offer everything from fresh fruit and vegetables to imported Russian caviar, toys, clothes, furniture, Czech crafts, electrical spare parts and even second-hand cars.

OPENING HOURS

MOST OF PRAGUE'S shops are open from 8am to 6pm Monday to Friday and until 1pm on Saturdays. However, they are often more flexible than that, as many shops rely almost entirely on tourists for their trade. The more expensive gift shops have adapted their opening hours to the needs of their Western customers and often do not open until 10am. They also close much later in the evening.

Food stores open earlier, most of them at 6am – reflecting the early working day of many locals – and close at around 7pm. Most shops also take a break for lunch, which can vary from any time between noon and 3pm. Department stores and the big shopping centres also open early but tend to close later, often around 8pm.

All the shops are at their most crowded on Saturdays and for stress-free shopping it's often better to wander around the shops during the week. Prague's markets are generally open early every morning weekday but have varied closing times.

A set of Russian dolls available from one of the many street stalls

One of the many antique shops in Bridge Street in the Little Quarter

HOW TO PAY

YOU WILL FIND that most staple goods, such as food, are much cheaper than comparable items in the West. However, with more multi-nationals, such as Benetton, moving into the city, prices are slowly starting to rise.

Never assume you can pay by credit card. The major ones *(see p222)* are often only accepted in the larger, more tourist-orientated shops and a very few department stores. Most shops will only accept payment in Czech crowns. Ignore any requests, polite or otherwise, to pay for your goods using Pounds Sterling, American Dollars or with German Marks, as

this is now illegal. The total price should always include Value Added Tax (this is 5 or 23% of the total price, depending on what is being sold), although all food is exempt from this. There is no tax-free shopping in Prague.

SALES AND BARGAINS

FOLLOWING THE examples of the newly arrived Western stores, sales are becoming more popular. As a result, it is now quite normal for clothes to be sold off cheaper at the end of each season. There is also an increasing number of post-Christmas sales in the shops found around Old Town Square, Wenceslas Square, Na příkopě and 28. října.

If you want fresh vegetables, fruit, meat or other perishable goods, buy them at the beginning of the day, when the best quality goods are still on sale. There is no point in waiting till the end of the day in the hope of getting bargains, as is the case in Western shops that reduce prices to get rid of perishable items.

DEPARTMENT STORES

THE WIDEST selection of goods can be found in the large, modern department stores. There are about ten at present, although more are planned for the future.

The best-known and most frequently visited department store, **Kotva** (The Anchor), lies in the centre of the city. It was built in 1975 and its four storeys offer a wide range of Western goods, particularly fashion and electronics, with the bonus of an underground car park. But compared to many Western department stores, Kotva, along with its competitors, has a smaller selection of goods than you may be accustomed to – with the exception of food such as smoked meats, for example. Prices charged for some of the more luxurious items on sale, such as famous perfumes, can often be equivalent to the Western ones.

Another popular store is **Tesco**. This opened in 1996 and has a good selection of Czech and western products. The city's oldest department store is **Bílá Labut'** (The White Swan) in Na poříčí. It was opened shortly before the occupation of Czechoslovakia in 1939 and was the first building in Prague to have an escalator. It has since been refurbished, and now

Two figurines decorate the façade of a chemist in the Old Town

specializes in furniture and interior accessories. **Krone**, also supplies a good range of products and is conveniently situated near Můstek metro.

In most supermarkets you are not allowed to go through the turnstiles unless you have a supermarket basket or trolley, and for these you need to queue behind each check-out counter. This system is to make sure the store does not become overcrowded.

MARKETS AND MALLS

PRAGUE'S MARKETS offer a vast range of goods in a friendly atmosphere where bargaining is all part of the fun. The largest market in the city, **Prague Market**, is in Holešovice. It was converted from a former slaughterhouse. The market now sells fresh fruit and vegetables, all kinds of poultry as well as fish, textiles, flowers, elec-

tronics and even second-hand cars and vehicle parts. These are all sold in several large halls and in outdoor stalls. The market is generally open from Monday to Friday, 6am to 5pm. In Havelská, right in the centre of the city, is the small **Havel Market**, which mainly sells fresh fruit and vegetables. Other well-known markets in Prague include **Prague Flea Market**, **Smíchov Market** and a small one in the street V kotcích. Remember that some of the goods sold at all these markets, especially the mass of clothes and shoes, can be of very poor quality.

Western-style shopping malls can now be found in Prague. **Vinohrady Pavilion** has been recently reopened as a shopping mall, following extensive modernization, as has **Koruna Palace**.

STREET STALLS

HUNDREDS OF street stalls and wandering street vendors appear during the summer around Charles Bridge, the Old Castle Steps, Na příkopě and Old Town Square. Usually run by young Czechs, they sell a huge variety of goods. Most stalls have handmade items such as jewellery, pottery, carved wooden toys, puppets, Russian dolls, models of Prague's houses, and Czech crafts. Recently many have started to sell Communist and Soviet memorabilia such as medals, watches, caps and uniforms.

A second-hand bookshop in Karlova Street

What to Buy in Prague

THE INCREASINGLY LARGE selection of goods available in Prague's shops means that everyday items, such as food, books, camera film and toiletries are easily available, and you may find that imported clothing is a better buy here. Prague's more traditional products, such as Bohemian crystal, china, wooden toys and antiques make great souvenirs, and there are still some real bargains to be picked up. Increasingly popular are the more unusual goods which are sold by many of Prague's street vendors. These include Soviet army medals, Red Army uniforms, Russian dolls, wooden puppets, ceramics and a wide selection of jewellery. In general, prices are far lower than in the West.

GLASS AND CHINA

BOHEMIAN GLASS and china have always been ranked among the finest in the world. From huge, decorative vases to delicate glass figures, the vast selection of glass and china items for sale is daunting.

Crystal, glass, and china can be quite different depending on where they are made. Some of the best glass and china in Bohemia is produced at the Moser glassworks at Karlovy Vary and sold at the **Karlovy Vary China** shop and **Moser**. The large Crystalex glassworks at Nový Bor and Poděbrady produce some of the most highly-decorated glass, sold at **Crystal**. Other shops which sell a good selection of glass and china include **Bohemia Crystal, Dana-Bohemia**, and two outlets called **Glass**. However, prices are starting to reflect the increasing popularity of a number of the rarer items and bargains are harder to find. Remember that many of the modern pieces are just as lovely and much cheaper. Because of the fragile nature of the goods, many shops will pack anything you buy there. But if you go for a more expensive piece, it is worth looking into insurance before you leave Prague.

ANTIQUE SHOPS

ANTIQUES IN PRAGUE have always been considered a good buy, as prices are still generally lower than in the West. Antique shops that are well worth a look include

Dorotheum, and **Antique Clocks** sells exactly what it says and **Military Antiques** is a haven for all army fanatics. For goods over Kč1,000, check with the shop whether you will need a licence to export them. However, watch out for an increasing number of fakes which are now appearing on the market.

Prague also has several *bazar* shops which stock a range of items at cheaper prices. Items are often unusual and good bargains can be found. **Bazar B & P** is a small, popular shop full of second-hand goods. For furniture bargains **Bazar nábytku** is well worth a visit.

TRADITIONAL CRAFTS

THE TRADITIONAL manufacture of high-quality and hand-crafted goods still survives. The variety of the products available in the shops – hand-woven carpets, wooden toys, table mats, beautifully-painted Easter eggs, baskets, figurines in folk costumes, and ceramics – are all based on Czech and Moravian folk themes and then enriched with modern elements. You can buy them from many market stalls as well as a fair number of shops.

Czech Traditional Handi-crafts offers a huge choice of hand-carved toys. Other arts and crafts shops include **Souvenirs** and **Pottery Tupesy**. A number of street vendors around Old Town Square also sell a range of handmade items including jewellery and puppets.

BOOKS

THERE ARE numerous book-shops in Prague, but most of the books sold are in Czech. Foreign-language books are available in the specialist bookshops in the city centre.

One of the main bookshops is **U Černé Matky Boží**. Here you'll find a range of English-language books (including Czech works which have been translated into English) as well as a fair number of German and French editions. Another well-stocked outlet is the **Big Ben Bookshop**. Maps and guides to Prague in English can be bought at **Antikvariát Makovsky & Gregor**. Other specialist bookshops include **Orbis**, **Kanzelberger**, **Arbes Bookshop**, **Academia** and **Fišer's Bookshop**.

Prague also has second-hand bookshops – look in Golden Lane and Karlova Street – which stock some English-language books, and they all offer the visiting bibliophile hours of enjoyable browsing.

FOOD AND DELICATESSENS

PRAGUE'S SUPERMARKETS are well stocked with the basic foodstuffs *(see p207)*. For something special, there are a few delicatessens. **Delicacies** is a small shop with meat and fish counters. A specialist food shop, selling smoked sausage, cheeses and other local delicacies, is **Jan Paukert**. For freshly-baked bread visit the bakers around Wenceslas Square and Mostecká Street. **Bakery Bonal** sells a good selection of patisseries.

PHARMACIES

MOST PHARMACIES in Prague stock all modern medicines, but a prescription from a Czech doctor is needed to buy them. Check listings for addresses *(see directory for 24-hour pharmacies)*. Toiletries can be bought at a drugstore.

DIRECTORY

DEPARTMENT STORES

Anchor
KOTVA
Náměstí Republiky 8.
Map 4 D3.
24 80 11 11.

Krone
Václavské náměstí 21.
Map 4 D5.
24 23 04 77.

Tesco
Národní 26. **Map** 3 B5.
24 22 79 71.

White Swan
BÍLÁ LABUŤ
Na poříčí 23.
Map 4 D3.
24 81 13 64.

MARKETS AND MALLS

Havel Market
Havelské náměstí.
Map 3 C4.

Koruna Palace
Václavské náměstí 1.
Map 3 C5.
24 21 95 26.

Prague Flea Market
PRAŽSKÁ BURZA
Výstaviště (Exhibition Ground).

Prague Market
Bubenské nábřeží 306.
Prague 7.
80 09 45.

Smíchov Market
Náměstí 14. října 15.
Map 3 C4.
57 32 11 01.

Vinohrady Pavilion
Vinohradská 50. **Map** 6 F1.
22 09 71 11.

GLASS AND CHINA

Bohemia Crystal
ČESKÝ KŘIŠTÁL
Národní 19. **Map** 3 B5.
26 44 36.
One of several branches.

Dana-Bohemia
GLASS, CHINA, CRYSTAL
Národní 43. **Map** 3 A5.
24 21 46 55.
One of several branches.

Crystal
Karlova 14.
Map 3 A4.
26 64 25.
One of several branches.

Glass
SKLO
Malé náměstí 6.
Map 3 B4.
24 22 84 59.
Staroměstské náměstí 26–27.
Map 3 C3.
24 22 97 55.

Karlovy Vary China
KARLOVARSKÝ PORCELÁN
Pařížská 2.
Map 3 B2.
24 81 10 23.

Moser
Na příkopě 12.
Map 3 C4.
24 21 12 93/
24 21 12 94.

ANTIQUE SHOPS

Antique Clocks
STAROŽITNOSTI UHLÍŘ
Mikulandská 8.
Map 3 B5.
29 41 70.

Bazar nábytku
Libenský ostrov.
66 02 93 10.

A.D. Starožitnosti
Skorepka 8, Prague 1.
Map 3 B4.
24 23 46 96.

Military Antiques
Charvátova 11.
Map 3 C5.
24 94 67 30.
One of several branches.

Bazar B & P
Nekázanka 17.
Map 4 D4.
24 21 05 50.

Dorotheum
Ovocný trh 2.
Map 3 C4.
24 22 20 01.

GIFTS AND SOUVENIRS

Czech Traditional Handicrafts
Karlova 26.
Map 3 A4.
22 22 04 33.

Hračky Traditional Toys
Pohořelec 24.
Map 1 B3.

Pottery Keramika Tupesy
Truhlářská 9.
Map 4 D3.
231 11 56.

Souvenirs Dům u Bílého Jednorožce
Staroměstské náměstí 15
Map 3 B3.
231 17 34.

BOOKS

Antikvariát Makovsky & Gregor
Kaprova 9.
Map 3 B3.
232 83 35

Arbes Bookshop
ARBESOVO KNIHKUPECTVÍ
Štefánikova 26.
Prague 5.
54 03 01.

Big Ben Bookshop
Malá Štupartská 5.
Map 3 C3.
24 82 65 65.

Fišer's Bookshop
FIŠEROVO KNIHKUPECTVÍ
Kaprova 10.
Map 3 B3.
232 07 33.

U Černé Matky Boží
Celetná 34.
Map 3 C3.
24 21 11 55.

Knihkupectuí Academia
Václavské náměstí 34.
Map 4 D5.
24 22 35 11.

Orbis
Václavské náměstí 42.
Map 4 D5.
24 21 73 35.

Kanzelberger
Václavské náměstí 4.
Map 4 D5.
24 21 92 14.

FOOD AND DELICATESSENS

Bakery Bonal
Václavské náměstí 57.
Map 4 D5.
24 21 49 36.

Bakeshop
U Kolkovně 2 .
Map 3 C3
232 01 95.

Delicacies
ZLATÝ KŘÍŽ
Jungmannovo náměstí 19.
Map 3 C5.
24 09 86 32.

Jan Paukert
Národní 17.
Map 3 B5.
26 64 44.

PHARMACIES

It is not usual for pharmacies to have individual names, so look out for **Léky** (drugs) or **Lékárna** (pharmacy).

Národní 35.
Map 3 B5.
24 23 00 86.

Malé náměstí 13.
Map 3 B4.
24 22 54 70.

Václavské náměstí 64.
Map 3 C5.
22 21 14 23.

Lékárna v Anděla
Stefanikova 6,
Prague 5.
253 70 39.

ENTERTAINMENT IN PRAGUE

SINCE THE VELVET REVOLUTION, Prague's entertainment programme has become increasingly varied. Whether you prefer opera to jazz or mini-golf to a football match, the city has plenty to offer. Movie buffs can choose from many of the latest Hollywood blockbusters, a lot of them in English with subtitles. For the adventurous, mime and fringe theatre are both thriving. Prague has a great musical tradition, which includes symphony orchestras, opera, musicals, jazz and folk music. Concerts are performed throughout the year, in venues which range from Baroque palaces to public parks and gardens. Even if you don't speak Czech, you can still enjoy the city's cultural offerings. Some plays can be seen in English, and for many types of entertainment, music, dance and sport, a knowledge of the language isn't necessary at all.

Street musicians entertaining the crowds

PRACTICAL INFORMATION

THE BEST PLACE to look for information about what's on and where in Prague, is in the two English-language newspapers, *Prognosis* and *The Prague Post (see p219)*. Both of the newspapers offer comprehensive details of the best entertainment and cultural events which will be of interest to an English-speaking audience. Those events that are in English or have translation facilities are marked. Other sources of information are the leaflets given out at the ticket agencies in the city like **Melantrich** or **PIS** *(see p211)*. These are generally printed in Czech, English and German. You can also use the free booklets *Přehled* and *The Month in Prague* printed in English and available from any **PIS** office. For a comprehensive rundown of events, buy *Culture in Prague*, a detailed monthly publication listing information on a variety of local exhibitions, concerts and theatre.

Theatre signs strung along Celetná Street

BOOKING TICKETS

TICKETS CAN be bought in advance from the box office at most entertainment venues. You can also book tickets in advance by writing to, or ringing, the venue. Remember that many of the city's box offices may not have any English speakers available. The more popular events tend to become heavily booked up in advance by tour groups – particularly during the summer – and by season-ticket holders. However, standby tickets are usually available about an hour before performances. If this isn't practical and you want to be sure of a ticket on a particular day, it is better to buy your tickets at one of the many booking agencies in the city. The drawback to using agencies

PUPPET THEATRE

Puppetry has a long tradition in Prague and is still strongly represented. The most famous puppet show in the city is held at the **Spejbl and Hurvínek Theatre** *(see p214)*. The show revolves around Daddy Spejbl and his reprobate son Hurvínek. Other puppet theatres include the **National Marionette Theatre** *(see p214)*, which uses all-string marionettes featured in regular performances for children at weekends. The **Theatre in the Old Town** *(see p214)* and the **Children's Little Sun Club** *(see p214)* also put on puppet shows occasionally. Check listings magazines *(see p218)*.

Theatre puppets

is that commission on these tickets can be high, sometimes doubling the original price. Your hotel receptionist may also be able to get you tickets.

TICKET PRICES

TICKET PRICES are still very cheap compared to Western prices, except for certain performances, most notably during the Prague Spring Festival *(see p50)*. Prices range from around Kč100 for a small fringe production or puppet theatre to up to Kč1,500 for a performance of an internationally-famous orchestra. Paying for your tickets by credit cards is rarely, if ever, accepted by any entertainment venue.

TICKET TOUTS

THERE HAS BEEN a recent spate of counterfeit tickets on sale, especially for the larger rock concerts. To be safe, always buy your tickets at reputable agencies or at the venue itself.

LATE-NIGHT TRANSPORT

PRAGUE'S METRO *(see p234)* stops running shortly after midnight, while the normal bus and tram service ends around 11:30pm. Then the city's extensive night bus and tram service takes over. Timetables are displayed at each stop. Night trams and buses are regular and efficient and it is likely that there will

Members of the Opera Mozart *(see p214)* performing *Così Fan Tutte*

be a tram or bus stop near your hotel. Taxis provide the most certain form of late-night transportation, but beware of unscrupulous drivers trying to overcharge you *(see p237)*. Always try to walk a little way from the

Sparta Stadium *(see p215)*

theatre before you hail a cab, the fare will probably be a lot cheaper. Ask your hotel before you go out what the best transport options are.

MUSIC FESTIVALS

THE MOST famous music festival of all is the Prague Spring Music Festival *(see p50)*, held annually between May and June. Hundreds of international musicians come to Prague to take part in the celebrations. Other music festivals in the city include the Mozart Festival *(see p51)*, which takes place during the summer months, and the International Jazz Festival *(see p52)*, which is held during the autumn.

A view of the Rudolfinum auditorium *(see p214)*

BOOKING AGENTS

Bohemia Ticket International
Malé Nàmèsti 13. **Map** 3 B4.
[24 22 78 32.
Na Příkopě 16. **Map** 4 D4.
[24 21 50 31.

Ticketpro
Salvátorská 10. **Map** 3 B3.
[1051/24 81 40 20.

CK Intercontact
Karmelitská 27. **Map** 2 E4.
[57 53 25 62.

Lucerna
Štěpánská 61. **Map** 5 C1.
[24 21 20 03.

Melantrich
Václavské náměstí 38.
Map 4 D5.
[24 21 50 18.

Pragotour
Staroměstské Nám.1.
Map 3 B3.
[24 48 25 62.

Prague Information Service (PIS)
Staroměstské náměstí 1.
Map 3 B3.
[24 48 25 62.
Na Příkopě 20. **Map** 4 D4.
[26 40 22.

Prague Tourist Centre
Rytířská 12. **Map** 3 C4.
[24 21 22 09.

Top Theatre Tickets
Zatecka 1. **Map** 3 B3.
[232 25 36.

Variety of Entertainment

PRAGUE HAS ALWAYS BEEN known for its artistic heritage. Theatre has played an important role in the city's cultural development, and recently the range of entertainment has expanded considerably. Many new theatre groups have emerged, especially more experimental ones. In general, the theatre season runs from September to June. During the summer, open-air performances are given in Prague's gardens and parks. The city also has a strong musical tradition, including great musicians and performers such as Mozart, Smetana and Dvořák. For those who prefer to dance till dawn, relax to the sound of jazz or take in a movie: you'll find plenty to entertain you in this inexpensive city.

ENGLISH-LANGUAGE PERFORMANCES

MANY THEATRES in Prague have started to stage a number of English-language productions – especially in the summer months. Even if the play is not performed in English, many theatre venues have installed simultaneous translation facilities. For more details, check in the listings magazines (see p219).

MAJOR THEATRES

PRAGUE'S FIRST permanent theatre was built in 1738, but the city's theatrical tradition dates from the Baroque and Renaissance periods.

The **National Theatre** (see p156) is Prague's main venue for opera, ballet and plays. The neighbouring New Stage is another important venue. It is also the main stage for the multi-media **Laterna Magika** company, which is one of Prague's best-known theatre groups as well as being at the forefront of European improvisational theatre.

Other major theatres in the city include the "stone theatres". These gained importance during the 18th century and include the **Vinohrady Theatre**, the **Estates Theatre** (see p65) – one of the most respected in Prague – and the **Prague Municipal Theatre**, an acting company whose plays appear in turn at the **ABC Theatre**, the **Comedy Theatre** and the **Rokoko Studio of Drama**. The **Kolowrat Theatre** is based in the Kolowrat Palace.

FRINGE THEATRES

THESE ORIGINATED during the 1960s and won renown for their fight against the status quo. The groups are still very innovative and largely experimental. They perform in small theatres, and many of Prague's best actors and actresses have developed their skills while working for some of these companies.

Fringe theatres include: the **Dramatic Club**, well known for its supporting ensemble; the **Ypsilon Studio**, with one of the finest acting companies in the city; **Theatre Na Fidlovačce**, stages a mix of musicals and straight drama; the large **Theatre Below Palmovka**, renowned for its mix of classical and modern plays and the **Theatre in Celetná**. One of Prague's most spectacular theatrical and music venues is **Křižík's Fountain**, at the Exhibition Ground, where classical concerts are held and full orchestras perform to stunning lightshows.

PANTOMIME, MIME AND "BLACK THEATRE"

SOME OF THE MOST popular theatre entertainment in Prague is Black Theatre (where black-clad actors move objects against a dark stage without being seen – a stunning visual spectacle), pantomime and mime. None of three requires any understanding of Czech and all are strongly represented. The **Bomiel Pantomime** is well worth a visit if you enjoy this rigorous and expressive discipline. **Jiří Srnec's Black Theatre** is one of the major venues for black theatre performance.

DANCE

IN PRAGUE, opera and ballet companies traditionally share the **National Theatre**, where the permanent ballet company is based. You can also watch ballet at the **Estates Theatre** and at the **Prague State Opera**. Musicals tend to be popular in Prague, and these are performed by some of the modern dance groups.

CLASSICAL MUSIC

THE MAIN CONCERT venues for classical music are the **Rudolfinum** (see p84) and the Smetana Hall, found in the **Municipal House** (see p64). Other permanent concert halls include the **Atrium in Žižkov**, a converted chapel, the **Clementinum** and the imposing **Congress Centre Prague**. **Bertramka** is another venue with the added attraction of being the place where Mozart stayed when he was in Prague.

MUSIC IN CHURCHES AND PALACES

CONCERTS PERFORMED in the numerous churches and palaces around Prague are extremely popular. Many of these buildings are closed to the public, so this is the only chance to see inside them. Major churches include the **Church of St James** (see p65); the **Church of St Nicholas** (see p128) in the Little Quarter; the **Church of St Nicholas** (see p70) in the Old Town; the **Church of St Francis** in Knights of the Cross Square (see p79); **St Vitus's Cathedral** (see p100) and **St George's Basilica** (see p98). Among the other venues included are the **National Museum** (see p147); the **Lobkowicz Palace** (see p99) and the **Sternberg Palace** (see p112). It's worth checking the listings magazines (p219) for the specific dates and times of concerts.

OPERA

DURING THE 20th century, opera has become very popular in Prague, and there are now two major opera companies in the city. One company performs solely in the **National Theatre** *(see pp156–7)* and the other in the **State Opera**. The latter presents all its performances in the language in which they were written, usually Italian, while the National Theatre has more Czech translations of the operas. The **Music Theatre in Karlín** puts on classical operettas and musicals only. More innovative pieces are staged by the **Lyra Pragensis**, while the **Mozart Opera** offers modern music programmes.

NIGHTCLUBS

EVEN THOUGH nightlife in Prague is not as extensive as in other European capitals, it is rapidly catching up. Since 1989 there have been great changes, so that now visitors have a wider choice of night-clubs, discos and cabaret.

The biggest club in the city is the **Lucerna Bar** which offers a varied programme in an unusual basement ballroom in the beautiful but run down Lucerna building. The **Praga Variety** has a disco and revue programme and is one of Prague's more popular venues. The **Eden-Palladium Dance Club** is the largest disco in Prague. **Zlat´y Strom** offers techno/house together with 70's, 80's and 90's dance tunes until 5 am in a medieval cellar setting. The trendier clubs include **Radost FX**, where the city's most affluent are attracted by a constant diet of techno/house and plush decor, together with **Obvodní Kulturní dům Vltavská** and **Nasa**.

ROCK AND POP CLUBS

LOVERS OF ROCK MUSIC are well served in Prague. There are a large number of popular rock venues, generally small clubs and cafés, which host a variety of different groups. There is a thriving indigenous scene – Prague's own rock bands play both their own compositions as well as cover versions of more famous numbers, many singing in English. Higher-profile, more internationally renowned Western bands also play in Prague occasion-ally. The **Rock Café**, and the **Uzi rock-bar**, both very popular venues, offer regular concerts followed by discos. Other venues include the **Futurum Rock Club**, open to the early hours; the **Junior Club na Chmelnici**, whose indie bands begin at 7:30pm. For lovers of nostalgia, **Classic Club** plays an hour of the most popular 1960s classics.

JAZZ

THE ROOTS OF JAZZ in Prague can be traced not only to the American tradition but also to the pre-war heyday of Prague's famous jazz players, such as Jaroslav Ježek. Prague's many jazz clubs play all forms, from Dixieland to swing. One of the leading and most popular jazz venues in the city is the **Jazz Club Reduta**, which has daily jazz concerts at around 9pm. The popular **Metropolitan Club** holds late-night concerts until 3 or 4am. At the **Agharta Jazz Centrum**, you can hear a high standard of playing while eating in its café. **Umaleho Glenna** has regular live blues, jazz and funk, and the **120 Days Club** plays a mixture of jazz, blues, rock and folk. **Malostranská beseda** is the venue for more traditional jazz. For serious enthusiasts, the International Jazz Festival *(see p52)* during October attracts talent.

ETHNIC MUSIC

A SMALL NUMBER of clubs and bars in Prague offer ethnic music. **The Palác Akropolis** hosts diverse daily performances in an atmospheric converted 20's theatre building. A variety of bands can be seen from around the world in an atmospheric setting, at the **House of Culture**.

GAY AND LESBIAN VENUES

PRAGUE'S FEW gay venues tend to cater mainly for men, though the buds of a lesbian scene are just beginning to peep through; *Amigo* magazine will give you up-to-date listings. The **A Club** has become very much the headquarters of the lesbian scene. Other popular gay places include **Aqua 2000**, the disco **Gejzeer**, and the cellar bar **Friends**.

CINEMAS

ALTHOUGH PRAGUE doesn't have all the latest Holly-wood blockbusters, more than 80 per cent of the films shown are recent US productions and a third of them have Czech subtitles. The listings magazines *(see p219)* show which films are on and in what language. Most major cinema screens are situated around Wen-ceslas Square, including **Hvězda**, **Lucerna** and **Blaník**; others are listed in the directory *(see p215)*. The **Illusion** and the **Bio Konvikt Ponrepo** cinemas show old films. For a cinema restaurant, visit **Evald**.

SPORTING VENUES

IN CENTRAL PRAGUE, sports facilities are not extensive, so you may have to travel a little further out if you feel like some exercise. Golf, mini-golf or tennis are on offer at the **Motol**, the **Exhibition Ground** *(see p162)* and **Štvanice Island**. Swimming pools are also further out, including two at **Divoká Šárka** and **Kobylisy**. There are beautiful natural lakes at **Lhotka** and **Šeberák** and a whole range of water sports is now on offer at **Hostivař Reservoir** and **Imperial Meadow**.

The main spectator sports are soccer and ice hockey. Sparta Praha, the top soccer team, play at **Sparta Stadium** in Letná, while ice hockey matches are held in the sports hall at the Exhibition Ground.

DIRECTORY

THEATRES

Bomiel Pantomime
Lávka Theatre,
Novotného lávka 1.
Map 3 A4.
(24 21 47 97.

**Children's Little
Sun Club**
DĚTSKÝ KLUB SLUNÍČKO
Vojtíškova 1783, Prague 4.
(792 20 74.

Dramatic Club
ČINOHERNÍ KLUB
Ve Smečkách 26.
Map 6 D1.
(96 22 21 23.

Estates Theatre
STAVOVSKÉ DIVADLO
Ovocný trh. **Map** 3 C3.
(24 22 85 03.

**Jiří Srnec's Black
Theatre**
ČERNÉ DIVADLO
JIŘÍHO SRNCE
U Lékárny 597,
15600 Prague 5.
(57 92 18 35.

Kolowrat Theatre
DIVADLO KOLOWRAT
(IN ESTATES THEATRE)
Ovocný trh.
Map 3 C3.
(24 90 14 48.

Křižík's Fountain
KŘIŽÍKOVA FONTÁNA
Výstaviště, Prague 7.
(20 10 32 80,
20 10 32 95.

Laterna Magika
Národní 4. **Map** 3 A5.
(24 91 41 29.

National Theatre
NÁRODNÍ DIVADLO
Národní 2.
Map 3 A5.
(24 91 34 37.

**National
Marionette
Theatre**
NÁRODNÍ DIVADLO
MARIONET
Žatecká 1.

Map 3 B3.
(232 34 29.

**Prague Municipal
Theatre,
ABC Theatre**
MĚSTSKÁ DIVADLA
PRAŽSKÁ DIVADLO ABC
Vodičkova 28.
Map 3 C5.
(24 21 25 85.

**Prague Municipal
Theatre,
Comedy Theatre**
MĚSTSKÁ DIVADLA
PRAŽSKÁ, DIVADLO
KOMEDIE
Lazarská 1. **Map** 5 B1.
(24 22 24 84.

**Prague Municipal
Theatre,
Rokoko Studio
of Drama**
MĚSTSKÁ DIVADLA
PRAŽSKÁ ČINOHERNÍ
STUDIO-ROKOKO
Václavské náměstí 38.
Map 4 D5.
(24 21 28 37.

Reduta Theatre
DIVADLO REDUTA
Národní 20.
Map 3 B5.
(24 91 22 46.

**Spejbl and
Hurvínek Theatre**
DIVADLO SPEJBLA A
HURVÍNKA
Dejvická 38.
(312 27 04.

**Theatre in
Celetná**
DIVADLO V CELETNÉ
Celetná 17.
Map 3 C3.
(232 68 43.

**Theatre below
Palmovka**
DIVADLO POD
PALMOVKOU
Zenklova 14,
Prague 8.
(66 31 17 08.

**Theatre in the
Old Town**
DIVADLO U DLOUHÉ
Dlouhá 39.
Map 3 C3.
(24 82 68 07.

**Theatre Na
Fidlovačce**
DIVADLO NA FIDLOVAČCE
Křesomyslova 625,
Map 6 E5.
(41 40 40 40.

Vinohrady Theatre
DIVADLO NA
VINOHRADECH
Náměstí Míru 7.
Map 6 F2.
(24 25 76 01.

Ypsilon Studio
STUDIO YPSILON
Spálená 16. **Map** 3 B5.
(24 94 71 19.

MUSIC VENUES

Atrium in Žižkov
ATRIUM NA ŽIŽKOVĚ
Čajkovského 12, Prague 3.
(627 04 53.

Bertramka
BERTRAMKA MUZEUM
W A MOZARTA
Mozartova 169, Prague 5.
(54 38 93.

Church of St James
KOSTEL SV. JAKUBA
Málá štupartská.
Map 3 C3.

**Church of St
Nicholas (Old
Town)**
KOSTEL SV. MIKULÁŠE
Staroměstské náměstí.
Map 3 B3.

**Church of St
Nicholas**
KOSTEL SV. MIKULÁŠE
Malostranské náměstí.
Map 2 E3.

Church of St Francis
KOSTEL SV. FRANTIŠKA
Křižovnické náměstí.
Map 3 A4.

Clementinum
ZRCADLOVÁ SÍŇ
KLEMENTINA
Mariánské náměstí 10.
Map 3 B3.

Lobkowicz Palace
LOBKOVICKÝ PALÁC
Jiřská 1, Pražský hrad.
Map 2 E2.

Lyra Pragensis
Václavskéé náměstí 16.
Map 4 D5.
(222 22 02 92.

Mozart Opera
OPERA MOZART
Novotného Làvka 1.
Map 3 B3.
(21 08 22 88.

**Music Theatre in
Karlín**
HUDEBNÍ DIVADLO V
KARLÍNĚ
Křižíkova 10.
Map 4 F3.
(21 86 81 11.

**Congress Centre
Prague**
KONGRESOVÉ CENTRUM
PRAHA
5. května 65,
Prague 4.
(61 17 27 11.

National Museum
NÁRODNÍ MUZEUM
Václavské náměstí 68.
Map 6 D1.
(24 49 71 11.

Prague State Opera
STÁTNÍ OPERA PRAHA
Wilsonova 4.
Map 6 E1.
(26 53 53.

Rudolfinum
RUDOLFINUM –
DVOŘÁKOVA SÍŇ
Alšovo nábřeží.
Map 3 A3.
(24 89 31 11.

St George's Basilica
BAZILIKA SV. JIŘÍ
Jiřské náměstí,
Pražský hrad.
Map 2 E2.

St Vitus's Cathedral
CHRÁM SV. VÍTA
Pražský hrad.
Map 2 D2.

Sternberg Palace
ŠTERNBERSKÝ PALAC
Hradčanské náměstí 15.
Map 1 C3.
(20 51 46 34.

NIGHTCLUBS

Caliente
Vejvocla 6.
Map 4 E3.
24 22 15 36.

Disco Kobra
Zlatniká 4.
Map 4 E2.
232 91 57.

Discoteka Zlatý Strom
Karlova 6. **Map** 3 A4.
22 22 04 41.

Eden-Palladium Dance Club
U Slavie 1.
72 73 63 06.

Lucerna Bar
Vodičova 36.
Map 5 C1.
24 21 71 08.

Nasa
Konviktská 6
Map 3 C5.
24 23 81 71.

Obvodní Kulturní dům Vltavská
Bubenská 1.
87 96 83.

Praga Variety
VATIETĚ PRAGA
Vodičkova 30. **Map** 3 C5.
24 21 59 45.

Radost FX
Bělehradská 120.
Map 6 E2.
24 25 47 76.

ROCK AND POP CLUBS

Classic Club
Pařižská 4. **Map** 3 B3

Futurum Rock Club
Zborovská 7. **Map** 2 F5
54 71 00.

Hrob
Sokolovská 144.
Map 4 F2
684 02 63.

Junior Club na Chmelnici
Akropolis,
Kubelíkova 27.
22 71 22 87.

Klub Lávka
Novotného lávka 1.
Map 3 A4.
22 22 21 56.

Meloun
Michalská 12.
Map 3 B4.
23 24 01 26.

Roxy
Dlouhá 33.
Map 3 C3.
248 11 09 51.

Rock Café
Národní 20.
Map 3 B5.
249 144 16.

Swamp
Újezd 5/598.
Map 2 E4.
53 00 02.

Uzi rock-bar
Legerova 44.
Map 6 D2.

JAZZ CLUBS

Agharta Jazz Centrum
Krakovská 5.
Map 6 D1.
22 21 12 75.

Jazz Club Reduta
Národní Třída 20.
Map 3 B5.
249 122 46.

Malostranská Beseda
Malostranské náměstí 21.
Map 2 E3.
53 90 24.

Metropolitan Jazz Club
Jungmannova 14.
Map 3 C5.
24 94 77 77

Umalého Glenna
Karmelitská 23.
Map 2 E4.
535 81 15.

ETHNIC MUSIC

House of Culture
OBVODNÍ KULTURNÍ DŮM VLTAVSKÁ
Bubenská 1. 87 96 83.

Palác Akropolis
Kubelíkova 27.
22 71 22 87

GAY AND LESBIAN CLUBS

A Club
Miličova 25.
22 78 16 23.

Aqua Club 2000
Husitská 7. **Map** 4 F4.
627 89 71.

Friends
Náoprstova 1. **Map** 3 A4.
221 63 54 08.

Gejzeer
Vinohradská 40. **Map** 6 F1.
222 51 60 36.

CINEMAS

Bio Konvikt Ponrepo
Bartolomějská 13.
Map 3 B5.
24 23 72 33.

Blaník
Václavské náměstí 56.
Map 6 D1.
24 03 21 72.

Budějovická Broadway
Budějovická 1667,
Prague 4.
61 38 22 97.

Evald
Národní Třída 28. **Map** 3 B5.
21 10 52 25

Hvězda
Václavské náměstí 38.
Map 4 D5.
24 21 68 22.

Illusion
Vinohradská 48.
Map 6 F1.
22 52 03 79.

Kotva
Naměstí Republiky 8.
Map 4 D3.
24 82 83 16.

Lucerna
Vodičkova 36
Map 3 C5.
24 21 69 72

Perštýn
Na Perštýně 6.
Map 3 B3.
21 66 84 32.

Praha
Václavské náměstí 17.
Map 4 D5.
26 20 35.

64 U hradeb
Mostecká 21.
Map 2 E3.
53 50 06.

SPORTING VENUES

Divoká Šárka
Prague 6.

Exhibition Ground
VÝSTAVIŠTĚ
Sports stadium, Prague 7.

Hostivař Reservoir
Prague 10.

Imperial Meadow
CÍSAŘSKÁ LOUKA
Prague 5.

Kobylisy
Prague 8.

Lhotka
Prague 4.

Motol
V Úvalu 84, Prague 5.

Šeberák
Prague 4.

Sparta Stadium
Milady Horákové,
Prague 7.

Štvanice Island
Ostrov Štvanice 1125,
Prague 7.

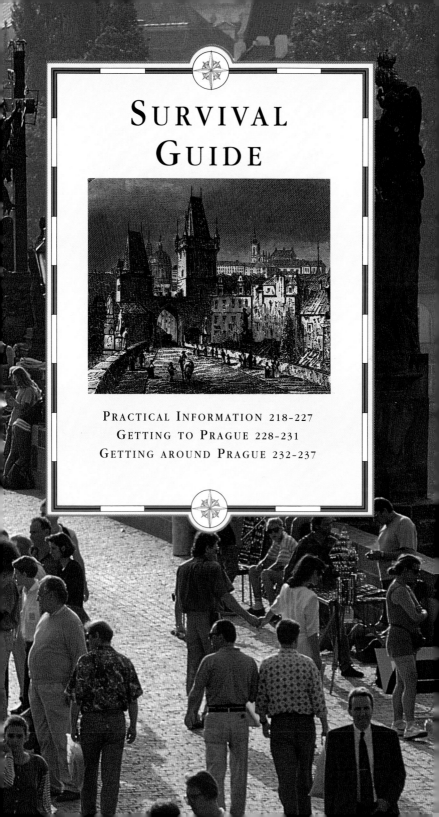

SURVIVAL
GUIDE

PRACTICAL INFORMATION

SINCE THE recent political upheavals, Prague has become far more open to visitors. The city has responded well to the enormous influx of tourists, and facilities such as hotels, banks, restaurants and information centres have improved considerably. Even so, a little forward planning is always worthwhile. Reading up about a sight, checking it is open and how best to get there, can save a lot of time

A Martin Tours sightseeing bus

and inconvenience. Prague's transport system is straightforward and most of the city's sights are within walking distance. In general, prices are still considerably lower than in the West, but a few of the more up-market restaurants and hotels are priced according to Western rather than Czech wallets. Despite a small increase in petty crime, especially pickpocketing, Prague is still safer than the majority of Western cities.

TOURIST INFORMATION

THERE ARE a number of tourist information offices ranging from specialized agencies to the state-owned **Čedok**. These can provide advice on anything from accommodation and travel to restaurants and guided tours. Many employ English speakers and print English language publications. The efficient **Prague Information Service (PIS)** is the city's best tourist information point. It has three offices in the city centre and it provides visitors with maps, advice, listings *(see pp210–11)* and other types of information in English, German and Czech. To help you find your way around the city, **Kiwi** has a large selection of maps and guides in English.

Čedok street sign

TIPS FOR TOURISTS

IN PRAGUE, there are enough English speakers to make booking a room, buying a ticket or ordering a meal relatively simple. A smattering of German may also help, as many Czechs have a working knowledge of the language.

One of the best times to visit Prague is during the summer, although it can be rather

crowded. Other busy times of the year are Easter and major Catholic festivals *(see pp50–53)*. The main sights, such as the Old Town Square, are always packed during these periods, but the crowds give Prague a carnival atmosphere. Street entertainers, buskers and small street stalls spring up around the most popular attractions. If the crowds do get too much, just turn off into one of the smaller streets and you are almost guaranteed peace and quiet. Bring a light raincoat for the summer and some warm, woolly clothes for the rest of the year.

OPENING HOURS

THIS GUIDE lists the opening hours for the individual museums, galleries and churches. Most of the city's major sights can be seen throughout the year, but many of Prague's gardens and the castles outside the city are only open from 1 April to 31 October. Visiting hours are normally from 9am to 5pm, daily, but the final admission times can often be as much as an hour earlier. A number of major museums and castles are also closed every Monday, so be sure to check before visiting them. The National Museum is closed on the first Tuesday of

Entry tickets for some of Prague's major tourist sights

the month and the Jewish Museum is closed on Friday afternoons and on Saturdays.

Opening hours of Prague's shops vary widely. Some businesses are open between 7am and 6pm, Monday to Friday, and 8am to noon on Saturdays. Some department stores *(see p208)* are open until 4pm on Saturdays and a few Sundays before Christmas.

The main office of the Prague Information Service in the street Na příkopě

A horse-drawn carriage in the Old Town Square

Prague does not have any standard late-night shopping, although many of the more expensive tourist shops stay open until around 10pm. Banks open from 8am to 4pm, Monday to Friday. Restaurants, cafés and bars all have varied opening hours *(see pp188–9)*. Most of the city's bars open from 10am and as there are no licensing laws, often stay open until everyone leaves.

LISTINGS AND TICKETS

THERE ARE some 160 galleries and 40 museums scattered throughout the city, and to find out what's on it is best to look in a listings paper. The English-language newspaper *The Prague Post* gives detailed listings of most events and exhibitions. Available from newsstands in the city centre, it also give tips for the visitor and informative articles on Prague, its politics and its people. The **PIS** has a free monthly English-language listings book.

The price of entry tickets for museums varies widely, from Kč20 to around Kč100. Most churches are free, with a collection box at the door. Tickets for entertainment events can be bought from the booking agencies in the city, or at the venue itself. Some of Prague's hotels can get you tickets, or try a large travel agent in the centre.

SIGHTSEEING TIPS

A GOOD WAY to see Prague is to take a sightseeing tour. Many firms offer trips around Prague's major sights as well as outings to castles such as Karlstein and Konopiště *(see pp166–7)*. Tours usually start from Náměstí Republiky (Republic Square) and from the upper part of Václavské náměstí (Wenceslas Square). These trips can be expensive but prices vary, so it is worth checking what's on offer before you make a booking.The Jewish Museum *(see p87)* organizes trips around the Jewish Quarter. For those on a tight budget, **PIS** offers some of the cheapest tours.

A trip on tram No. 91, run by the Museum of Municipal Mass Transport, is one of the cheapest and best city centre tours. It starts off at the Exhibition Ground *(see pp176–7)* and travels around the Old Town, the New Town and the Jewish Quarter. It runs from Easter to the end of October every weekend and public holiday. Tickets can be bought on board. Sightseeing trips in horse-drawn carriages (fiacres) are run from the Old Town Square, and in summer, a "fun train" from Mostecká Street runs through some of the loveliest parts of Hradčany and the Little Quarter.

A street sign showing the services offered by Pragotur

INFORMATION CENTRES AND TOUR OPERATORS

Akasi
Václavské náměstí 17. **Map** 4 D5.
☎ *24 23 61 18.*
FAX *24 94 90 02.*

American Express
Václavské náměstí 56. **Map** 6 D1.
☎ *24 21 99 92.*
FAX *22 21 11 31.*

Arstour
28. října 14. **Map** 3 C4.
☎ *24 21 99 92.*
FAX *24 21 88 05.*

Čedok
Na příkopě 18. **Map** 3 C4.
☎ *24 19 71 11.*
FAX *232 16 56.*
Rytířská 16. **Map** 3 C4.
☎ *26 36 97.*
FAX *26 27 96.*

Tourist information centre

Kiwi
Jungmannova 23. **Map** 3 C5.
☎ *24 94 84 53.*
FAX *26 24 55 55.*

Martin Tours
Štěpánská 61.
Map 5 C1.
☎ *24 21 24 73.*
FAX *24 22 54 37.*

Pragotur
Staroměstské Náměstí 1.
Map 3 B3.
☎ *24 48 25 62.*
FAX *24 48 23 80.*

Prague Information Service – PIS
Na příkopě 20.
Map 3 C4.
☎ *26 40 22.*
Staroměstské náměstí 22.
Map 3 B3.
☎ *24 48 25 62.*

Thomas Cook
Národní 28.
Map 3 B5.
☎ *21 10 53 71.*
FAX *24 94 90 02.*

Personal Security and Health

A T PRESENT PRAGUE suffers from a shortage of police officers. However, compared to many Western cities, Prague is still relatively safe. If you do need help from the police you will find them generally very helpful to the tourist population. If you should need emergency medical care during you stay in Prague, it will be given free. There is also a number of English-speaking services available, including health centres, pharmacies and dentists, as well as US and British information centres.

A Prague police sign

ADVICE FOR VISITORS

P RAGUE IS A SAFE and un-threatening city to walk around. Violent crimes against tourists in the city centre are rare. The main crime problems that affect tourists are petty pilfering from cars, hotels and pockets; violence with robbery is very unusual. Using your common sense should help you to avoid Prague's only real plague – its pickpockets. The crowded summer months are a favourite time for these thieves. Always remember to keep your bag in sight and avoid carrying your passport, wallet and valuables in your back pocket or an open bag. Thieves do tend to operate around the popular sights, such as Charles Bridge, and many use diversionary tactics,

Municipal police badge

State police badge

one knocking into you while the other steals your belongings. It is very unlikely that anything stolen will ever be recovered. Never leave anything of value in your car. Car alarms have proved not to be a deterrent. Try and park your car in an underground car park, especially if you are driving a foreign make. Always take out adequate insurance before visiting Prague, as it is difficult to arrange once there. Report any thefts to the police for future insurance claims. Avoid getting drawn into a street card game known as shells. It is a classic con game. Women may encounter a few stares and comments, but this is about as far as sexual harassment will go. However, one place to try and avoid at night if you are a woman

alone, is Wenceslas Square. Most men will assume you are one of the city's growing band of prostitutes. Prostitution is rife and has increased considerably since 1989. Although it is illegal, the police tend to turn a blind eye. A growing practice among many of the city's prostitutes is to drug their client's drink and then steal everything he has on him.

It is an unwritten law that you should carry your passport at all times and although you are unlikely to be asked to produce it, having it could save a lot of problems. Before you travel take photocopies of all essential documents as replacing them can be difficult and time-consuming.

THE POLICE AND SECURITY SERVICES

I N PRAGUE you will come across several kinds of policemen and women and members of various security services. Report any problems to a uniformed state police officer at a police station. The main stations are marked on the Street Finder maps (see pp238–45). The state police carry guns and can arrest a suspect. They patrol the streets on foot or drive green and white patrol cars. The municipal police are the other main security force, have greater powers, and are divided into different sections.

Traffic police ensure the smooth running of traffic and regulate parking, speeding and drink driving. Fines for illegal parking and speeding are huge. It is illegal to drive with any alcohol in your bloodstream. Occasionally the police have a clamp down on drink driving and if you are caught, the penalties are

A male state police officer

A municipal police officer

A female state police officer

A "black sheriff"

State police patrol car

Prague ambulance

severe. The traffic police are also responsible for car clamping and collecting the fines *(see pp232–3)*. Finally, if you have a traffic accident, you must immediately ring **Road Accidents**. It is against the law to move anything before the police get there.

There are also a number of private security guards. These are often called "black sheriffs" (many of them actually wear black uniforms) and tend to guard banks and be used as security at football matches and so on. They are also armed but should only use their guns in self-defence. Many are also former members of the hated Communist secret service and most Czechs try to steer clear of them; it is strongly advised that you do too.

Pharmacy sign

HEALTH CARE

Health care in Prague is divided into state and private care. If you need emergency treatment it will be provided free of charge. But all non-essential treatment has to be paid for there and then. So make sure you have adequate medical insurance before you arrive in Prague and a credit card or

enough traveller's cheques to pay – don't forget the receipt for your insurance claim.

Your hotel should be able to put you in touch with a local doctor, but if you need more prompt service, Prague's emergency services are on call 24 hours a day and you can call an ambulance if necessary. Hospitals with casualty units are marked on the Street Finder maps *(see pp238–45)*.

There are also 24-hour pharmacies (lékárna) *(see p209)* and a **First Aid/ Emergency Dental Care Centre** giving advice and simple remedies. If you want an English-speaking doctor, visit **Fakultní Poliklinika** in the New Town, or else go to the **Diplomatic Health Centre** for foreigners at Na Homolce. You will need to take a passport and a means of payment if you use these.

Those with respiratory problems should be aware that between October and March, sulphur dioxide levels in Prague regularly exceed the World Health Organization's accepted levels – often by up to three times. With increasing car ownership and a lack of money for alternative fuels, this seems unlikely to decrease in the near future.

DIRECTORY

EMERGENCY NUMBERS

Ambulance
Rychlá lékařská pomoc
(155.

Police
Tísňové volání policie
(158.

Fire
Tísňové volání hasičů
(150.

MEDICAL CENTRES

Diplomatic Health Centre
Nemocnice Na Homolce
Roentgenova 2.
(52 92 21 46.

Fakultní Poliklinika
Karlovo Nám 32. Map 5 B3.
(24 90 41 11.

First Aid/ Emergency Dental Care
První pomoc zubní
Palackého 5. Map 3 C5. *(7am–7pm Mon–Fri, 24hrs Sat, Sun.)*
(24 94 69 81.

First Medical Clinic
Vyšehradská 35. Map 5 B4.
(29 22 86.

24-hour Pharmacy
Štětánikova 6.
(57 32 09 18, 53 70 39.
ᴹ Anděl.

GENERAL HELP

American Cultural Centre
Americké Kulturní středisko
Hybernská 7a. Map 4 D3.
(24 23 10 85/24 21 98 44.

British Council
Britské kulturní oddělení
Národní 10. Map 3 B5.
(21 99 11 11.

Car Breakdown Service
Havarijní služba pro motoristy
(1044.

Lost and Found
Ztráty a nálezy
Karoliny Světlé 5. Map 3 A5.
(24 23 50 85.

Road Accidents
Dopravní nehody
(42 41 41.

Money, Banks and Currency Exchange Offices

A bureau de change sign in Prague

Today Prague is a relatively cheap city to visit. In the past few years, hundreds of banks and bureaux de change have been established, some staying open all night. For the lowest charges and, unfortunately, the longest queues, it is best to change money in a bank. Credit cards are becoming more accepted, but never assume that you can pay with them. Traveller's cheques can only be changed in banks.

BANKING

Hundreds of private banks and bureaux de change have been opened in Prague since 1989. The large, modern banks – generally found outside the city centre – all open between 8am and 5pm Monday to Saturday. The banks may not close at lunch, but many exchange tills do. Lunch hour varies from around 12:30pm to 2:30pm. There are always long queues at the exchange tills so make sure you get there well before closing time. Bureaux de change are found in tiny shops throughout the city. However, despite offering much better exchange rates than the banks, their commission charges are huge, often as high as 12% compared to the bank's 1%. The main advantage of these exchange offices is their convenience. Many are open late every day, some offer a 24-hour service, and queues are rare.

Most of the larger hotels will also change foreign currency for you, but again commission rates may be very high. If you find you have some Czech currency left over from your stay, you can only reconvert your money if you have kept your transaction slips. Komerční bank, located on Na

příkopě, and the airport bank, will reconvert your extra crowns for a small commission. Finally, never change your money on the black market. As well as being illegal the rate is not any higher than banks or exchanges and it is likely you'll be given notes that are not legal tender.

An automatic teller machine for dispensing cash

CREDIT CARDS

Paying by credit card is becoming more popular. Even so, only the larger hotels, restaurants, international car hire agencies and a few of the more expensive tourist shops accept them as a matter of course. The majority of businesses in Prague do not recognize credit cards at all. Even if a shop or restaurant window sports a credit card sign, do not assume they will take them as payment – always ask before you have eaten your meal. The cards most often accepted are: American Express, VISA, Master Card and Access. Most banks will allow cash advances (up to your limit) on your card.

Façade of the Československá Obchodní bank

CASH AND TRAVELLER'S CHEQUES

CURRENCY COMES in Czech crowns and hellers. There are 100 hellers to the crown. It is now legal to bring Czech currency into and out of the Czech Republic. Traveller's cheques are by far the safest alternative to carrying cash. It is best to take well-known brands – American Express, Thomas Cook, for example – although it is unlikely that the major banks will refuse any. Traveller's cheques are not accepted as currency by any shops or restaurants and must be changed at exchanges or banks. Keep receipts if you want to change crowns back to foreign notes. The American Express office *(see p225)* sells and cashes traveller's cheques. They don't charge commission for cashing their own cheques.

Banknotes

Czech banknotes are now in circulation in the denominations Kč20, Kč50, Kč100, Kč200, Kč500, Kč1,000, Kč2,000 and Kč5,000.

Coins

Coins come in the following denominations: 10, 20 and 50 hellers; Kč1, Kč2, Kč5, Kč10, Kč20 and Kč50. All the coins have the Czech emblem, a lion rampant, on one side.

Kč5,000 note

Kč2,000 note

Kč1,000 note

Kč500 note

Kč200 note

Kč100 note

Kč50 note

Kč20 note

10 hellers

20 hellers 50 hellers

1 crown (Kč1)

2 crowns (Kč2)

5 crowns (Kč5)

10 crowns (Kč10)

20 crowns (Kč20)

50 crowns (Kč50)

Telephone and Postal Services

T HE CZECH telephone and postal service, Telecom, has undergone a major modernization programme. Digital phones have replaced the older coin-operated ones, and the postal service has become much more efficient. But there have been a few problems in the transition, and patience is sometimes needed when using the phone.

Old Post Office sign

USING PUBLIC TELEPHONES

A LTHOUGH THERE are a large number of public phones on street corners and near metro stations, there is a high incidence of vandalism. To make sure you have a working phone, it is better to use one in a post office.

International calls can be made more easily from a post office, a private phone or your hotel. At most major post offices you have to leave a deposit, make the call and then pay what you owe to the attendant. In hotels, you can usually get a direct line but commission charges on the call are often exorbitant. Remember also that international calls are extremely expensive, no matter what time of day you phone. But they are at least somewhat cheaper after 7pm, and also on Saturdays and Sundays.

There is an increasing number of modern phonecard telephones in Prague. You can buy the cards (*Telefonní karta*) for these phones from most tabáks and newsstands.

The dialling tone is a short note followed by a long one; the ringing tone consists of long regular notes while the engaged signal has short and rapid notes. Remember that many people in Prague are still connected to a party line and that, because of this, a number can remain engaged for a long time.

PROBLEM NUMBERS

I F YOU HAVE problems getting through to a number in Prague, it is very likely that the number has changed due to the modernization of the phone system. To check, ring the directory and ask for an English speaker.

USING A COIN-OPERATED TELEPHONE

1 Lift the receiver and wait for the dialling tone.

2 Insert either a 1, 2 or 5 crown coin in the slot (the older orange phones only accept Kč1 coins).

3 The digital display shows how much credit is left. If you need to insert more money, the message *Vložte mince* appears.

4 When the words *Volte číslo* come up, dial the number then wait to be connected.

5 When you have finished speaking replace the receiver. Any coins that were unused are returned here. These phones do not give change.

Kč1   Kč2   Kč5

Coins that can be inserted in the newer coin-operated phones

USING A PHONECARD TELEPHONE

1 Lift the receiver and wait for the dialling tone.

2 The message *Vložte telefonní kartu*, asks you to insert your card. The display also shows you how much credit you have left on your phonecard.

3 When the words *Volte číslo* appear, dial the number and wait to be connected.

By pressing this small button on the phone at any time during your call, you can have an English translation of the instructions.

Emergency numbers

4 The card is ejected automatically when it runs out of credit.

100 telefonních jednotek

Telecom phonecards are available at 50, 80, 100 and 150 units

POST OFFICES

THERE ARE A number of post offices in Prague *(see Street Finder on pp238–49).* The best and largest one is the **Main Post Office** in Jindřišská just off Wenceslas Square. It has a huge variety of services and some, such as sending telegrams, operate for 24 hours a day. It also has a large phone room where you can make international calls. This service operates from 7am to 11pm.

This post office has recently undergone a complete refurbishment, and is now astonishingly modern and straightforward to use, with easy-access information in English. Take a ticket when you enter the building and then follow the number on it to the correct booth, which will be indicated by an electronic display.

New Post Office sign

Much to the delight of locals, the former long queues have at last been replaced by swift and efficient service.

USEFUL ADDRESSES

Main Post Office
Jindřišská 14. **Map** 4 D5.
📞 21 13 11 11.
📞 61 00 44 44 (general information).

American Express
Václavské náměstí 56.
Map 4 D5.
📞 24 21 99 92.

DHL
Klimentská 46. **Map** 4 D2.
📞 1030.

REACHING THE RIGHT NUMBER

	Dial
• Internal (Czech) directory enquiries	120
• Prague directory enquiries and the operator	120
• International exchange and to make a collect call *(ask for an English-speaker)*	0132
• Prague from elsewhere in the Czech Republic	02
• International call followed by the country code	00
• International directory enquiries	0149

• **In case of emergencies ring 158**

Tobacconist's, where you can also buy stamps and phonecards

SENDING A LETTER

THE POSTAL SERVICE is now fast, efficient and cheap, although prices for all the post office services are expected to increase slightly in the future.

There is no first or second class mail in the Czech Republic, but the majority of letters usually arrive at their destination within a few days.

If you want to send something more valuable through the post, use the registered mail service, which is reliable and efficient. Aerogrammes abroad do not exist.

Postcards or letters can be posted in the many orange post boxes scattered around Prague. Both take around five working days to arrive in England and about a week to get to America.

Stamps can be bought from post offices, newsagents or tabáks – who will also tell you what stamps you need. All parcels and registered letters need to be handed in at a post office.

For emergency parcels and packages, you can use an international courier service, such as **DHL**.

POSTE RESTANTE

POSTE RESTANTE letters are delivered to the Main Post Office in Jindřišská Street. Go to window 28 (open Monday to Friday 6:30am to 8pm and Saturday 6:30am to 1pm) with your passport or other official identification. The **American Express** office will also hold mail and parcels for up to a month for anyone who is a registered card holder.

Post letters in side flap

Old-style post box attached to a wall

Post your letters in the top flap

Collection times of the mail

One of the new-style post boxes

A selection of stamps for letters and postcards from the Czech Republic

Additional Information

Visitors resting around the Jan Hus Monument in the Old Town Square

DISABLED TRAVELLERS

FACILITIES FOR THE disabled are few and far between. Occasionally you will come across a ramp at the entrance to a building to allow the disabled easier access, but this is the exception rather than the rule. There are few organizations that campaign for the disabled and those that do are hampered by public inertia and a lack of money. But these attitudes are slowly changing and, although transport around the city is a major problem, groups do now exist who can help you with advice, sightseeing tours, accommodation and getting around the city. Two of the best organizations to contact are: the **Czech Association of Persons with Disabilities** and the **Prague Wheelchair Association**.

Czech Association of Persons with Disabilities

Karlínské náměstí 12.
Map 5 B2.
(24 81 69 76/24 81 59 15.

Prague Wheelchair Association

Benediktská 6.
Map 4 D3.
(24 82 72 10/24 82 60 78.

CUSTOMS REGULATIONS AND IMMIGRATION

A VALID PASSPORT is needed when entering the Czech Republic. British nationals must

International Student Identity Card

have a ten-year passport – a visitor's passport is not valid – but visas are not needed to enter. At present, New Zealand, Canadian, and Australian passport holders still need visas. These are valid for a month and can be obtained from your nearest Czech embassy or consulate before you travel. When you apply for your visa, your passport has to be be valid for at least eight more months.

When you arrive at the airport, customs allowances per person are 2 litres (3.6 pints) of wine, 1 litre (1.8 pints) of spirits, 250 cigarettes or equivalent tobacco products. Goods under Kč3,000 in value can be imported duty-free.

You can take in as much foreign currency as you like. But if you want to reconvert Czech crowns into your own currency you have to produce legal cash-transaction slips. It is against the law to take any Czech currency worth above Kč100 out of the country. If

you want to export authentic antiques you will have to obtain a special licence (*see Shopping pp206–7*).

STUDENT INFORMATION

IF YOU ARE ENTITLED to an International Student Identity Card (ISIC), it is worth getting one before travelling to Prague. Admission charges into most of Prague's major tourist sights are cheaper on production of a valid ISIC card. Students can also get cheaper coach travel, and while in the country, train travel. There are a couple of youth hostels in the centre of the city (*see Where to Stay, pp182–9*). For further up-to-date information about what is available contact the tour operator **Universitas Tour**, which arranges accommodation, food, sports and cultural facilities.

Universitas Tours

Jednota Youth Hostel,
Opletalova 38. **Map** 4 D5.
(26 04 26. **FAX** 24 21 22 90.

NEWSPAPERS, TV, RADIO

PRAGUE HAS A number of newspapers including two weekly English-language ones, *The Prague Post* and *Prague Business Post*. They are both well produced and

The two English-language newspapers published in Prague

provide useful tips for visitors to the city as well as up-to-date and informative pieces on Prague, its people and politics. The former includes a good leisure supplement, *Night and Day*.

Most of the newsstands that are around Wenceslas Square and other popular tourist spots sell the main European papers and the *International Herald Tribune*. These are usually a day old – with the exception of *The Guardian*, whose European edition is actually published in Germany.

There is a larger choice of television in Prague than ever before. Western films are

A two-prong and a three-prong plug adaptor for use in Prague

interspersed with well-made nature programmes and classic Czech films. The stations also show a few soap operas, like *Dallas*.

CNN, the US news channel, broadcasts weekdays on CT3 from 11:30pm to 9:55am and 12:30pm to 4pm. However, schedules are liable to change.

You can listen to the BBC World Service on 101.1FM, but one of the most popular radio stations is Europe II on 88.2MHz playing a blend of mainstream pop. Club VOA on 106.2FM has a similar mix of music with English news. Others include, Radio I on 91.9MHz, Radio Golem on 90.3MHz and Radio Bonton on 99.7MHz. Reception can be very bad outside the city. You can also listen to the BBC on the internet at
W www.bbc.co.uk/

CONVERSION CHART

Imperial to Metric
1 inch = 2.54 centimetres
1 foot = 30 centimetres
1 mile = 1.6 kilometres
1 ounce = 28 grams
1 pound = 454 grams
1 pint = 0.6 litre
1 gallon = 4.6 litres

Metric to Imperial
1 millimetre = 0.04 inch
1 centimetre = 0.4 inch
1 metre = 3 feet 3 inches
1 kilometre = 0.6 mile
1 gram = 0.04 ounce
1 kilogram = 2.2 pounds
1 litre = 1.8 pints

ELECTRICAL ADAPTORS

THE ELECTRICITY SUPPLY in Prague is 220V AC and two-pin plugs are used. For British or US plugs, an adaptor is needed. This will have to be bought before leaving home.

PRAGUE TIME

PRAGUE IS ON Central European time – Greenwich Mean Time (GMT) plus 1 hour. From the end of March until the end of September, summer time is in effect – this is GMT plus 2 hours.

RELIGIOUS SERVICES

Anglican
St. Clement's; Klimentská 18.
Map 4 D2. (231 00 94 .
11am Sun.

Baptist
Baptist Church of Prague;
Vinohradská 68. **Map** 6 F1.
(24 25 46 46. 11am Sun.

Hussite Church
Church of St. Nicholas;
Staroměstské náměstí.
Map 3 C3. (23 22 589.
10:30am Sun.

Interdenominational
International Church;
Peroutkova 57.
(33 32 56 91.
10:30am daily (in English).

Jewish
Old-New Synagogue *(see pp88–9)*.
Jerusalem Synagogue;
Jeruzalémská 7. **Map** 4 E4.
(in Czech) 8:45am Sat,
sundown Fri.

Methodist-Evangelical
Ječná 19. **Map** 5 C2.
(57 53 00 20.
3pm Sun.

Roman Catholic
Services are held in many
churches. Some are:
Dominican Priory; Husova 8.
Map 3 B4.
(24 22 02 35, 24 21 84 39.
7am, 6:30pm daily; 8:30,
10:30am, noon, 6:30pm Sun.

Church of St. Joseph; Josefská 8.
Map 2 E3.
(57 31 52 42.
11am Sun.

A Roman Catholic service

GETTING TO PRAGUE

PRAGUE IS LOCATED at the heart of Europe and – apart from the Czech Republic's lack of motorways – has good transport connections with the rest of the continent. There are direct flights every day from most of Europe's major cities and, via ČSA, from Newark, in the USA. However, there are no direct flights from Australia. International coach transport is efficient and cheap. But the journey is about 20 hours from London compared to an hour and a half by air. International rail transport is a popular method of travelling to Prague, but trains tend to get booked up early, especially in the summer. The main train station (Hlavní nádraží) is close to Wenceslas Square and the city centre and, except for the airport, other major points of arrival are also fairly central.

ČSA aircraft

AIR TRAVEL

THERE ARE 40 international airlines which now fly to Prague airport. If you are flying from the United States, **Delta Air** operate scheduled flights from the east coast of America. But these are not direct flights – there is a stopover in Frankfurt. There are no Australian or New Zealand carriers flying to Prague, although you can fly **British Airways** with a stop in London. Other airlines include **Air France**, **KLM**, **Air Canada** and **Czechoslovak Airlines (ČSA)**. It takes about one and a half hours to fly from London to Prague and about nine hours from the east coast of America – not including the stopover.

DISCOUNT FARES

BECAUSE OF the increasing popularity of Prague as a tourist destination, many new airlines are starting to fly to the city. Increased competition has led to a significant drop in the price of flights.

Charter flights have been introduced by a few agents. They are set to become more popular and it is well worth investigating their availability. Remember that these can be subject to last-minute changes and cancellations. Check the ads in the travel sections of major papers for special fares.

APEX (advanced purchase) tickets can be good buys, but they have stringent conditions attached to them. These include having to book your ticket at least a month in advance and severe penalties if you cancel your flight.

If you ring well in advance, airlines will quote you the standard fare, but the price may be lowered nearer the time if seats remain unsold – this is rarely the case in the summer months. Students, senior citizens and regular business travellers may all be able to get discounts. Children under two (who do not occupy a separate seat) pay 10% of the adult fare. Remember fares are more expensive in July and August. If you do manage to get a cheaper deal, ensure that you will get a refund if your agent goes out of business.

Porters at Ruzyně

AIRLINE OFFICES

Air Canada
Revoluční 17. **Map** 4 D3.
☎ 24 89 27 32, 24 89 27 37.

Air France
Václavské náměstí 10. **Map** 3 C5.
☎ 24 22 71 64.

British Airways
Ovocný Trh 8. **Map** 3 C3.
☎ 22 11 44 44.

Czechoslovak Airlines (ČSA)
Na Celní 5, Prague 1.
☎ 20 10 41 11.

Delta Airlines
Národní 32. **Map** 3 B5.
☎ 24 94 67 33.

KLM
Na Příkopě 13. **Map** 3 C4.
☎ 24 21 69 50.

Lufthansa
Pařížská 28. **Map** 3 B3.
☎ 24 81 10 07.

The recently modernized interior of Ruzyně Airport

RUZYNĚ AIRPORT

PRAGUE'S ONLY international airport, Ruzyně, is 15 km (9 miles) northwest of the city centre. Although small, the airport is modern, clean, efficient and functional. Built in 1936, it was modernized during the 1960s and now boasts all the facilities you would expect from an international airport: 24-hour exchange facilities; car rental offices; a small duty-free shop; restaurants; post office and a left-luggage office.

The airport was bought by Air France in 1992 and is presently undergoing further

The airport forecourt, where buses and taxis pull up

modernization, including the addition of a business class lounge. Other changes include a newly opened catering facility. The quality of the

Sign for passport control

food at the airport's restaurants and of the in-flight food on ČSA airlines has improved dramatically – a trained French chef has now been employed to oversee all the preparation of both the traditional Czech and international dishes.

TRANSPORT FROM THE AIRPORT TO THE CITY

THE AIRPORT is linked to the city centre by a regular, efficient bus service run by ČSA. The buses leave from immediately outside the arrivals building. A timetable is available from the airport information office, listing hourly departures, but buses usually leave every half hour, departures often connecting with an incoming flight. You pay the driver on board in crowns and after a 30-minute journey arrive at the ČSA Vltava

Airport bus stop (letiště means airport)

Two of the car rental agencies at Ruzyně airport

terminal in Revoluční Street (see Street Finder, map 4). There is also a bus, No. 119, which is cheap, but takes longer to get to the city as it stops more frequently and terminates further out at Dejvická metro station (see inside back cover). Buy your ticket in advance from the machine in the Arrivals area. You can also take a taxi; the rank is in front of the terminal. Ask at the information booth how much you should expect to pay to the city and use it as a guide.

PRAGUE'S EUROPEAN AIR CONNECTIONS

Prague, situated at the centre of Europe, has good flight connections to most major European cities. It can be reached in less than two and a half hours on direct flights from all the airports marked on the map.

Helsinki
Stockholm
St Petersburg
Moscow
Riga
Manchester
Copenhagen
Hamburg
Amsterdam
Berlin
Hanover
Warsaw
London
Düsseldorf
Brussels
Frankfurt
PRAGUE
Ostrava
Kiev
Paris
Stuttgart
Munich
Brno
Tatry
Košice
Zurich
Vienna
Bratislava
Geneva
Budapest
Milan
Zagreb
Bucharest
Madrid
Barcelona
Rome
Sofia
Istanbul
Athens

The spacious interior of the railway station, Masarykovo Nádraži

TRAVELLING BY TRAIN

PRAGUE IS CONNECTED by rail to all the major capitals of Europe. Rail travel can be an enjoyable, if rather slow, way to travel to and from Prague. International trains have dining cars and couchettes, and tickets are cheaper than air fares. The railways in the Czech Republic are run by the State (České Dráhy – ČD).

The façade of Hlavní nádraží

There are information offices at stations, but they may not have English speakers. PIS and Čedok (see p219), will help you with timetables and prices. There are two types of train run by ČSD. The fastest ones are the rychlík (express) trains. These stop at the major towns and you have to pay a small supplement to travel on them. The very slow trains are Osobní (passenger trains). These stop at every station and often travel as slowly as 30 km/h (20 mph). International trains are the fastest, but get delayed at borders. Tickets can

be bought at stations in advance or on the day, but trains tend to get booked up. If you do want to buy a ticket just before your train leaves, be warned that queues at ticket booths can be very long. When you buy your ticket, specify exactly where and when you want to go, whether you want a single or return and what class of ticket you want. First class carriages exist on all trains and guarantee you a seat. In the time-table, an 'R' in a box by a train number means you must have a seat reserved on that train. An 'R' without a box means a reservation is recommended. If you are caught in the wrong carriage, you have to pay an on-the-spot fine.

TRAIN STATIONS

THE BIGGEST and busiest railway station in Prague is Hlavní nádraží (see p34) which is only a five-minute walk from the city centre. In the 1970s, the original Art Nouveau structure was enlarged and a modern departure hall now dominates the whole terminal. The station is large, efficient and clean with a good-sized, inexpensive, 24-hr left-luggage office in the basement.

The nearby luggage lockers are convenient and very cheap but are often broken into. There are also food stalls, bureaux de change and a number of booking and information services in the departure hall.

The other rail stations in the city are Masarykovo nádraží – Prague's oldest terminal, the newly-built and modern Holešovice Station and the smallest, Smíchov Station.

TRAVELLING BY COACH

COACH CONNECTIONS from Prague to many of the major European cities can be infrequent and are often very booked up. However, many of these coach routes are much cheaper, and often faster, than the slower trains. The city's main bus terminal is Florenc, situated on the eastern edge of the New Town. The majority of long-haul, internal coach routes are still run by the large State bus company (Česko-slovenská státní automobilová doprava – ČSAD). During the summer months there are hundreds of coach trips to all the major coastal resorts in southern Europe. These get booked up quickly by Czechs, so buy your ticket in advance and be sure to reserve yourself a seat. International bus timetables are confusing; check with PIS (see p218) for more detailed information. Coach travel is cheap, but long-haul journeys can be uncomfortable and are slower than train or air.

A uniformed ČSD railway porter

Passengers boarding a long-haul coach

PRAGUE'S MAJOR RAIL AND COACH STATIONS

The major points of arrival by train and coach are all fairly central and easily accessible by metro – the nearest metro to each terminal is shown in the boxes along with more detailed travel information.

KEY

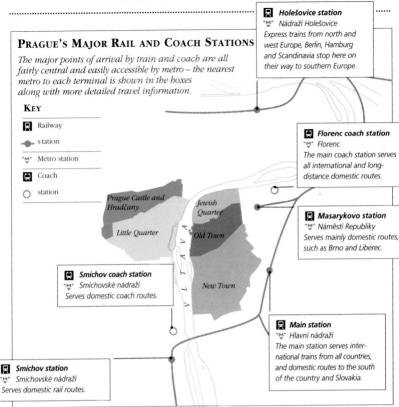

🚆 Railway
— station
Ⓜ Metro station
🚌 Coach
○ station

🚆 Holešovice station
Ⓜ *Nádraží Holešovice*
Express trains from north and west Europe, Berlin, Hamburg and Scandinavia stop here on their way to southern Europe.

🚌 Florenc coach station
Ⓜ *Florenc*
The main coach station serves all international and long-distance domestic routes.

🚆 Masarykovo station
Ⓜ *Náměstí Republiky*
Serves mainly domestic routes, such as Brno and Liberec.

Prague Castle and Hradčany
Jewish Quarter
Little Quarter
Old Town
New Town

VLTAVA

🚌 Smíchov coach station
Ⓜ *Smíchovské nádraží*
Serves domestic coach routes.

🚆 Main station
Ⓜ *Hlavní nádraží*
The main station serves international trains from all countries, and domestic routes to the south of the country and Slovakia.

🚆 Smíchov station
Ⓜ *Smíchovské nádraží*
Serves domestic rail routes.

A Czech motorway sign

TRAVELLING BY CAR

To DRIVE A CAR in the Czech Republic you must be at least 18. Most foreign driving licences are honoured; these include all Canadian, US and EC ones – New Zealand and Australian drivers should get an International Driving Licence. If you bring your own car to Prague, there are a few things which by law you must carry with you at all times. The documents needed are: a valid driver's licence, vehicle registration card, a hire certificate or, if you are borrowing the car, a letter signed by the owner and authorized by a recognized body, such as the AA or RAC, giving you permission to drive it and a Green Card (an international motoring certificate for insurance). Other items you have to carry at all times are a set of replacement bulbs, red warning triangles and a first-aid kit. You also have to display a national identification sticker. It is compulsory to wear seatbelts if fitted, and children under 12 are not allowed to travel in the front seat. When you are driving it is strictly forbidden to have any alcohol in your blood – penalties are severe if you are caught drink driving. There are few motorways in the Czech Republic, although there are good connections to Bratislava and Brno, and more major routes are currently under construction.

Road signs are clear and easy to follow. The speed limit on motorways is 130 km/h (81 mph); on dual and single carriageways 90 km/h (56 mph) and in urban areas 50 km/h (31 mph). The traffic police patrolling the roads are very vigilant, and any infringements are dealt with harshly – expensive cars from abroad are an obvious target (foreigners have to pay any fines immediately). There are also occasional road blocks to catch drunken drivers.

The popular, Czech-made Skoda car

GETTING AROUND PRAGUE

THE CENTRE OF PRAGUE is conveniently small and most of the sights can be reached comfortably on foot. But to cross the city quickly or visit a more remote sight, the public transport is efficient, clean and cheap. It is based on trams, buses and the underground (metro) system, all of which are run by the Prague Transport Corporation (Dopravní-podnik). Throughout this guide, the best method of transport

Walking around the city

is given for each sight. The metro and trams serve the city centre, while buses are used to reach the suburbs. The entire system is simple to use – only one ticket is needed for all three forms of transport. Bus, tram and metro routes are found on city maps, available at most city centre tabáks, bookshops and newsagents; or refer to the map on the inside back cover of this guide.

DRIVING A CAR

MOST VISITORS ARE better off not driving around the centre of Prague. The city's complex web of one-way streets, the large number of pedestrianized areas around the historic core of the city and a very severe shortage of parking spaces make driving very difficult. Prague's public transport system is a much more efficient way of travelling around the city centre.

If you do decide to use a car, remember that on-the-spot fines for traffic violations are common, especially if you are caught driving in one of the city's restricted areas, such as Wenceslas Square. Prague's motorists have become less disciplined and caution is often needed, You must drive on the right and the law states that both driver and front- and back-seat passengers should wear seat belts, if they are fitted. The speed limit in the city is 50 km/h (31 mph) unless a sign indicates otherwise. Traffic signs are similar

One-way traffic and No stopping except for supply lorries

to those in Western Europe. Cars can be useful for seeing sights outside the city. But car rental is expensive and public transport is almost as efficient getting out of the city as in it (see pp228–31).

PARKING

CAR PARKING SPACES in the city centre are scarce and the penalties for illegal parking, harsh. Many parking areas are restricted and the only places to park legally on

Pedestrian zone

PRAGUE ON FOOT

Walking around Prague is the most enjoyable way to see the city. But it can also be rather hazardous: it is well known that the only drivers to stop for people at pedestrian crossings are foreigners. Some crossings are controlled by traffic lights, but be sure to cross only when the green man is flashing and even then, check the road carefully. Those crossings without lights are largely ignored by drivers. Remember that trams run in the centre of the road and go in both directions, which can be confusing. They also travel at high speeds, occasionally coming upon you unawares. With the uneven cobbled streets, steep hills and a mass of tram lines, flat comfortable shoes are strongly recommended.

Pedestrian crossing

Street or square name and Prague district

Street number **City registration number**

Pedestrian traffic lights in Prague

the street are in front of the New Town Hall in Karlovo náměstí, in Na Florenci and at Hlavní station. Unfortunately, car theft is rife, and expensive Western cars are a favourite target. It is safer to park in an official – preferably underground – car park *(see the Street Finder pp244–9)*. But these are expensive and tend to get full early on in the morning. Many parking spaces are reserved for office workers and disabled drivers. Parking at central hotels is limited, with only a few spaces allocated. It is better to park at one of the guarded car parks at the edge of the city and use public transport. Parking meters are rare in Prague but traffic wardens are not.

Parking sign

TOWING AND CLAMPING

MANY PRAGUE LOCALS park on the pavement. But ignoring *No Parking* signs may well mean that you find your car has been towed away or clamped. Both the municipal and the private firms that patrol the city are vigilant and ruthless with illegally parked cars, especially with foreign cars. If your car has disappeared, ring 158 to find out if it has been towed away or stolen. To reclaim your towed-away car, you have to go to one of the parking lots (the police will tell you which one) and pay a hefty fine before the car is released. Wheel clamping is becoming very

Prague's colourful clamp, also known as the Denver Boot

popular. You must pay a fine of several hundred crowns at a police station (the ticket on your windscreen will tell you the address) and return to your car to wait for the clamp to be removed.

THE TRANSPORT SYSTEM

The best and quickest way to get around the city centre is by metro or tram. Prague's rush hours are between 6am and 8am and 3pm and 5pm, Monday to Friday. But more trains, trams and buses run at these times, so crowding is not a problem. Some bus routes to the suburbs only run during these peak hours. From 1 July to 31 August a summer timetable operates and the entire transport system is reduced.

There is a Transport Information Office at Muzeum metro (7am–9pm Mon–Fri); English is spoken.

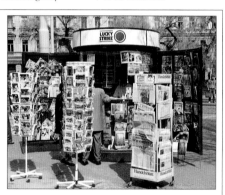

One of the many newsstands in Wenceslas Square

TICKETS

Paying on the transport system relies on the honour system, with periodic checks by plain-clothes ticket inspectors who levy an on-the-spot and large fine if you don't have a valid ticket. There is one ticket for use on the entire system – bus, tram and metro.

Buy the ticket before you travel and stamp or punch it yourself in the machines provided, or you will be travelling illegally. You can buy single ride tickets, from tabák stores and metro stations. There are automatic ticket machines in the metros *(see p234)*. Charges vary according to type of journey: up to 15 minutes with no changes (or 30 minutes and four stops on the metro), or up to 60 minutes with the possibility of changing your route. Children under six travel free and 6- to 15-year-olds travel half price. You can also buy network tickets *(síťová jízdenka)*. These offer unlimited rides on buses, trams and metro for periods ranging from 24 hours to 30 days.

Short-term network tickets, for unlimited travel within the city

Adult single tickets, priced by type and length of journey

Travelling by Metro

T HE UNDERGROUND RAILWAY, known as the metro, is the
quickest, most comfortable and widely used form
of transport in Prague. Managed by the Prague Transport
Corporation (see p232), its construction began in 1967.
It has three lines, A, B and C, three junctions and 50
stations. The straightforward layout and clear signs make
finding your way around the system very easy.

The metro sign for
Mùstek metro station

FINDING YOUR WAY
AROUND THE METRO

M ETRO ENTRANCES are not
always easy to spot.
Look for a sign displaying
the 'M' within an upside-
down triangle (see right).
The street entrance will
normally lead you down a
flight of steps. A high-
pitched bleep (for the blind)
at some entrances can also
help to guide you.

Once you have purchased
your ticket and passed
through the unmanned ticket
barriers, continue down the
fast-moving escalators to the
trains. At the bottom of each
escalator is a long central
corridor with a platform on
either side for trains
travelling in either direction.
Signs suspended from the
ceiling indicate the direction
of the trains (see opposite
page). The edges of the

platforms are marked with a
white, broken line which
should not be crossed until
the train stops. The metro
doors open and close automatically, giving a recorded
message when they are
about to close. During the
journey the name of the next
station is announced in
Czech.
  Maps of the underground
system can be found above
each metro door.
  Line A is the most useful
for tourists, because it covers
all the main areas of the city
centre – Prague Castle, the
Little Quarter, the Old Town
and the New Town – as well
as the main shopping area
around Wenceslas Square.
  Displayed above some
seats are disabled signs.
These seats should be given
up for the elderly, disabled,
and those with small
children.

The spacious interior of Mùstek metro station

AUTOMATIC
TICKET MACHINES

You can buy transport
tickets at designated
ticket sellers (see p233)
or at the automatic
ticket machines in the
metro station. The ticket
machines, and tickets
themselves, may vary in
design and colour, but
they are still applicable
to all forms of transport.
The machine offers a
choice of tickets at
varying prices, for adults,
children, bicycles and
other bulky items. Once
it has been validated, a
single-journey ticket is
valid for an hour.

1 Check which
price band is the
right one to meet
your requirements,
then press the
appropriately
labelled button.

3 If you are happy
that you have
selected the right
type of ticket, then
press the výdej
button to confirm
your choice. (If you
are unsure, press the
button labelled
storno and start the
process again.)

2 The visual display
unit confirms which
type of ticket you are
in the process of
selecting.

4 When you have
confirmed your
choice of ticket, insert
coins into this slot. Most
machines give change.

5 Collect your ticket,
and any change that
may be due to you, from
the large slot at the base
of the machine.

MAKING A JOURNEY BY METRO

1 The letters, each in a different colour, indicate the three metro lines. The number above the letter is the time it takes to get from one end of the line to the other.

This metro map can be bought from most metro stations, tabáks and news-agents. A metro map has also been included at the end of this book.

2 To decide which line to take, find your destination on the *Street Finder (see pp244–9)*, its nearest metro station and then plot your route on a metro map.

The central corridor with platforms either side and signs indicating the direction of trains

3 You can use single-journey tickets *(left)*, or a network ticket *(below)* which give you unlimited travel for a set period of time, and are also valid for buses and trams *(see p233)*. Generally, a child's ticket costs half that of an adult's.

5 This sign, hanging from the ceiling, is visible when you come down the escalator. It shows the direction of the trains on each platform. This one says that the train's final station *(Stanice)* on the left is Nové Butovice, so from the metro map you know the train is travelling west.

4 Before going down the escalators, you must stamp a single-journey ticket in one of these machines. If the ticket has not been stamped, it is not valid and you will have to pay a fine if caught. Do not stamp tourist tickets.

"Stanice" means station

"Směr" means direction

Name of station

6 This sign along the central platform indicates the station on line A where you are (white circle) and those stations where you can transfer to the other lines (C and B). For stations to the left of the white circle follow the arrow to the left, and vice-versa for stations to the right.

The white circle indicates which station you are in

7 Once you are at your stop, follow the exit signs *(Výstup)* leading out of the metro system.

Travelling by Tram

Trams are Prague's oldest method of public transport. Horse-drawn trams appeared on the streets in 1879, but by 1891 the first electric tram was in operation. After the metro, the tram system is the fastest and most efficient way of getting around the city. Some lines only operate in the rush hour and there are a number of night trams, all of which pass by Lazarská in the New Town.

TRAM TICKETS

The tram system is run by the Prague Transport Corporation (see p230). Tram tickets are also valid for the metro and buses (see p233).

You have to buy your ticket before you board a tram. Once you have entered, you will see two or three small punching machines on metal poles just inside the door. Insert your ticket and it will be stamped automatically.

If you do not punch your ticket it is not valid and, if you are caught by a ticket inspector, you will have to pay an on-the-spot fine (see p233). A single-journey ticket is valid for one journey only (see p233), however long.

At every tram stop there is a timetable – the stop underlined is where you are standing. All the stops below that line indicate where that tram is heading.

Trams run every 10 to 20 minutes. The doors open and close automatically and each stop is announced by a recorded message in Czech. After the metro closes, a small number of night trams run every 40 minutes or so. These trams (numbers 51 to 58) are marked by blue numbers at the tram stop.

Tram Signs
These are found at every tram stop and tell you which trams stop there, and in what direction each tram is going.

Tram logo

ANDĚL

Name of the tram stop

The direction each tram is heading in

Numbers indicate which trams stop here

One of the new trams on the streets of Prague

USEFUL TRAM ROUTES

These three tram routes are the most useful for getting around the centre of Prague. They pass many of the major sights on both sides of the Vltava, so are also a cheap, pleasant way of sightseeing.

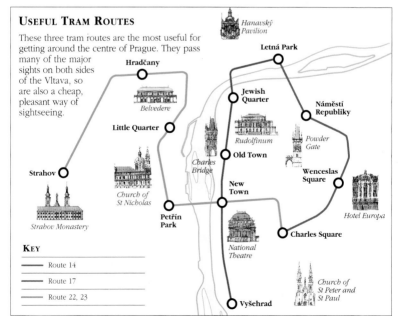

Hanavský Pavilion

Letná Park

Hradčany

Belvedere

Jewish Quarter

Náměstí Republiky

Little Quarter

Rudolfinum

Powder Gate

Strahov

Charles Bridge

Old Town

Wenceslas Square

Church of St Nicholas

New Town

Hotel Europa

Strahov Monastery

Petřín Park

Charles Square

National Theatre

Church of St Peter and St Paul

Vyšehrad

KEY

— Route 14
— Route 17
— Route 22, 23

Travelling by Bus

YOU ARE UNLIKELY to use a bus unless you want to visit the outer suburbs. By law, buses are not allowed in the city centre (they produce noxious fumes and the streets are too narrow), so they transport people from the suburbs to tram and metro stops outside the centre.

Bus stop logo

BUS TICKETS

A typical public bus in Prague

AS WITH THE TRAM, you must always buy a ticket before you board a bus. Tickets are available from all the usual agents (see p233). Once

again, you must validate your ticket in the punching machine on the bus. If you buy a single-journey ticket, it is only valid for one journey. Each time you change bus, you will have to buy a new ticket, unless you have a tourist ticket (see p233). The doors open and close automatically and the end of the boarding period is signalled by an irritating high-pitched signal. You are expected to give up your seat for the elderly and disabled.

Bus timetables are located at every stop. They have the numbers of all the buses that stop there and the timetable for each route. Unlike in most other capitals, buses nearly always run on time. The frequency varies considerably. In the rush hour there may be 12 to 15 buses an hour, at other times as few as three.

Throughout the night there are 12 buses which go to the outer areas not served by the tram and metro system.

Travelling by Taxi

FOR VISITORS TO PRAGUE taxis are a useful but often frustrating form of transport. Until 1989 all taxis belonged to the Prague Transport Corporation but they are now all privately owned and run. Unfortunately there are more and more unscrupulous taxi drivers who are out to charge as much as they can get away with, so it's worth taking a few simple precautions.

An illuminated taxi sign

TAXI FARES

One of the many taxi ranks in the centre of the town

AS SOON AS you enter a taxi there is a minimum charge. After that, by law the fare should increase at a set rate per kilometre. However, this set charge is rarely, if ever, adhered to and taxis can be a very expensive way of getting around the city. Taxi meters can be set at four different rates but for journeys in the city it should be set at one (the cheapest). However, rather than depend on the meters –

they are often rigged – it is a wise move to negotiate a fare you think is reasonable before you enter the cab. Vigorous bargaining can often bring the price down. Few taxi drivers speak more than the most rudimentary English, so communication can be difficult. Unless your Czech pronunciation is good, write down your destination for them in Czech. At night, charges will increase, sometimes by 200 or even 300 per

Taxi receipts, if requested, are required to be given by law.

The distance travelled	Amount charged

cent. Be sure surcharges are included in the figure you negotiate beforehand. If problems do arise at the end of the journey, ask for a receipt before you pay. This will normally deter drivers from trying to overcharge you. Avoid taxis around the main tourist sights, these can often be the worst offenders. Despite occasional problems, taxis are a safe form of transport and women should feel comfortable alone in them.

The meter displays your fare and surcharges.

Fare	Surcharges	Rate

STREET FINDER

THE MAP REFERENCES given for all the sights, hotels, restaurants, bars, shops and entertainment venues described in this book refer to the maps in this section. A complete index of street names and all the places of interest marked, can be found on the following pages. The key map (right) shows the area of Prague covered by the *Street Finder*. This map includes sightseeing areas, as well as districts for hotels, restaurants, pubs and entertainment venues.

In keeping with Czech maps, none of the street names in the index or on the Street Finder have the Czech word for street, *ulice*, included (though you may see it on the city's street signs). For instance, Celetná ulice appears as Celetná in both the index and the Street Finder. The numbers preceding some street names are dates. In our index we ignore the numbers, so that 17. listopadu (17 November), is listed under 'L'.

KEY TO STREET FINDER	
▢	Major sight
▢	Places of interest
◼	Other building
ᴹ	Metro station
🚆	Train station
🚌	Coach station
🚋	Tram stop
🚞	Funicular railway
⛴	River boat boarding point
🚕	Taxi rank
P	Car park
ℹ	Tourist information office
✚	Hospital with casualty unit
🛡	Police station
✝	Church
✡	Synagogue
⊠	Post office
⚊	Railway line
	One-way street
▪▪	City wall
	Pedestrian street

SCALE OF MAP PAGES

```
0 metres        200
|=========|          1:10,000
0 yards         200
```

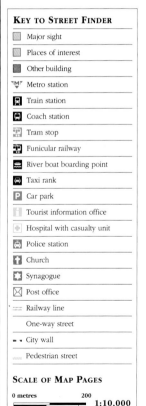

View of the Little Quarter, Hradčany and Prague Castle from the Old Town Bridge Tower

Aerial view of the
Baroque Church of
St Nicholas in the Old
Town Square, from the
tower at the top of the
Old Town Hall

2 **3** **4**

NÁBŘEŽÍ EDVARDA BENEŠE

V L T A V A

DY HORÁKOVÉ

NA FRANTIŠKU

REVOLUČNÍ

*Jewish
Quarter*

DOVA

Karlův most

SMETANOVO NÁBŘEŽÍ

Old Town

WILSONOVA

*Little
Quarter*

NÁRODNÍ

UJEZD

5 **6**

metres 500

ŽITNÁ

ANGLICKÁ

yards 500

SLEZSKÁ

KORUNNÍ

New Town

JEČNÁ

SOKOLSKÁ

LEGEROVA

V L T A V A

RAŠÍNOVO NÁBŘEŽÍ

SVORNOSTI

RADLICKÁ

SVOBODOVA

VNISLAVOVA

SEKANINOVA

JAROMÍROVA

KŘESOMYSLOVA

The imposing twin
towers of the Church of
St Peter and St Paul on
top of Vyšehrad rock

Street Finder Index

THE ORDER OF THE NAMES in the index is affected by the *háček*, the accent like an inverted circumflex (*háček* means "little hook"). In the Czech alphabet, **č**, **ř**, **š** and **ž** are treated as separate letters. Street names beginning with **ř**, for example, are listed after those beginning with **r** without an accent.

Churches, buildings, museums and monuments are marked on the Street Finder maps with their English and Czech names. In the index, both forms are listed. However, English names for streets and squares, such as Wenceslas Square, do not appear on the maps. Where they are listed in the index, the Czech name is given in brackets in the form that appears on the map.

USEFUL WORDS	
dům	house
hrad	castle
kostel	church
klášter	convent, monastery
most	bridge
nábřeží	embankment
nádraží	station
náměstí	square
sady	park
schody	steps
třída	avenue
ulice	street
ulička	lane
zahrada	garden

1

VÁCLAVSKÉ NÁMĚSTÍ

M Muzeum

WASHINGTONOVA

WILSONOVA

Státní opera
State Opera

Národní muzeum
National Museum

ČELAKOVSKÉHO SADY

ČELAKOVSKÉHO SADY

VE SMEČKÁCH

KRAKOVSKÁ

MEZIBRANSKÁ

ŠPANĚLSKÁ

MÁNESOVA

NA SMETANCE

ITALSKÁ

POLSKÁ

RIEGROVY SADY

VINOHRADY

ANNY LETENSKÉ

MÁNESOVA

VINOHRADSKÁ

BLANICKÁ

ŽITNÁ

ANGLICKÁ

SLEZSKÁ

2

SOKOLSKÁ

LEGEROVA

HÁLKOVA

V TŮNÍCH

MIKOVCOVA

VOCELOVA

BĚLEHRADSKÁ

LONDÝNSKÁ

ITALSKÁ

RUBEŠOVA

ŘÍMSKÁ

BALBÍNOVA

SKŘETOVA

P

ŘÍMSKÁ

ŠUBERTOVA

SIBIŘSKÁ

KORUNNÍ

JEČNÁ

MELOUNOVA

NÁMĚSTÍ I. P. PAVLOVA
M I.P. Pavlova

JUGOSLÁVSKÁ

NÁMĚSTÍ MÍRU

Náměstí Míru

M

BLANICKÁ

Muzeum Antonína Dvořáka
Dvořák Museum

LUBLAŇSKÁ

TYLOVO NÁMĚSTÍ

P

RUMUNSKÁ

LONDÝNSKÁ

AMERICKÁ

URUGUAYSKÁ

FRANCOUZSKÁ

VARŠAVSKÁ

3

NA BOJIŠTI

KE KARLOVU

Restaurace U Kalicha
Chalice Restaurant

TYRŠOVA

SOKOLSKÁ

LEGEROVA

KOUBKOVA

FÜGNEROVO NÁMĚSTÍ

LUBLAŇSKÁ

BRUSELSKÁ

BĚLEHRADSKÁ

ŠAFAŘÍKOVA

BELGICKÁ

ZÁHŘEBSKÁ

AMERICKÁ

MASARYKA

MÁCHOVA

KOPERNÍKOVA

APOLINÁŘSKÁ

KE KARLOVU

WENZIGOVA

UZVONAŘKY

JANA

NA KLEOVCE

NAD PETRUSKOU

4

BOŽENY NĚMCOVÉ

POD ZVONAŘKOU

POD NUSELSKÝMI SCHODY

PERUCKÁ

PERUCKÁ

HORSKÁ

POD KARLOVEM

EKANINOVA

OLDŘICHOVA

JAROMÍROVA

Botič

SVATOPLUKOVA

NUSELSKÝ MOST

P

ŠPITÁLNÍHO

SARAJEVSKÁ

REJSKOVA

NA FOLIMANCE

ZÁVIŠOVA

BĚLEHRADSKÁ

NA OSTRŮVKU

5

KŘESOMYSLOVA

Botič

KŘESOMYSLOVA

NÁMĚSTÍ BRATŘÍ SYNKŮ

General Index

Acknowledgments

DORLING KINDERSLEY wishes to thank the following people who contributed to the preparation of this book.

MAIN CONTRIBUTOR

Vladimír Soukup was born in Prague in 1949. He worked for the daily newpaper, *Evening Prague*, for 20 years, eventually becoming Deputy Chief Editor. He has written a wide range of popular guides to Prague.

ADDITIONAL CONTRIBUTORS

Ben Sullivan, Lynn Reich.

EDITORIAL AND DESIGN

MANAGING EDITOR Carolyn Ryden; MANAGING ART EDITOR Steve Knowlden; SENIOR EDITOR Georgina Matthews; SENIOR ART EDITOR Vanessa Courtier; EDITORIAL DIRECTOR David Lamb; ART DIRECTOR Anne-Marie Bulat; PRODUCTION CONTROLLER Hilary Stephens; PICTURE RESEARCH Ellen Root; DTP DESIGNER Salim Qurashi; CONSULTANT Helena Svojsikova; MAPS Caroline Bowie, Simon Farbrother, James Mills-Hicks, David Pugh (DKCartography).

Russell Davies, Fay Franklin, Alistair Gunn, Elaine Harries, Charlie Hawkings, Jan Kaplan, Dr Tomáš Kleisner Susannah Marriott, Robert Purnell, Helen Townsend, Daphne Trotter, Christopher Vinz.

ADDITIONAL PHOTOGRAPHY

DK Studio/Steve Gorton, Otto Palan, M Soskova, Clive Streeter, Alan Williams.

t = top; tl = top left; tc = top centre; tr = top right; cla = centre left above; ca = centre above; cra = centre right above; cl = centre left; c = centre; cr = centre right; clb = centre left below; cb = centre below; crb = centre right below; bl = bottom left; b = bottom; bc = bottom centre; br = bottom right; d = detail.

Works of art on the pages detailed have been reproduced with the permission of the following copyright holders: Aristide Maillol *Pomona* 1910 © ADAG, Paris, and DACS, London, 1998: 164cr; Oskar Kokoschka *Charles Bridge and Hradcany* 1935 © DACS 1998: 164bl; Pablo Picasso *Self-Portrait* 1907 © Succession Picasso/DACS 1998: 165tl. Gustav Makarius Tauc (An der Aulenkaut 31, Wiesbaden, Germany) under commission of the Minorite Order in Rome: 35br.

The publishers are grateful to the following individuals, companies and picture libraries for permission to reproduce photographs or to photograph at their establishments:
ARCHEOLOGICKÝ ÚSTAV ČESKÉ AKADEMIE VĚD: 20t; ARCHIV FÜR KUNST UND GESCHICHTE, BERLIN: 17b, 18tl (d), 18tr, 18bc(d), 18br(d), 19tl(d), 19tc(d), 19tr(d), 19c(d), 19bc(d), 20clr, 20bl, 23cb(d), 29cla(d), 32t(d), 32bl, 34ca(d), 35ca(d), 35bl, 43tl, 50b(d), 105cr, 118t, Erich Lessing 28ca(d), 31bl(d), 88c, 89cb, 106c; ARCHÍV HLAVNIHO MESTA. PRAHY (CLAM-GALLASÙV PALÁC): 23cl, 24bl, 28bl, 28br, 30b, 33clb, 33bc, 72t, 136br, 137br(d), 138ca, 168c. BILDARCHIV PREUSSISCHER KULTURBESITZ: 4t(d), 19bl(d), 29br, 34bc, 68tr, 104bl(d); BRIDGEMAN ART LIBRARY, London: Prado, Madrid 29t; Rosegarten Museum, Constance 26ca.
ČESKÁ TISKOVÁ KANCELÁR: 19br, 35cbr, 195cr; ČSA: 228t; JEAN-LOUP CHARMET: 18bl(d), 21c, 31br, 33t, 33tl, 33br(d), 34tr(d), 34bl, 62c, 69tc; ZDENEK CHRAPPEK: 50c; COMSTOCK: Georg Gerster: 10; JOE CORNISH: 58–9, 60, 148br. MARY EVANS PICTURE LIBRARY: 9, 59, 138cb, 181, 217. GRAFOPRINT NEUBERT: 31clb, 38clb, 116c. ROBERT HARDING PICTURE LIBRARY: Michael Jenner 128tl; Christopher Rennie 24ca, 103tr; Peter Scholey 30t, 129tl; HUTCHISON LIBRARY: Libuše Taylor 51b, 52t, 175tl, 197c. THE IMAGE BANK: Andrea Pistolesi 14b; Courtesy of ISIC, UK: 226c.
KANCELÁŘ PREZIDENTA REPUBLIKY: 20–1, 21tr, 21bl, 21br, 22c; KARLŠTEJN: 25tl; Vladimír Hyhlík 24–5, Oldrich Karasek 135b; KAREL KESTNER: 35cbl; KLEMENTINUM: 23tl; Prokop Paul 22t; THE KOBAL COLLECTION: 35tl; DALIBOR KUSÁK: 164bl, 166–7 all, 16–9 all.
IVAN MALÝ: 210t, 211t; MUZEUM HLAVNÍHO MĚSTA PRAHY 32–3; MUZEUM POŠTOVNÍ ZNÁMKY: 149cl; NÁRODNÍ FILMOVÝ ARCHIV: 34br; NÁRODNÍ GALERIE V PRAZE: 24br, 40b; Oto Palen 38 cla; Grafická sbírka 26t, 27bl, 31t, 67b, 69c, 100t, 102b, 121t, 125cb, 129br, 138b, 157cb, 175b, 178b; Klášter sv. Anežky 39tr, 83t, 92–3 all, 133b; Klášter sv. Jiří 16, 37br, 38t, 97br, 106–7 all except 106c, 108–9 all, Šternberský palác 38ca, 112–3 all, 114–5 all, Veletržní Palac 164–5 all; Zbraslav 40b; NÁRODNÍ MUZEUM V PRAZE: Vlasta Dvořáková 20clb, 26–7, 26bl, 26bc, 26br, 27t, 27cl, 27cr, 27br, 29bl, 39cb, 75b, 72b, Jarmila Kutová 20c, 22bl, Dagmar Landová 28bc, 126c, Muzeum Antonína Dvořáka 39b, Muzeum Bedřicha Smetany 32ca, Prokop Paul 75b, Tyršovo muzeum; 34cb, 149bl; NÁRODNÍ TECHNICKÉ MUZEUM: Gabriel Urbánek 41t.
OBRÁZÁRNA PRAŽSKÉHO HRADU: 98b; ÖSTERREICHISCHE NATIONALBIBLIOTHEK, WIEN: 25clb, 26cb. PIVOVARSKÉ MUZEUM: 196tr, 196c; BOHUMÍR PROKÙPEK: 25bl, 30t, 120c, 121c, 121bl, 163b. REX FEATURES LTD: Alfred 35tr, Richard Gardener 232t. SCIENCE PHOTO LIBRARY: Geospace 11, 38crb; SOTHEBY'S/ THAMES AND HUDSON: 104c; STÁTNÍ ÚSTREDNI ARCHIV: 23b; STÁTNÍ ÚSTAV PAMÁTKOVÉ PÉČE: 23tc; STÁTNÍ ŽIDOVSKÉ MUZEUM: 39ca, 85t, 85c, 90t; SVATOVÍTSKÝ POKLAD, PRAŽSKÝ HRAD: 14t, 21tl, 24t, 24cb, 28t, 40tr. UMĚLECKOPRÙMYSLOVÉ MUZEUM V PRAZE: 39tl, 40tl, 149c, 149br, Gabriel Urbánek 28clb, 41b; UNIVERZITA KARLOVA: 25tr. PETER WILSON: 4b, 191t, 216–7, 238. ZEFA: 33cra. Front endpaper: all special or additional photography except (centre) JOE CORNISH.

DORLING KINDERSLEY SPECIAL EDITIONS

Dorling Kindersley books can be purchased in bulk quantities at discounted prices for use in promotions or as premiums. We are also able to offer special editions and personalized jackets, corporate imprints, and excerpts from all of our books, tailored specifically to meet your own needs.

To find out more, please contact:
(in the United Kingdom) – SPECIAL SALES, DORLING KINDERSLEY LIMITED, 9 HENRIETTA STREET, COVENT GARDEN, LONDON WC2E 8PS; TEL. 020 7753 3572;

(in the United States) – SPECIAL MARKETS DEPARTMENT, DORLING KINDERSLEY PUBLISHING, INC., 95 MADISON AVENUE, NEW YORK, NY 10016.

Phrase Book

IN EMERGENCY

Help!	Pomoc!	*po-mots*
Stop!	Zastavte!	*za-stav-te*
Call a	Zavolejte	*za-vo-ley-te*
doctor!	doktora!	*dok-to-ra!*
Call an	Zavolejte	*za-vo-ley-te*
ambulance!	sanitku!	*sa-nit-ku!*
Call the	Zavolejte	*za-vo-ley-te*
police!	policii!	*poli-tsi-yi!*
Call the fire	Zavolejte	*za-vol-ey-te*
brigade!	hasiče	*ba-si-che*
Where is the	Kde je	*gde ye*
telephone?	telefón?	*tele-fohn?*
the nearest	nejbližší	*ney-blish-ee*
hospital?	nemocnice?	*ne-mots-nyitse?*

COMMUNICATION ESSENTIALS

Yes/No	Ano/Ne	*ano/ne*
Please	Prosím	*pro-seem*
Thank you	Děkuji vám	*dye-ku-ji vahm*
Excuse me	Prosím vás	*pro-seem vahs*
Hello	Dobrý den	*do-bree den*
Goodbye	Na shledanou	*na s-ble-da-no*
Good evening	Dobrý večer	*dob-ree vech-er*
morning	ráno	*rah-no*
afternoon	odpoledne	*od-po-led-ne*
evening	večer	*ve-cher*
yesterday	včera	*vche-ra*
today	dnes	*dnes*
tomorrow	zítra	*zeet-ra*
here	tady	*ta-di*
there	tam	*tam*
What?	Co?	*tso?*
When?	Kdy?	*gdi?*
Why?	Proč?	*proch?*
Where?	Kde?	*gde?*

USEFUL PHRASES

How are you?	Jak se máte?	*yak-se mah-te?*
Very well,	Velmi dobře	*vel-mi dob-rzhe*
thank you.	děkuji.	*dye kuyi*
Pleased to meet you.	Těší mě.	*tyesh-ee mye*
See you soon.	Uvidíme se	*u-vi-dyee-me-se-*
	brzy.	*br-zi*
That's fine.	To je v	*to ye vpo-*
	pořádku.	*rzhabdku*
Where is/are...?	Kde je/jsou ...?	*gde ye/yso ...?*
How long does	Jak dlouho to trvá	*yak dlo bo tr-va*
it take to get to..?	se dostat do..?	*se do-stat do...?*
How do I get to...?	Jak se	*yak se*
	dostanu k ..?	*do-sta-nu k ..?*
Do you speak	Mluvíte	*mlu-vee-te*
English?	anglicky?	*an-glits-ki?*
I don't understand.	Nerozumím.	*ne-ro-zu-meem*
Could you speak	Mohl(a)* byste	*mohl- (a) bis-te*
more slowly?	mluvit trochu	*mlu-vit tro-khu*
	pomaleji?	*po-maley?*
Pardon?	Prosím?	*pro-seem?*
I'm lost.	Ztratil(a)*	*stra-tyil (a)*
	jsem se.	*ysem se.*

USEFUL WORDS

big	velký	*vel-kee*
small	malý	*mal-ee*
hot	horký	*bor-kee*
cold	studený	*stu-den-ee*
good	dobrý	*dob-ree*
bad	špatný	*shpat-nee*
well	dobře	*dob-rzhe*
open	otevřeno	*ot-ev-rzhe-no*
closed	zavřeno	*zav-rzhe-no*
left	do leva	*do le-va*
right	do prava	*do pra-va*
straight on	rovně	*rov-nye*
near	blízko	*blee-sko*
far	daleko	*da-le-ko*
up	nahoru	*na-bo-ru*
down	dolů	*do-loo*
early	brzy	*br-zi*
late	pozdě	*poz-dye*
entrance	vchod	*vkbod*
exit	východ	*vee-kbod*
toilets	toalety	*toa-leti*
free, unoccupied	volný	*vol-nee*
free, no charge	zdarma	*zdar-ma*

MAKING A TELEPHONE CALL

I'd like to place a	Chtěl(a)* bych	*khtyel(a) bikh*
long-distance call.	volat	*vo-lat me-zi-*
	meziměstsky.	*mye-stski*
I'd like to make a	Chtěl(a)* bych	*khtyel(a) bikh*
reverse-charge call.	volat na účet	*volat na oo-chet*
	volaného.	*volan-eh-bo*
I'll try again later.	Zkusím to	*skus-eem to*
	pozdějí.	*poz-dyey*
Can I leave	Mohu nechat	*mo-bu ne-kbat*
a message?	zprávu?	*sprab-vu?*
Hold on.	Počkejte.	*poch-key-te*
Could you speak	Mohl(a)* byste	*mo-bl (a) bis-te*
up a little, please?	mluvit hlasitěji?	*mluvit bla-si-tyey?*
local call	místní hovor	*meest-nyee bov-or*

SIGHTSEEING

art gallery	galerie	*ga-ler-riye*
bus stop	autobusová	*au-to-bus-o-vah*
	zastávka	*za-stab-vka*
church	kostel	*kos-tel*
garden	zahrada	*za bra-da*
library	knihovna	*knyi-bov-na*
museum	muzeum	*muz-e-um*
railway station	nádraží	*nah-dra-zhee*
tourist	turistické	*tooristi-tske*
information	informace	*in-for-ma-tse*
closed for the	státní	*staht-nyee*
public holiday	svátek	*svah-tek*

SHOPPING

How much does	Co to stojí?	*tso to sto-yee?*
this cost?		
I would like ...	Chtěl(a)* bych ...	*khtyel(a) bikh...*
Do you have ...?	Máte ...?	*maa-te ...?*
I'm just looking.	Jenom se dívám.	*ye-nom se dyee-vahm*
Do you take	Berete kreditní	*be-re-te kred-it*
credit cards?	karty?	*nyee karti?*
What time do	V kolik	*v ko-lik*
you open/	otevíráte/	*o-te-vee-rah-te/*
close?	zavíráte?	*za vee rah-te?*
this one	tento	*ten-to*
that one	tamten	*tam-ten*
expensive	drahý	*dra-bee*
cheap	levný	*lev-nee*
size	velikost	*vel-ik-ost*
white	bílý	*bee-lee*
black	černý	*cber-nee*
red	červený	*cber-ven-ee*
yellow	žlutý	*zblu-tee*
green	zelený	*zel-en-ee*
blue	modrý	*mod-ree*
brown	hnědý	*bnyed-ee*

TYPES OF SHOP

antique shop	starožitnictví	*sta-ro zbit--nyits-tvee*
bank	banka	*banka*
bakery	pekárna	*pe-kabr-na*
bookstore	knihkupectví	*knib-kupets-tvee*
butcher	řeznictví	*rzbez-nyits-tvee*
camera shop	obchod	*op-kbot*
	s fotoaparaty	*sfoto-aparabti*
chemist		
(prescriptions etc)	lékárna	*leb-kab-rna*
chemist (cosmetics,		
toiletries etc)	drogerie	*drog-erye*
delicatessen	lahůdky	*la-boo-dki*
department store	obchodní dům	*op-kbod-nyee doom*
grocery	potraviny	*pot-ra-vini*
glass	sklo	*sklo*
hairdresser		
(ladies)	kadeřnictví	*ka-derzb-nyits-tvee*
(mens)	holič	*bo-lich*
market	trh	*trkb*
newsstand	novinový	*no-vi-novee*
	stánek	*stah-nek*
post office	pošta	*posb-ta*
supermarket	samoobsluha	*sa-mo-ob-slu-ba*
tobacconist	tabák	*ta-babk*
travel	cestovní	*tses-tov-nyi*
agency	kancelář	*kantse-laarzb*

Alternatives for a female speaker are shown in brackets.

STAYING IN A HOTEL

Do you have a vacant room?	Máte volný pokoj?	*mah-te vol-nee po-koy?*
double room	dvoulůžkový pokoj	*dvo-loozh-kovee po-koy*
with double bed	s dvojitou postelí	*sdvoy-to pos-telee*
twin room	pokoj s dvěma postelemi	*po-koy sdvye-ma pos-tel-emi*
room with a bath	pokoj s koupelnou	*po-koy s ko-pel-no*
porter	vrátný	*vraht-nee*
hall porter	nosič	*nos-ich*
key	klíč	*kleech*
I have a reservation.	Mám reservaci.	*mahm rez-ervatsi*

EATING OUT

Have you got a table for ...?	Máte stůl pro ...?	*mah-te stool pro ...?*
I'd like to reserve a table.	Chtěl(a)* bych rezervovat stůl.	*khtyel(a) bikh rez-er-vov-at stool*
breakfast	snídaně	*snyee-danye*
lunch	oběd	*ob-yed*
dinner	večeře	*vech e-rzhe*
The bill, please.	Prosím, účet.	*pro-seem oo-chet*
I am a vegetarian.	Jsem vegetarián(ka)*.	*ysem veghe-tariahn(ka)*
waitress!	slečno	*slech-no*
waiter!	pane vrchní!	*pane vrkh-nyee!*
fixed price menu	standardní menu	*stan-dard-nyee men-u*
dish of the day	nabídka dne	*nab-eed-ka dne*
starter	předkrm	*przhed-krm*
main course	hlavní jídlo	*hlav-nyee yeed-lo*
vegetables	zelenina	*zel-en-yin-a*
dessert	zákusek	*zah-kusek*
cover charge	poplatek	*pop-la-tek*
wine list	nápojový lístek	*nah-po-yo-vee lee-stek*
rare (steak)	krvavý	*kr-va-vee*
medium	středně udělaný	*strzhed-nye ud-yel-an-ee*
well done	dobře udělaný	*dobrzhe- ud-yel-an-ee*
glass	sklenice	*sklen-yitse*
bottle	láhev	*lah-hev*
knife	nůž	*noozh*
fork	vidlička	*vid-lich-ka*
spoon	lžíce	*lzhee-tse*

MENU DECODER

biftek	*bif-tek*	steak
bílé víno	*bee-leh vee-no*	white wine
bramborové knedlíky	*bram-bo-ro-veh kne-dleeki*	potato dumplings
brambory	*bram-bo-ri*	potatoes
chléb	*khlebb*	bread
cibule	*tsi-bu-le*	onion
citrónový džus	*tsi-tron-o-vee dzhuus*	lemon juice
cukr	*tsukr*	sugar
čaj	*chay*	tea
čerstvé ovoce	*cher-stveh-o-vo-ce*	fresh fruit
červené víno	*cher-ven-eh vee-no*	red wine
česnek	*ches-nek*	garlic
dort	*dort*	cake
fazole	*fa-zo-le*	beans
grilované	*gril-ov-a-neh*	grilled
houby	*bo-bi*	mushrooms
houska	*bous-ka*	roll
houskové knedlíky	*bo-sko-veh kne-dleeki*	bread dumplings
hovězí	*bov-ye-zee*	beef
hranolky	*bran-ol-ki*	chips
husa	*bu-sa*	goose
jablko	*ya-bl-ko*	apple
jahody	*ya-bo-di*	strawberries
jehněčí	*ye-bnye-chee*	lamb
kachna	*kakb-na*	duck
kapr	*ka-pr*	carp
káva	*kah-va*	coffee
krevety	*krev-et-i*	prawns
kuře	*ku-rzhe*	chicken
kyselé zelí	*kis-el-eh zel-ee*	sauerkraut
maso	*ma-so*	meat
máslo	*mah-slo*	butter
minerálka	*min-er-abl-ka*	mineral water
šumivá/ nešumivá	*sbum-i-vah/ ne-sbum i-vab*	fizzy/ still
mléko	*mleb-ko*	milk
mořská jídla	*morzh-skab-yeed-la-*	seafood
ocet	*ots-et*	vinegar
okurka	*o-ku-rka*	cucumber
olej	*oley*	oil
párek	*paa-rek*	sausage/frankfurter
pečené	*petsb-en-eh*	baked
pečené	*pech-en-eh*	roast
pepř	*peprzh*	pepper
polévka	*pol-eh-vka*	soup
pomeranč	*po-me-ranch*	orange
pomerančový džus	*po-me-ran-ch-- o-vee dzhuus*	orange juice
pivo	*pi-vo*	beer
rajské	*rayskeh*	tomato
ryba	*rib-a*	fish
rýže	*ree-zhe*	rice
salát	*sal-at*	salad
sůl	*sool*	salt
sýr	*seer*	cheese
šunka	*sbun-ka*	ham
vařená/ uzená	*varzh-enah u-zenab*	cooked smoked
telecí	*te-le-tsee*	veal
tuna	*tu-na*	tuna
vajíčko	*va-yee-chko*	egg
vařené	*varzh-en-eb*	boiled
vepřové	*vep-rzho-veb*	pork
voda	*vo-da*	water
vývar	*vee-var*	broth
zelí	*zel-ee*	cabbage
zelenina	*zel-enyina*	vegetables
zmrzlina	*zmrz-lin-a*	ice cream

NUMBERS

1	jedna	*yed-na*
2	dvě	*dvye*
3	tři	*trzbi*
4	čtyři	*chti-rzbi*
5	pět	*pyet*
6	šest	*sbest*
7	sedm	*sedm*
8	osm	*osm*
9	devět	*dev-yet*
10	deset	*des-et*
11	jedenáct	*ye-de-nabtst*
12	dvanáct	*dva-nabtst*
13	třináct	*trzbi-nabtst*
14	čtrnáct	*chtr-nabtst*
15	patnáct	*pat-nabtst*
16	šestnáct	*sbest-nabtst*
17	sedmnáct	*sedm-nabtst*
18	osmnáct	*osm-nabtst*
19	devatenáct	*de-va-te-nabtst*
20	dvacet	*dva-tset*
21	dvacet jedna	*dva-tset yed-na*
22	dvacet dva	*dva-tset dva*
23	dvacet tři	*dva-tset trzbi*
24	dvacet čtyři	*dva-tset chti-rzbi*
25	dvacet pět	*dva-tset pyet*
30	třicet	*trzbi-tset*
40	čtyřicet	*chti-rzbi-tset*
50	padesát	*pa-de-sabt*
60	šedesát	*sbe-de-sabt*
70	sedmdesát	*sedm-de-sabt*
80	osmdesát	*osm-de-sabt*
90	devadesát	*de-va-de-sabt*
100	sto	*sto*
1,000	tisíc	*tyi-seets*
2,000	dva tisíce	*dva tyi-see-tse*
5,000	pět tisíc	*pyet tyi-seets*
1,000,000	milión	*mi-li-ohn*

TIME

one minute	jedna minuta	*yed-na min-uta*
one hour	jedna hodina	*yed-na bod-yin-a*
half an hour	půl hodiny	*pool bod-yin-i*
day	den	*den*
week	týden	*tee-den*
Monday	pondělí	*pon-dye-lee*
Tuesday	úterý	*oo-ter-ee*
Wednesday	středa	*strzbe-da*
Thursday	čtvrtek	*chtvr-tek*
Friday	pátek	*pab-tek*
Saturday	sobota	*so-bo-ta*
Sunday	neděle	*ned-yel-e*

Alternatives for a female speaker are shown in brackets.

COUNTRY GUIDES

AUSTRALIA • CANADA • FRANCE • GREAT BRITAIN
GREECE: ATHENS & THE MAINLAND • THE GREEK ISLANDS
IRELAND • ITALY • JAPAN • MEXICO
PORTUGAL • SCOTLAND • SINGAPORE
SOUTH AFRICA • SPAIN • THAILAND
GREAT PLACES TO STAY IN EUROPE
TASTE OF SCOTLAND

REGIONAL GUIDES

BARCELONA & CATALONIA • CALIFORNIA
FLORENCE & TUSCANY • FLORIDA • HAWAII
JERUSALEM & THE HOLY LAND • LOIRE VALLEY
MILAN & THE LAKES • NAPLES WITH POMPEII & THE
AMALFI COAST • PROVENCE & THE COTE D'AZUR • SARDINIA
SEVILLE & ANDALUSIA • SICILY • VENICE & THE VENETO

CITY GUIDES

AMSTERDAM • BERLIN • BRUSSELS • BUDAPEST
CRACOW • DELHI, AGRA & JAIPUR • DUBLIN
ISTANBUL • LISBON • LONDON • MADRID
MOSCOW • NEW YORK • PARIS • PRAGUE • ROME
SAN FRANCISCO • STOCKHOLM • ST PETERSBURG
SYDNEY • VIENNA • WARSAW • WASHINGTON, DC

NEW FOR SPRING 2001

BALI & LOMBOK • BOSTON • CHICAGO
CRUISE GUIDE TO EUROPE AND THE MEDITERRANEAN
GERMANY • NEW ENGLAND • NEW ZEALAND

FOR UPDATES TO OUR GUIDES, AND INFORMATION ON
DK TRAVEL MAPS & PHRASEBOOKS

VISIT US AT
eyewitnesstravel.dk.com